# INTELLECTUALS IN HISTORY

## THE *NOUVELLE REVUE FRANÇAISE*
## UNDER JEAN PAULHAN, 1925-1940

# FAUX TITRE

Etudes
de langue et littérature françaises
publiées

sous la direction de Keith Busby,
M.J. Freeman, Sjef Houppermans,
Paul Pelckmans et Co Vet

No. 93

Amsterdam - Atlanta, GA 1995

# INTELLECTUALS IN HISTORY

## THE *NOUVELLE REVUE FRANÇAISE* UNDER JEAN PAULHAN, 1925-1940

## MARTYN CORNICK

∞ The paper on which this book is printed meets the requirements of "ISO 9706:1994, Information and documentation - Paper for documents - Requirements for permanence".

ISBN: 90-5183-797-6 (CIP)
©Editions Rodopi B.V., Amsterdam - Atlanta, GA 1995
Printed in The Netherlands

*For Helen, Jack and Susanna*
*and in memory of my mother and father*

# CONTENTS

|  |  | Page |
|---|---|---|
| Introduction | | 1 |
| Chapter 1 | Anatomy of a review: the *Nouvelle Revue française* and Jean Paulhan, 1920-1940 | 11 |
| Chapter 2 | Catalyst for intellectual *engagement*: the serialization of *La Trahison des clercs* | 47 |
| Chapter 3 | Idealism or militancy?  Radicalism, antifascism and the *NRF* | 69 |
| Chapter 4 | A fatal attraction: the *NRF* and Franco-German *rapprochement* | 97 |
| Chapter 5 | The 'great glow in the East': the *NRF*, Gide and the Soviet Union | 123 |
| Chapter 6 | The *NRF*, the Jewish question and anti-Semitism | 149 |
| Chapter 7 | Resisting delusion: the *NRF* and the drift into war | 181 |
| In conclusion | | 201 |
| Bibliography | | 207 |
| Index | | 219 |

# Introduction

*Tout ce qui a paru depuis vingt-cinq ans dans les lettres de neuf et de puissant sortait de la NRF. [...] La NRF continue et vous verrez se former en elle tout ce qui comptera dans la littérature de demain.*[1]

This book aims to fill a gap in our knowledge of French cultural history between the wars. It is concerned with the relatively unexplored middle ground of French intellectual life, terrain occupied by liberal writers and their monthly review, the *Nouvelle Revue Française*. These personalities were the leading representatives of the French radical-republican intellectual tradition, and were exposed to new ideological and political conditions which evolved after the First World War. The nature of the intellectual tradition they represented led them to confront a dichotomy between 'idealism and militancy', between non-involvement and political *engagement*. In this way they conformed to French 'intellectual practice' as summarized by Sudhir Hazareesingh:

> The tradition of intellectual practice which dominated the political horizon for most of the modern era in France rested on two pillars. The first was a moralistic concern with abstract principles of truth and justice, which was ultimately derived from classical republican philosophical concerns. The second was a conception of the universality of reason, which regarded the possession of a certain level of cultural authority [...] as a sufficient qualification for intervention in the political arena.

**N.B.:**   Place of publication is Paris unless otherwise stated.

1      J. Paulhan, 'Présentation de la *NRF* à *Radio-37*', in *Oeuvres complètes*, vol. IV, Cercle du Livre Précieux, 1969, p. 363.

The mutually reinforcing effects of these principles produced a tradition of intellectual universalism. On one hand, French intellectuals were persistently drawn outside the circle of their specialized knowledge as a result of their disposition to view the political sphere through the prism of general moral principles. On the other hand, their authority for making evaluative judgements about the temporal world rested on an underlying appreciation of the interdependence of the worlds of culture and politics. The net result was a fluid conception of the socio-professional identity of the intellectual, who could simultaneously perform the role of a thinker, a producer of culture, an adviser to the prince, and a political activist.[2]

This book will examine the importance of national and international issues for these liberal intellectuals, and how they responded to them.

There are three principal motives informing this study. Firstly, in the cultural history of twentieth century France, the *Nouvelle Revue Française* — hereafter referred to as the *NRF* — is singled out as the exemplar of literary reviews.[3] To consider the *NRF* *solely* as a literary review, however, is to take a too narrow view. It is rightly judged to be the pinnacle of literary creativity and innovation in modern France, so much so that many of the review's pages have been reproduced either in anthology form or in separate volumes.[4] The *NRF* acquired this unparalleled reputation early in its life. In 1920 the nationalist *Revue critique des idées et des livres*, welcoming the reappearance of its rival after the war in June 1919, printed a generous tribute:

> Vers 1950, l'historien des lettres, s'il cherche à se faire une idée des mouvements profonds qui orientaient celles-ci aux alentours de la guerre, n'aura fait qu'un vain travail tant qu'il n'aura pris connaissance des collections de la *Nouvelle Revue Française*. [...] Nulle part il ne trouvera aussi concentré cet appétit d'invention et d'originalité qui est un des plus remarquables mérites de la *Nouvelle Revue Française*.[5]

Writing in 1940, the American critic Justin O'Brien paid the review another glowing compliment: 'No other single periodical will afford historians of the future such a vast panorama of literary activity in France during the years

---

2  See S. Hazareesingh, *Political traditions in modern France*, Oxford: OUP, 1994, pp. 52-53.

3  For instance, see J.-F. Sirinelli, writing in René Rémond's *Notre siècle de 1918 à 1991*, Fayard, 1991, p. 247.

4  See P. Hebey's selection *L'Esprit NRF*, Gallimard, 1990. A number of special numbers ('Hommages') devoted to authors including André Gide, Marcel Proust, Valery Larbaud and Jean Paulhan have also been republished.

5  *Revue critique des idées et des livres*, 27, 25 January 1920, p. 117.

1909 to 1939'.[6] Many of the authors closely associated with the *NRF* have indeed found lasting renown: among the most celebrated names are those of André Gide, André Malraux, Jean-Paul Sartre, Albert Camus, and the roll-call could be extended to include dozens of less famous but none the less worthy authors, such as Roger Martin du Gard, Jean Grenier, Jean Schlumberger, Marcel Jouhandeau, Francis Ponge, Roger Caillois and many more. The review, with its distinctive off-white cover and red lettering, was required reading for successive generations of aspiring French students, some of whom have acknowledged its rôle in their education. One such student was François Mitterrand, who recalled: 'À dix-sept ans [...] j'avais eu mon évolution personnelle et je lisais Gide, Claudel, la *NRF*...'.[7] Its appeal was surprisingly broad, and was read even by those intellectuals who, like Robert Brasillach, chose a very different political course, and ended up in front of a firing squad after the Liberation for 'intelligence with the enemy'.[8]

The intention of this work is to show that the *NRF* did not shy away from the historical and political realities of the two interwar decades, quite the contrary: its pages were opened to discussions focusing on the implications of events. Considering the growth of interest in French intellectual history, the rôle of the *NRF* as a forum, as a means of propagating ideas and reputations, and as a major intersection of intellectuals' networks, is of great significance, and deserves detailed attention.[9] As the cultural historian Jean-François Sirinelli explains, 'les comités de rédaction des revues sont, pour le chercheur [...] un balcon offrant une vue imprenable sur la sociabilité des intellectuels'.[10] The *NRF* is all the more important because intellectuals and writers sought the recognition that came from having their work published in its pages. Régis Debray, who salutes the contribution of the *NRF* to a 'golden age' of publishing in France, stresses that 'l'imprimatur *NRF*, c'était l'adoption par une famille, sinon l'incorporation à un ordre'.[11] The events of the 1920s and 1930s were so important for intellectuals that the *NRF* should be viewed in a perspective which gives as much emphasis to its

6    J. O'Brien, '*La NRF dans l'histoire des lettres*, par L. Morino, Paris, Gallimard, 1939', in *Romanic Review*, vol. 31, 1940, p. 194.

7    *Le Nouvel Observateur*, 18-24 November 1968, p. 8.

8    See Brasillach's *Notre avant-guerre*, Plon, 1941, p. 33.

9    See especially J.-F. Sirinelli, 'Le hasard ou la nécessité? Une histoire en chantier: l'histoire des intellectuels', *Vingtième siècle*, 9, January-March 1986, pp. 97-108; P. Ory and J.-F. Sirinelli, *Les intellectuels en France, de l'affaire Dreyfus à nos jours*, A. Colin, 1987; and N. Racine and M. Trebitsch (eds.), 'Sociabilités intellectuelles', *Cahiers de l'IHTP*, no. 20, March 1992.

10    J.-F. Sirinelli, *Intellectuels et passions françaises. Manifestes et pétitions au XX$^e$ siècle*, Fayard, 1990, p. 14.

11    R. Debray, *Le pouvoir intellectuel en France*, Ramsay, 1979, p. 79.

status as a platform for, and even a catalyst of, intellectual debate as to its prominence in literary creativity. Any survey of the intellectual history of interwar Europe would be incomplete without reference to the pages of the *NRF*.

Secondly, to ignore the rôle played by the *NRF* in intellectual debates in France is to provide only a partial picture of intellectuals' activity in the interwar period. In his history of French intellectuals after the Liberation, Tony Judt looks back at the 1930s and writes:

> Intellectuals of the "center" were rare. Those few men who would speak after Munich in defense of the Republic and against fascism did so in the name of values that they continued to hold in spite of the Third Republic and its shortcomings but that they had mostly ceased to associate with that political regime and its institutional forms.[12]

If one examines more closely the debates in the interwar *NRF*, the cultural organ *par excellence* of the French centrist Radical Party, then one finds that these intellectuals of the "centre" did indeed question and reassess those values which they had long held dear: ultimately, however, the review would resist temptations from a number of quarters and rally to the defence of the French Republic. Writers and intellectuals (particularly those associated with the *NRF*) did not adopt committed points of view without much prior reflection; neither did they do so in a vacuum. Again, intellectuals in France acted within a set of parameters specific to its culture:

> The republican intellectual tradition was [...] predicated upon the existence of a set of core political beliefs and values, but also on a generalized belief that the possession of a certain level of professional authority in a given cultural field was in itself a sufficient qualification for public intervention in the political world. This was, and indeed remains, one of the distinctive features of the structure of political life in France.[13]

Intellectuals in interwar France *were* important figures: rightly or wrongly they carried influence in political circles, and they were listened to by opinion makers and the public. Their status during these years lent weight to their pronouncements and invested them with a conviction which they might not have had otherwise; their views were certainly not treated lightly. The

---

12    T. Judt, *Past imperfect. French intellectuals 1944-1956*, Berkeley, Los Angeles, Oxford: University of California Press, 1992, p. 16.

13    S. Hazareesingh, *Political traditions in modern France*, p. 52.

temperament and background of the personalities involved, among them André Gide, Jean Schlumberger, Julien Benda, Ramon Fernandez and Roger Martin du Gard, to name only the most important, further helped to ensure that intellectual and political questions of national and international scope were treated. Thanks to such personalities (and thanks to Jacques Rivière, Paulhan's predecessor), the *NRF* was already sensitive to questions which were not, strictly speaking, 'literary'. The *NRF* was influential because it was located at the intersection of a number of important networks, or *milieux*, including political parties (the Radical Party in particular), the world of education (teachers, students and the École Normale Supérieure) and the world of publishing; and it was the recognized home of many luminaries of the cultural world. It could not help but stand out as an authoritative tribune for the expression and exchange of opinion.

The third motive underlying this study is to illuminate the rôle of Jean Paulhan, the editor of the *NRF* between 1925 and 1940. Paulhan is, quite simply, a neglected figure in French intellectual and cultural history: all too often he is treated dismissively as an *éminence grise* without explanation of why he may or may not have been a shadowy figure, and without properly examining his contribution. As Michel Trebitsch has argued, it is time to 'demythologize' such 'heroic' figures at the centre of reviews, and to offer a true evaluation of their contribution to cultural history.[14] In addition to organizing each monthly issue, Paulhan's prime duty as editor was to act as an intermediary between the review and the members of a team of contributors whose political views were often more polarized than their aesthetic ones. One of the most arresting aspects of Paulhan's direction of the *NRF* is precisely the manner in which he balanced the review, aesthetically as well as politically, around a centre of gravity that is identifiably radical-republican and liberal. In short, as described above, Paulhan and the *NRF* operated within the parameters set by the predominant radical-republican political culture. Yet simultaneously Paulhan encouraged a critical consciousness which, from time to time, was focused upon the very ideology which had produced it. Clashes were sometimes inevitable, but the *NRF* never truly suffered from the occasional release of internal tensions. It is important to see, rather, how Paulhan managed to exploit these tensions and debates, usually to the commercial benefit of the review.

During the interwar period the *NRF* became increasingly subjected to the forces of history. Far from expunging it of 'non-literary' content, Paulhan

---

14    M. Trebitsch, preface to 'Sociabilités intellectuelles', p. 20.

opened it up to consideration of the issues of the day, sometimes under coercion and sometimes under his own volition. Here the issues are examined thematically in a chronological, or historical, sequence. They reflect an interest not only in domestic politics, but are also largely determined by international relations and events. The first chapter outlines the 'anatomy' of the *NRF*, focusing on its organizational features and personnel. This forms a prelude to the following thematic chapters: chapter 2 assesses the impact of the serialization of Julien Benda's seminal essay on the responsibilities of intellectuals, *La Trahison des clercs*, and chapter 3 examines the attitudes of the review's contributors towards the political character of the Third Republic and the question of ideological renewal. The impact on *NRF* intellectuals of the revolutionary upheavals elsewhere in Europe was deeply felt; the themes of reconciliation and fellow-travelling are examined in the case of Germany in chapter 4 and in chapter 5 in the case of the Soviet Union. Chapter 6 analyses the Jewish question as it was reflected in the review through the prism of French anti-Semitic traditions and contemporaneous influences. It was partly inevitable that the editor should allow the *NRF* to reflect the preoccupations of his contributors; later on, however, as will be outlined in chapter 7, when it was perceived that peace must not be bought at any price, Paulhan steered the review towards an overtly partisan position, even making clear his own views on the matter in its pages. This was not done merely to introduce new content, but out of sheer conviction.

The *NRF* is both the subject and the primary source of this study: it is both *history* and *text*.[15] Even a rapid scan through the review over the years 1920 to 1940 reveals much regarding the questions of the day. However, a close reading and detailed analysis of each number reveals a great deal more. As the period progresses, contemporary preoccupations permeate its pages ever more, and their traces are detectable in every *genre* of text, whether articles, serialized novels, regular features, book reviews, extracts from other reviews or topical items. To have considered the pages of the *NRF* alone would have resulted in a rather limited view which, of necessity, is broadened by examining the pages of the other periodicals it engaged in debate, including its life-long enemy *Action française* and its satellites, like the *Revue universelle*, and friendlier rivals, such as *Europe*. Finally, the picture is completed, and the focus becomes sharper, thanks to Jean Paulhan's correspondence. As editor Paulhan wrote ceaselessly to a wide range of

---

15      This distinction is noted by John King in *'Sur'. A study of the Argentine literary journal and its rôle in the development of a culture 1931-1970*, Cambridge: CUP, 1986.

contributors and associates. These letters – whether unpublished[16] or published[17] – provide a privileged insight into the way editorial policy was conceived and shaped, and they shed light on the motives for including or excluding material which might have been or which was politically sensitive. We learn a great deal about why certain texts were unacceptable. In their own right these letters stand as one of the last great collections of literary correspondence in France, in the tradition of Voltaire or Diderot or Hugo. Not only do they provide evidence about the day-to-day tasks and dilemmas of arguably the century's most influential cultural impresario, they also provide the cultural historian with insights into the motivations behind intellectuals' reactions to issues raised by the rapid succession of events during the interwar years.

Of course Paulhan's rôle amounts to more than simply fulfilling the duties of an editor of a monthly review. Yet at the beginning of his career there his responsibilities at the *NRF* were primarily organizational, and he and his contributors were subjected to the 'mechanics' of the review, to its fixed periodicity. Paulhan relished his task as editor, and any discussion of the *NRF* would be incomplete without an examination of the various elements of the organization and policy of the *NRF*. This forms a prelude to the ensuing thematic study.

---

16    Reference to unpublished correspondence in footnotes is shown by the letters AP (Archives Paulhan), AR (Archives Rivière), BD (Bibliothèque Littéraire Jacques Doucet), and Fonds RMG (the Fonds Roger Martin du Gard, Bibliothèque Nationale, Département des Manuscrits). Where dates are approximate, square brackets are used. For full details of this unpublished correspondence, see section I of the bibliography.

17    The most important volumes of published correspondence are: J. Paulhan, *Choix de lettres*, I. *1917-1936. La littérature est une fête*, Gallimard, 1986; *Choix de lettres*, II. *1937-1945. Traité des jours sombres*, Gallimard, 1992 (hereafter referred to as *JPC* 1 or 2). See also J. Paulhan and J. Grenier, *Correspondance 1925-1968*, préface de Roger Judrin, Quimper: Calligrammes, 1984; J. Paulhan and F. Ponge, *Correspondance 1923-1968*, 2 vols, Gallimard, 1986, and J. Paulhan, 'Correspondance', in *NRF*, May 1969, 'Jean Paulhan, 1884-1968', pp. 988-1041. A complete list is given in section II of the bibliography.

8

## Acknowledgements

I should like to express my warmest gratitude to the following for their assistance and cooperation in my researches:

- Mme Jacqueline F. Paulhan, who has always shown great generosity in allowing me access to her father-in-law's correspondence held in the Paulhan Archive.
- M Alain Rivière, who allowed me to read and quote from his father's unpublished correspondence with Jean Paulhan.
- M Claude Martin, founder of the Association des Amis d'André Gide, and former editor of the *Bulletin des Amis d'André Gide*, for his informative conversations during a visit to Lyon, and for his recommendations.
- M Jean-Pierre Dauphin, of Les Editions Gallimard, for his advice, as well as for showing me copies of material on the *NRF* which otherwise would have remained inaccessible.
- Mme Dominique Aury, former secretary to Jean Paulhan and Marcel Arland, of Les Editions Gallimard, for access to the whole voluminous correspondence between Jean Paulhan and Jean Grenier.
- Pascal Mercier and Vincent Wackenheim, for their stimulating conversation, and for an introduction to the late Auguste Anglès, whose comments were so encouraging.
- Mr Herbert R. Lottman, author of *La Rive Gauche*, for his time and advice.
- Mme Grüner-Schlumberger and M Daniel de Coppet for granting permission to consult the correspondence of Jean Paulhan to Jean Schlumberger and Roger Martin du Gard respectively.
- M François Chapon and Mme Nicole Prévot of the Bibliothèque Littéraire Jacques Doucet, Paris, for their patient assistance during visits to the library where much of Paulhan's unpublished correspondence is conserved.
- The staff of the Bibliothèque de Documentation Internationale et Contemporaine, Université de Paris-X, Nanterre, for their assistance and guidance.

- Mme Florence Callu of the Département des Manuscrits, Bibliothèque Nationale, Paris, for her assistance and guidance.

Earlier versions of chapters 2, 3 and 7 have appeared respectively in *French Cultural Studies*, *Nottingham French Studies* and *Modern and Contemporary France*.

Finally, I am grateful to Peter Morris, Nicholas Hewitt, Olivier Corpet and Sophie Levie for reading part or the whole of the manuscript at various stages.

Martyn Cornick
Department of European Studies
Loughborough University
December 1994

**A note about references and abbreviations:**

Reference to unpublished correspondence in footnotes is shown by the letters AP (Archives Paulhan), AR (Archives Rivière), BD (Bibliothèque Littéraire Jacques Doucet), and Fonds RMG (the *Fonds Roger Martin du Gard*, Bibliothèque Nationale, Département des Manuscrits). Where dates are approximate, square brackets are used. For full details of the unpublished correspondence, see section I of the bibliography.

**Abbreviations used:**

| | |
|---|---|
| AEAR | Association des écrivains et des artistes révolutionnaires |
| AP | Archive Paulhan (private) |
| AR | Archive Rivière (private) |
| BD | Bibliothèque littéraire Jacques Doucet |
| *CAG* | *Cahiers André Gide* (i.e. the 'Cahiers de la Petite Dame', by Maria Van Rhysselberghe: Vol. 1, *1918-1929*, vol. 2, *1929-1937*, and vol. 3, *1937-1945*, in *Cahiers André Gide* 4, 5 and 6, published respectively in 1973, 1974 and 1975 by Gallimard. |
| *CJP* | *Cahiers Jean Paulhan* (Gallimard) |
| CVIA | Comité de vigilance des intellectuels antifascistes |
| Fonds RMG | The *Fonds Roger Martin du Gard*, Département des Manuscrits, Bibliothèque Nationale, Paris |
| *JPC* 1 or 2 | Jean Paulhan, *Choix de lettres*, I and II (Gallimard, 1986 and 1992) |

# Chapter 1

## Anatomy of a review: the *Nouvelle Revue française* and Jean Paulhan (1920-1940)

*Dans une revue, c'est tout différent. On y voit la littérature qui se forme et s'invente et tâtonne entre mille dangers. On y prend part. On s'y reprend à plusieurs fois. C'est qu'une revue n'a de prix que si l'on y voit, à côté de quelques auteurs consacrés (comme on dit) de jeunes écrivains qui recommencent la littérature à leurs risques et périls. On y voit les lettres à l'état naissant.* [1]

*Une des charmes de la NRF, un des secrets de sa persistante jeunesse fut de s'accorder de temps en temps une fugue dans les vignes du Seigneur. Elle tituba quelque peu, à la suite de Gide, sous l'effet de la vodka communiste, et jamais elle ne sut refuser les elixirs que lui faisait goûter l'Ange du Bizarre. L'influence qu'elle a eue sur la vie des lettres pendant l'entre-deux-guerres, impliquait qu'elle entrât dans le jeu de son époque et ne nageât pas à contre-courant.* [2]

The exalted reputation of the interwar *NRF* was achieved partly because of the solid foundations laid down before the First World War by its founders. After an initial, unsuccessful, appearance under Eugène Montfort in 1908, the *NRF* was launched in February 1909 by André Gide, Jean Schlumberger, Henri Ghéon, Jacques Copeau, André Ruyters and Michel Arnauld, and it rapidly made its mark as an important new review.[3] Yet the lasting renown of the *NRF* was achieved through the skill, talent-seeking activities and networks of its editors, Jean Paulhan and, before him, Jacques Rivière.[4] It was

---

1    J. Paulhan, 'Présentation de la *NRF* au Club du Faubourg', *Oeuvres*, IV, p. 377.
2    J. Schlumberger, *Oeuvres*, II, p. 203.
3    This early phase has been studied in close detail by Auguste Anglès who, unfortunately, did not live to see the completion of his magisterial study *André Gide et le premier groupe de la NRF, 1890-1914*, 3 vol., Gallimard, 1978-1986.  See also M. Décaudin, 'L'année 1908 et les origines de la *NRF*', *Revue des sciences humaines*, 68, 1952, pp. 347-58, and, for the literary historical context, the same author's *La Crise des valeurs symbolistes: vingt ans de poésie française (1895-1914)*, Toulouse: Privat, 1960.
4    On Rivière's contribution, see J.-P. Cap (ed.), *Jacques Rivière-Jean Schlumberger, Correspondance 1909-1925*, Lyon: Centre d'études gidiennes, 1980, pp. 13-36.  A brief

difficult for them as editors to ignore the preferences and tastes of the remaining founders of the review, particularly André Gide and Jean Schlumberger, and still less could they exercise their editorial choices in a vacuum, because both were submitted to the commercial exigencies of Gaston Gallimard, publisher of the review and of the *NRF*-imprint.[5] It should not be forgotten that the editors' selections of material, both literary and non-literary, were ultimately determined by the intrinsic logic of the review, by its periodicity, by its 'mechanics'. To a large degree, the material published was subordinated to the mechanics of the review itself, and in this way, although it rarely chronicled or reported events throughout the period, it could – and did – reflect seriously upon the issues raised by those events.

**What was the *NRF*?**

When Paulhan became editor in April 1925, the *NRF* was a monthly subscription review appearing in 128-page issues.[6] The prewar series of the *NRF*, from its inception, had quickly attracted a substantial readership, at a time when some reviews were fortunate if they had a few dozen readers. In the first year alone, 1909 to 1910, the *NRF* had been printing 1,400 numbers a month; on the eve of war in 1914 (when it ceased publication for the duration), the subscription figure had itself risen to 1,400.[7] Because the overall print-run figure was normally double that of the regular subscription list, by mid-1914 the average printing would have been between 2,500 and 3,000 per month. After the resumption in June 1919 the same figure was quickly reestablished by Christmas of the same year.[8] Entering the New Year 1920 with some 1,500 subscribers, the *NRF* built on its success. In his study on its rival *Europe*, Joseph Kvapil notes that in 1923 the *NRF* had 2,000 subscribers.[9] After he took over in April 1925, Paulhan regularly kept Gide

---

outline and complete index of Rivière's review is provided in C. Martin, *La NRF de 1919 à 1925*, Lyon: Centre d'études gidiennes, 1983. The remainder of the interwar period is covered in the companion volumes, *La NRF de 1925 à 1934*, and *La NRF de 1935 à 1940*, 1976 and 1977.

5 See P. Assouline, *Gaston Gallimard, un demi-siècle d'édition française*, Balland, 1984.
6 During Paulhan's editorship, from 1925 to 1940, the *NRF* appeared in 180 issues (nos. 142-321) in 28,676 pages. The *NRF* progressed steadily from 128-page issues in 1925, to 144, then 160-page issues (until February 1937), 168 pages from March 1937, and eventually 182 pages in 1938-1939, until October 1939, when restrictions on paper reduced it to 144 pages.
7 A. Anglès, 'Le fonctionnement de la *NRF* (1909-1914)', *Bulletin des amis d'André Gide*, no. 61, January 1984, pp. 11-28.
8 'A nos abonnés' [October 1919], reproduced in *La NRF de 1919 à 1925*, p. xiv.
9 J. Kvapil, *Romain Rolland et les amis d'Europe*, Prague: Acta Universatis, 1971, p. 88. Pierre Gamarra confirmed that *Europe*'s print-run was double the subscription list (letter to the author dated 30 October 1981).

and Schlumberger informed of progress in reports that contained details of new subscriptions. In fact the review gained some 1,000 new subscribers during the first ten months of his editorship.[10] He could still lament, however, with some impatience, that 'nous sommes bien loin encore des 8 000 abonnés que nous devrions avoir'.[11] By 1927, a year of considerable expansion for the *NRF*, Paulhan celebrated by tabulating all the gains in subscriptions over an eight-year period:

> Il y a, dans les progrès de la *NRF*, un côté presque mécanique, qui est assez étonnant. Ainsi la *NRF* a gagné:
> en 1920: 100 abonnés
> 1921: 150 abonnés
> 1922 : 140 abonnés
> 1923 : 750 abonnés
> 1924 : 450 abonnés
> 1925 : 875 abonnés
> 1926 : 1100 abonnés
> (1927 : 900 abonnés).
> Or ces 'bonds' sont régulièrement dus à une oeuvre particulière.[12]

By 1928, the *NRF* was printing around 12,000 copies a month, a figure confirmed by Paul Léautaud, who also reported a print-run of 17,000 in 1931.[13] This success was not only due to the literary quality of the review, it is also explained by the fact that the *NRF*'s treatment of historical events gained readers. After his 'special number' on Munich, Paulhan wrote to tell Schlumberger that:

> La 'montée' continue: 100 abonnés de plus en décembre [1938], 260 en janvier-février [1939], 140 en février-mars. Je crois que le numéro de novembre [1938] est à l'origine de tout.[14]

Its stance against the Munich accords drew an extra 500 subscribers in just three months, and even during the war itself, the review continued to gain readers.

These figures show that in comparison to some of its competitors, the *NRF* was a medium-sized review, especially when viewed alongside *Commerce*, or *Bifur*, for example, both of which were more esoteric, more

10      'La *NRF* a gagné, depuis dix mois, un peu plus de mille abonnés'; JP to Gide, letter dated 27 February [1926], in *JPC* 1, pp. 109, 127.
11      JP to Schlumberger, letter dated 20 June 1925 (BD).
12      JP to Schlumberger [August 1927] (BD).
13      P. Léautaud, *Journal littéraire*, VIII, pp. 310-11.
14      JP to Schlumberger [March 1939] (BD). For further details, see below, chapter 7.

exclusively literary reviews. *Commerce* had a maximum print-run of 2,900 and some 800 subscribers, while *Bifur* claimed 400 subscribers and had a maximum print-run of 3,000.[15] *Mesures*, another review administered by Paulhan, declared a print-run of 1,800 and 1,200 in 1935 and 1937 respectively. Yet compared with high circulation general reviews, the *NRF* seems rather modest: for example, Plon's *Revue hebdomadaire* printed an average of 30,000 numbers a week, while the *Revue des Deux Mondes* had a twice-monthly print-run of 40,000 in 1931.[16]

### The arrival of Jean Paulhan at the *NRF*

Jean Paulhan officially became *directeur* of the *NRF* on 1 January 1935. He had, however, already been secretary of Rivière's review from 1920 to 1925, and editor-in-chief from 1926 to 1935, with Gaston Gallimard as nominal *directeur*. Before looking more closely at the make-up of the *NRF*, and how it evolved during Paulhan's editorship, we shall examine how he emerged as a suitable candidate to run such a review.

Paulhan's background and education suited his appointment to the *NRF*. His family had moved from Nîmes to Paris in 1894, when Jean was ten. His father, the philosopher Frédéric Paulhan, had 'beaucoup d'influence sur son fils qui parvint difficilement à se dégager de son emprise intellectuelle.'[17] These formative influences in the fields of philosophy and psychology led Jean to begin preparing the *agrégation de philosophie* in 1907, just prior to his departure for Madagascar in December of that year on a teaching appointment. He remained there from January 1908 to November 1910, when he returned to France. His letters to Guillaume de Tarde show how closely Paulhan kept in touch with Paris, from where he received a steady stream of reviews. Already in 1908 Paulhan and his friend were responsible for the *Psychologie* rubric of Alfred de Tarde's review *La Vie Contemporaine*.[18] Paulhan gained more experience in the review *Le Spectateur*, founded in April 1909. *Le Spectateur* was 'une revue de culture critique', and, according to Paulhan,

---

[15]   See S. Levie, *Commerce 1924-1932. Une revue internationale moderniste*, Rome: Fondazione Camillo Caetani, 1989, p. 50, and J. Leiner, in fascimile reprint of *Bifur*, J.-M. Place, 1976, p. XIII.

[16]   See R. de Saint-Jean, *Passé pas mort*, Grasset, 1983, p. 135, and Robert Aron, *Fragments de mémoire*, Plon, 1981, p. 28.

[17]   Notes by Jacqueline F. Paulhan, in 'Correspondance Jean Paulhan-Guillaume de Tarde, 1904-1920', *CJP* 1, Gallimard, 1980, p. 14.

[18]   Ibid., p. 57.

> il s'agissait d'une enterprise, une sorte de logique appliquée: une grammaire des idées qui cherche patiemment à mener quelques observations cohérentes et dégager quelques lois. *Le Spectateur* a courageusement vécu jusqu'en 1914.[19]

Such experiences apprenticed Paulhan in the planning and administration of reviews. After the war, he became *rédacteur-gérant* of *La Vie* from December 1919 until August 1920, by which time he had been officially appointed as secretary to Rivière at the *NRF*.[20] Just prior to the war in 1914, Paulhan had taken the entrance examination for the Ministère de l'Instruction Publique, in which, eventually, he would become a *rédacteur*. This post provided him with a network which would prove to be of great importance to the *NRF* circle, for not only did he manage to disseminate favourable propaganda throughout the educational administration on behalf of the review, he was also able to pass on information about vacant teaching posts to various contributors.

As a combatant during the early phase of the First World War, Paulhan was severely wounded. By 1916 he had still not fully recovered, and it was only in 1917 that he was able to assume the duties of interpreter and driving instructor for Madagascan troops. The war years gave him the opportunity to write, and, in 1917, he contacted André Gide indicating that he wished to dedicate to him an early version of the narrative *Progrès en amour assez lents*. During the period around his demobilization (21 March 1919), Paulhan involved himself more and more in the literary *avant-garde*: in 1918, he contributed to *Nord-Sud* (founded in 1917), associated with the group of writers who founded *Littérature*, and had an article published in the first issue.[21] And as far as direct contact with the *NRF* was concerned, Paulhan had (unsuccessfully) offered Jean Schlumberger a text as early as 1912, and had submitted (again unsuccessfully) a review in 1913.[22] He was not discouraged, and, believing rightly that the *NRF* might benefit from his position as *rédacteur* in the Ministère de l'Instruction Publique, he wrote to Gide before the reappearance of the *NRF* in 1919 offering his services. Gide replied:

---

[19] Ibid., p. 75, and J. Paulhan, *Les Incertitudes du langage*, Gallimard, 1970, pp. 116-117.

[20] For details on *La Vie*, see 'Jean Paulhan et Madagascar, 1908-1910', *CJP* 2, Gallimard, 1982, pp. 218-219.

[21] For details of these *avant-garde* networks, see 'Lettres de Jean Paulhan', *NRF*, June 1978, pp. 166-79, and *JPC* 1, pp. 22-23.

[22] JP to Schlumberger, letter dated 9 October 1912 (BD), and Rivière to Schlumberger, letter dated 7 August 1913, in J.-P. Cap (ed.), *Jacques Rivière-Jean Schlumberger, Correspondance 1909-1925*, p. 91.

Votre lettre m'emplit de joie. Je crois que vous êtes parfaitement
dans le vrai en pensant que la NRF est loin d'avoir trouvé tous
ses lecteurs, en estimant qu'une saine propagande pourrait faire
beaucoup et je ne puis vous dire avec quelle satisfaction je vous
vois soucieux d'y travailler.[23]

In 1919, therefore, Paulhan was already engaged at the NRF in a part-time
capacity, to help in organizing the 'propaganda effort' for the review; by
February 1920, his first text appeared in its pages.[24]

During the first half of 1920 came Paulhan's chance to move towards
the centre of the NRF. It was Rivière's family circumstances that helped to
bring him much closer to the review. On 2 February that year, Rivière urged
patience:

Je suis profondément touché par votre gentillesse. Je vais
étudier la question de savoir quel travail je pouvais vous
confier. Et si je ne me décidais pas tout de suite à vous appeler à
mon secours, je profiterais certainement de votre offre amicale
au moment des couches de ma femme, c'est-à-dire dans un mois
d'ici.[25]

By March 1920, Paulhan was engaged as an editorial assistant to help organize
material for the review, and kept in touch with his editor through regular
correpondence. Although removed from the operation, Rivière was able to
take a much needed rest while keeping a finger on the pulse of the NRF.
Paulhan's efforts were appreciated during this trying time, for he told Rivière
that Gaston Gallimard had made a provisional offer to engage him more
permanently. Rivière agreed:

Il faut que notre collaboration devienne régulière; elle peut nous
être infiniment profitable à tous deux, je crois; et je suis
convaincu qu'en tous cas elle aura pour la revue les effets
extrêmement précieux. J'examinerai, en rentrant, avec Gaston
Gallimard, les moyens de l'organiser pour ainsi dire légalement.
Il y aura bien quelques petites difficultés matérielles à vaincre;
mais nous les vaincrons.[26]

23     Gide to JP, letter dated 15 March 1919, in NRF, January 1970, p. 75.
24     La Guérison sévère, NRF, February 1920, pp. 201-33. His networks had served him
        well: Paulhan's text had been recommended to Rivière by Roger Allard, an
        acquaintance from before the war.
25     Rivière to JP, letter dated 2 February 1920 (AR).
26     Rivière to JP, letter dated 15 May 1920 (AR).

Consequently the name of Jean Paulhan appeared for the first time as *secrétaire* in the *NRF* for July 1920. Paul Valéry, already by this time one of the *NRF*'s most renowned contribuors, wrote to congratulate Paulhan:

> Je suis très heureux pour la *NRF* de vous y voir définitivement attaché. Un homme de votre conscience et de votre précision d'esprit est une acquisition très précieuse pour une revue. Et quant à vous, quant à la réaction sur vous-même de cette occupation, je suis sûr qu'elle ne sera pas sans conséquence pour votre oeuvre à venir. L'exercice presque perpétuel et aiguisé de responsabilités, du sens critique (qui est [...] la chose la plus rare de ce monde), vous servira certainement.[27]

Having been appointed officially as secretary, Paulhan's expertise and editorial talents blossomed and began to mature. He was able to influence his director by introducing young authors from the *avant-garde*: Aragon and Breton were among those invited to contribute. This interest in 'modernist' literature attracted Rivière too, anxious as he was to prevent the review from becoming too staid, an anxiety shared by André Gide.[28] Apart from his propaganda efforts, Paulhan's tasks as secretary were, by and large, no different from those which had fallen to Rivière when he had occupied the post from 1911 to 1914:

> Voici en gros en quoi consiste mes fonctions: 1. rassembler tous les mss. destinés au prochain numéro; 2. les envoyer à l'imprimeur; 3. recevoir les premières épruves en double, les répartir entre les différents auteurs, corriger celles qui me restent; 4. renvoyer le tout à l'imprimeur; 5. corriger les secondes épreuves; 6. envoyer ce qu'on appelle le bon à tirer.[29]

### Gide's review?

Clarification is necessary because confusion existed, and still persists, regarding Gide's rôle at the review. For a long time there was a tendency to regard Gide as the editor (*directeur*) of the *NRF*: even in 1935 Paulhan observed that 'Gide passe pour diriger la *NRF*.[30] Gide, however, was at no

---

27  Valéry to JP, letter dated 22 June 1920, *NRF*, August 1971, p. 19.
28  See, for instance, 'Reconnaissance à Dada', *NRF*, November 1920, pp. 216-37, and M.-R. Carré, 'La *NRF* et André Gide face à l'insurrection Dada', *French Review*, XXXIX, October 1965, pp. 57-68.
29  Rivière to his aunts, letter dated 17 December 1911, quoted in J.-P. Cap (ed.), *Jacques Rivière-Jean Schlumberger*, p. 19.
30  JP to Suarès, letter dated 7 January 1935, in *Correspondance Jean Paulhan-André Suarès, 1925-1940*, *CJP* 4, Gallimard, 1987, p. 107.

time editor or *directeur* of the review.[31]    The literary critic Robert Kanters
provides the most accurate summary of the position:

> [Gide] a été l'âme du mouvement littéraire le plus important de
> l'époque, celui de la *Nouvelle Revue française*, mais même une
> personnalité aussi complexe que la sienne ne peut exprimer
> toute la complexité d'une telle entreprise. [...] Elle n'eut que deux
> directeurs— Jacques Rivière et Jean Paulhan.[32]

At the time of its foundation in 1908-1909, Gide was listed among the
members of the *comité de rédaction*, along with the other founders.[33]  Yet
Jean Schlumberger clearly saw himself as the editor responsible for the
composition of each issue (with Rivière as his secretary from 1911): 'Pendant
deux ans c'est moi qui centralisai les manuscrits, qui m'efforçai d'équilibrer
les numéros, de les faire paraître à peu près pontuellement'.[34]  Gide, although
he had been enthusiastic about their new venture, was too infrequently in
Paris to assist with the month-to-month and day-to-day running of the
review.  What is undeniable, however, is that Gide was the inspiration for
much of what came to be known as the 'spirit of the *NRF*' (*l'esprit de la NRF*),
and that he personified this spirit.  In 1921 Gide himself complained in the
pages of the *NRF* that 'plus je me retire de la *NRF*, plus on croit que c'est moi
qui la dirige', showing that he wished to disassociate himself from the
misconception, enthusiastically propagated by opponents such as Henri
Massis and Henri Béraud, that the review was solely in his charge.[35]  It *is* true
that Gide, occasionally, did consider becoming director, for example just prior
to the reappearance of the *NRF* in 1918-1919.[36]  Again, later, after Rivière's
death in 1925, Gide was considered as a candidate, but Gaston Gallimard
considered him to be unsuited to the task.[37]

---

31    G. Brée, for example, mistakenly lists Gide as *'directeur'* of the review; see vol. 16 of
        *Littérature française, le XXe siècle, 2, 1920-1970*, Arthaud, 1978, pp. 77-78, 94.
32    R. Kanters, 'Le XXe siècle – de 1914 à 1940 – la relève', in *Neuf siècles de littérature
        française*, Delagrave, 1958, pp. 731-732.
33    See A. Anglès, *André Gide et le premier groupe de la NRF, 1890-1910*, esp. pp. 118ff.
34    J. Schlumberger, *Eveils*, in *Oeuvres*, VI, Gallimard, 1960, p. 381.
35    A. Gide, *Incidences*, Gallimard, 1924, p. 52.
36    The disputes arising from this are recounted in J.-P. Cap, 'La reprise de la *NRF* en 1919 à
        travers la correspondance de Jacques Rivière et de Jean Schlumberger', *Bulletin des amis
        de Jacques Rivière et d'Alain-Fournier*, no.1, 1976, pp. 27-9.  In 1939 Schlumberger
        reminded Paulhan that the group had been 'within a hair's breadth of breaking up'
        after the end of the First World War; Schlumberger to JP, letter dated 28 November
        1939 (AP).
37    F. Grover, 'Les années 30 dans la correspondance Gide-Paulhan', *Modern Language
        Notes*, 95, 1980, pp. 830-49 (pp. 831-833).

That Gide's inspirational rôle had little bearing upon the day-to-day running of the review is underscored by the fact that, as their correspondence shows, both Rivière and Paulhan, whether as secretary or editor, looked to Jean Schlumberger and *not* to Gide as their mentor and editorial advisor, for Schlumberger had had all the experience of composing and balancing each issue. Schlumberger's rôle, so little appreciated even today, was of great importance to Paulhan, who paid him this compliment: 'vous êtes à la *NRF* comme le tao, qui inspire sans se montrer, qui ordonne sans intervenir'.[38] All this helps to explain that when Rivière died on 14 February 1925, there was some confusion over who should become *directeur*. Although Gide's name was mentioned, his appointment was out of the question; Charles du Bos too had ambitions to succeed Rivière, but this idea was forcefully quashed by Schlumberger and Gide. Rumours spread that Rivière's widow Isabelle might be interested, and the critic Benjamin Crémieux also seems to have been a candidate.[39] In the event Gallimard himself assumed the title, a shrewd move, for at once he quickly ended the speculation, avoided offending unsuitable candidates, and passed the reins of the editorship to Paulhan, as editor-in-chief. And as though to vindicate Gallimard's choice, Paulhan prepared a special number in honour of Rivière that remains a model of this genre, and provides an impressive illustration of his powers of organization.[40]

It was only in December 1934 that Gallimard talked of handing the reins to Paulhan, who wrote to explain to Jean Grenier the ambiguities of the situation:

> G.G. [i.e., Gaston Gallimard] m'a demandé de m'appeler «directeur» de la *NRF*. Il y aurait eu de l'hypocrisie à refuser (puisqu'en réalité je fais ce que fait un directeur, et que G.G. connaît surtout la revue par les plaintes de ceux de ses auteurs dont on n'a pas assez parlé). Seulement, il y a aussi de l'hypocrisie à accepter parce que je ne puis pas faire de la *NRF* ce que je voudrais.[41]

From 1 January 1935, therefore, Paulhan's name was printed in the cover as *directeur* of the *NRF*. As the 1930s progressed, circumstances became such that the review reacted more and more to political and historical events, as

---

38  JP to Schlumberger, letter dated 3 August 1937 (BD).
39  For details, see C. Martin, *La NRF de 1925 à 1934*, pp. viii-ix; J.-P. Cap (ed.), *Jacques Rivière-Jean Schlumberger, Correspondance 1909-1925*, pp. 219-239, and J. Paulhan, 'Pages de carnet', *NRF*, August 1979, p. 189.
40  'Hommage à Jacques Rivière', *NRF*, April 1925, pp. 400-832.
41  JP to Grenier, letter dated 6 December 1934 (AP).

the following chapters will show. This trend made Paulhan's task no easier, and on several occasions he was driven to tell various correspondents of his frustrations as editor. Indeed, as the risk of war grew, Paulhan felt more and more isolated: he complained to his mentor Schlumberger that 'Gide et vous êtes véritablement trop absents, ces temps-ci, de la revue.'[42]

As editor Paulhan fulfilled two mutually dependent tasks: he prepared each issue of the review, and acted as intermediary between it and his frequently temperamental contributors, attempting to protect the interests of both to the detriment of neither. As far as the contributors were concerned, Paulhan was impresario, administrator, critic, arbitrator and conciliator. He deployed his skill, tact and patience in various attempts to reconcile the review with such 'difficult' personalities as Suarès, Claudel and Léautaud, but only after expending much time and effort in manoeuvring behind the scenes. By far his most important duty, however, was to plan and compose each issue.

What helped to establish the unique status of the *NRF* was its outwardly undogmatic appearance, which was, in fact, the result of a highly self-conscious and selective approach in the composition of each issue. Whatever material it published, Paulhan insisted that the same 'literary' criteria should be applied in the process. Moreover, due to its periodicity, a further key to imposing order on what appeared to be an eclectic monthly lay in planning ahead and in having the completed number printed and distributed on time. Thus, in order to fulfil the promise of publicity material that the review appeared on the first day of each month, Paulhan followed the *tableau d'ordre*, or working schedule (established under Rivière's editorship) and applied it even more rigorously. Copy had to be received so that, in normal circumstances, the layout of the review and the first proofs could be checked in time for the final instruction to the printer—the*bon à tirer* —to be given on the 20th day of each month. The final printing and binding took place between the 25th and 28th or 29th days of each month, and then the review was distributed. Late submissions could delay the issue of the *bon à tirer*, much to Paulhan's distress; he would sometimes even be obliged to travel to the printer, Paillart, at Abbeville, to correct the final proofs. The following letter to Schlumberger reveals much about Paulhan's devoted attention to the review:

> Je ne me souviens pas que Jacques [Rivière] ait jamais accepté
> une note plus tard que le 15 [du mois]. J'ai conservé son 'tableau

---

42    JP to Schlumberger [September 1938] (BD).

> d'ordre', suivant lequel les derniers *bons à tirer* doivent être donnés le 20. Il s'en suit nécessairement que les dernières pages à composer ont été envoyées à l'imprimerie le 15 le plus tard.
> Le tableau d'ordre est suivi à présent plus strictement que jamais. Aucun numéro, depuis un an, n'a paru avec un jour de retard. Mais je n'ai pu obtenir de Paillart l'organisation, et quand il y a lieu, les coups de collier nécessaires qu'en prenant de mon côté (et en tenant) les engagements qu'aucun manuscrit nouveau ne soit envoyé apres le 15. Un retard *d'un jour* [...] m'a obligé l'annee dernière, en août, à aller passer une journée à Abbeville pour corriger les épreuves sur place. A quoi s'ajoute: 1. qu'avril n'a que 30 jours; 2. que Paillart m'a averti, il y a un mois, que tout retard de ma part entraînerait pour le numéro un retard de *quelques* jours (à cause d'une nouvelle application des lois du travail: interdiction des heures supplémentaires, etc.).[43]

Just one or two days' delay could detemine whether certain items would be included or not, for later on in the 1930s, events tended to move with a rapidity which excluded the holding over of topical material until the next issue. Most importantly, regarding the treatment of politically and historically related questions in the *NRF*, Paulhan was often forced to alter the content of any given month's issue at short notice. Thus, replying to a complaint from Grenier, who was mystified by the non-inclusion of one of his *notes*, Paulhan explained:

> Il m'est difficile d'arrêter chaque mois tout mon numéro par avance parce que la dimension des articles peut varier au dernier moment dans d'assez grandes proportions. De sorte qu'il me faut souvent retirer de la mise en pages les notes qui sont le moins 'd'actualite'.[44]

The composition, but especially the balance of each number had always been an obsessive concern at the *NRF*: Auguste Anglès has shown this for the prewar years of the review, and Paulhan, having worked so closely with Rivière, continued this tradition. Yet in questions of selection and presentation, at least during the period after taking over from the more authoritarian Rivière, Paulhan did not assume sole responsibility for editorial choice. He appeares to have favoured the more collegiate approach that had been characteristic of the first review. As early as January 1926 he outlined to Schlumberger his idea for a two-tier editorial committee:

---

43    JP to Schlumberger [April 1926] (BD).
44    JP to Grenier, letters dated 28 May and 4 September 1935 (AP).

Je songe qu'au centre de la *NRF* d'aujourd'hui il faudrait le désintéressement et l'énergie d'un comité—et tout particulièrement pour ce qui touche à la «direction» des *notes*, au choix des auteurs nouveaux. Voici mon plan: un comité d'action se réunirait tous les sept ou tous les quinze jours— il pourrait comprendre [Marcel] Arland, [Ramon] Fernandez, [Bernard] Groethuysen, [Henri] Rambaud, un surréaliste ([Roger] Vitrac?), et moi. (Eventuellement: [André] Lhote, Gabriel Marcel, [Boris] de Schloezer, et [...] Jean Prévost.) Il existerait, d'autre part, un sur-comité, ou comité d'anciens, comprenant Gide, vous, [Jean] Giraudoux, [Jules] Romains, [Albert] Thibaudet, [Benjamin] Crémieux, [Félix] Bertaux, dont les membres seraient bienvenus à nos réunions, mais ne s'attireraient aucun reproche s'ils n'y venaient pas. D'ailleurs ces réunions ne seraient pas seulement consacrées à des discussions et à des échanges d'idées autour de la *NRF*. Je voudrais aussi qu'il y eût des communications des lecteurs.[45]

However desirable they may have been, such unwieldy sessions would have resembled seminars rather than editorial meetings. Accordingly, during 1927, the committee structure was pruned down to a more manageable caucus. A wide range of topics was covered at these more successful meetings:

Nous avons décidé de nous réunir un jour chaque mois— Arland, Crémieux, Fernandez et moi—; le matin un de nous fera une communication, l'après-midi on discutera de la *NRF*. C'était hier la première réunion; tout s'est fort bien passé, et le soir nous étions ravis. Je crois que cette fois nous tenons notre comité—mais je voudrais bien que de longtemps on ne songeât à lui donner d'autres membres que Gide, Gaston [Gallimard], vous et nous quatre. Le prochaine réunion aura lieu le 5 octobre [1927]. Crémieux doit lire un essai, peut-être une pièce.[46]

Remembering his own experiences at the *NRF*, Marcel Arland also talked of this 'cabinet de direction':

J'ai très bien suivi la *NRF* depuis environ 1920, j'ai collaboré depuis 1922. Mais intimement je n'en ai fait partie que lorsque Jean Paulhan a fait son petit cabinet de direction avec Benjamin Crémieux et Jean Schlumberger. Notre ami Jean Schlumberger, Fernandez et moi nous nous réunissions, nous parlions, nous discutions et vraiment on n'y allait pas de main morte et

---

45    JP to Schlumberger [January 1926] (BD).
46    JP to Schlumberger [July 1927] (BD).

lorsqu'on faisait une lecture d'un texte personnel, les autres ne se gênaient par pour critiquer.[47]

Much of the success of Paulhan's early years at the *NRF* is attributable to this committee structure, but as the years passed, Paulhan himself gradually became more independent, if not autocratic. During 1932, when Gide's commitment to the Soviet cause increased the political preoccupations of *NRF* intellectuals, Paulhan felt impelled to wield his own authority. In the late 1930s, particularly after Munich and throughout the phoney war (the *drôle de guerre*), as we shall see Paulhan steered the *NRF* very much according to his own firm convictions, feeling confident enough to ignore some of the strongly-voiced objections of his mentor Jean Schlumberger.

In his choices as editor, Paulhan was obliged to take account of factors which were commercially, or sociologically, determined. Greater impact could be made and more new subscriptions gained at certain times of the year. The covers and publicity brochures of the *NRF* show that the review was targeted specifically at the Christmas market (i.e., the *étrennes*). Special offers of books were made as an inducement for subscription renewal and for the purchase of gift subscriptions; the same was offered for the introduction of new subscribers. Paulhan was obliged to select material with these factors in mind: 'Si j'y tiens, c'est que la première *NRF* de l'année est composée avec plus de soin, ou plus d'amour—ou bien, observée plus attentivement—que les suivantes'.[48] So it was customary for new serializations to begin in January, and often the November, December and January numbers carried more pages, making the review appear more substantial. Not only was the Christmas and New Year market an important one, extra care also went into preparing the *rentrée* issues. This explains why some serials or other important texts started in August, September or October, running through until Christmas in time for subscription renewals. With these commercial factors in mind, Paulhan's committee proceeded to select and edit their material. And, as his correspondence shows, if there was a risk of disharmony between articles, one would be postponed in favour of another.

**Serials and composition**
Serialization in review form was of course a widely accepted practice of publishing, and the *NRF* was no exception: like its rivals, its leading pages

---

47    In *Valery Larbaud et la littérature de son temps,* actes du colloque Valery Larbaud, Klincksieck, 1978, p. 76.

48    JP to Suarès, letter dated 17 December 1932, in *CJP* 4, 1987, p. 44.

carried the serials. Authors could benefit from a well timed serialization, and enjoy further sales from the release of the volume. The review certainly benefited: popular serializations could, from time to time, double the print-run of the review, as in the case of Jean Giraudoux's novel *Bella*. In fact, large increases in new subscriptions were identifiably linked to specific serials:

> *Le no Proust* nous a valu en quatre mois (Janv.-Avril 1923) *450* abonnés nouveaux
> *Bella* (Oct. 25 à Janvier 26) *460* abonnés nouveaux
> *Le Voyage au Congo* (Oct. 26 à Janvier 27) *470* [abonnés nouveaux]
> Enfin: *Le Voyage au Congo* et *Le Temps retrouvé réunis* (Févr. 27 à Mai 27) *810* [abonnés nouveaux].[49]

Moreover, publishing in the interwar period was a very competitive business: it was not uncommon for reviews to outbid or out-manoeuvre one another in order to print the latest novel by the newest celebrity. Despite this commerical competitiveness, Paulhan attempted to respect established principles. He faced occasional criticism from some readers concerning the publication in the *NRF* of novels in incomplete or fragmentary form. Conscious for a long time of the storm of protest whipped up in 1925 over the partial publication of Gide's novel *Les Faux Monnayeurs* — 'cette publication fragmentaire m'a valu un tel courrier de reproches et d'injures'[50] —, Paulhan tried to make it a matter of principle never to repeat the same mistake, because he wished to avoid accusations that the review was little more than a promotional tool of the Gallimard publishing house. He would also invoke this policy when the refusal of certain contributions would prove delicate: sometimes he had difficulty in persuading authors that he was right.

As noted by Georges Raillard, the need to cut a novel or long work into extracts of relatively similar length, without necessarily being able to follow the chapter structure, was a practical and aesthetic problem which Paulhan constantly faced, much to his delight.[51] Gide for one commented that Malraux's *La Condition humaine* was ill-suited to publication in review form, while it cohered much better as a book, and objected forcefully to the serialization of Louis Aragon's seemingly interminable work *Les Voyageurs de l'Impériale*.[52] The key to balancing the *NRF*, however, was to find the

---

49   JP to Gide, in *JPC* 1, pp. 126-127.
50   JP to Schlumberger, letter dated 11 April 1938 (BD).
51   In *Jean Paulhan le souterrain*, ed. J. Bersani, Editions "10/18", 1976, p. 112.
52   See Gide, *Journal*, I, p. 1165, entry dated 10 April 1933; C. Moatti, 'Esthétique et politique: *Les Conquérants*, 1928-1947, ou les aventures d'un texte', in *Andre Malraux 5,*

'centre of gravity' of each instalment; this became a challenging and rigorous principle for Paulhan. In the final analysis he would palliate his rejections or alterations by insisting that he was acting in the best interests of the *NRF*.

Authors too would often express their misgivings about serialized publication, but, due sometimes to pressing financial anxieties, they were forced to accept this practice. This is well illustrated in Paulhan's correspondence. For example, Roger Martin du Gard exchanged a number of letters with Paulhan over the protracted negotiations regarding his play *La Gonfle*. Despite all the problems and complaints, however, Paulhan managed to satisfy the needs of both authors and readers; the continuing success of the review was proof enough that his choices were judicious and that his skills matched the 'balancing act' of the review.

## Regular features

The continuity of any review derives from its regular features, and in the adaptation of their presentation to a variety of needs including, in particular, readers' expectations and changes in editorial policy, and important historical events. Paulhan's duty to the *NRF* was to nurture and promote interest in the highly important critical section of the review. This section, which soon had found recognition and attracted applause, even from rivals such as Romain Rolland, enjoyed a solid reputation.[53] Schlumberger confirms that 'l'important, à nos yeux, c'était nos dernières pages, celles qui contenaient notre appareil critique.'[54]

## The *chroniques* and the *chroniqueurs*

The *chroniques*, or regular feature articles, expanded under the editorship of Paulhan. Out of the entire review, this was the part which assumed the most mechanical character, providing what sometimes became a tribune for expressing and exchanging the ideas of the most regular contributors. Moreover the *chroniques* formed the group of articles that most satisfied readers' expectations: each month they could rely on reading the *chroniqueurs* whatever the rest of the review had to offer. For the contributors, the *chroniques* offered a prestigious monthly outlet for their

---

'Malraux et l'histoire', ed. Walter G. Langlois, Minard, 1982, pp. 117-57; and Grover, 'Les années 30...', pp. 844-845.

53  'Le talent, les efforts pour toucher une tradition nouvelle, et le juste équilibre qu'ils tâchent de garder contre l'excès de liberté', were admired by Rolland. Quoted by B. Duchâtelet, 'André Gide and Romain Rolland', in *Série André Gide 7*, 'Le romancier', *Revue des lettres modernes*, Minard, 1984, pp. 196-202 (p. 197).

54  *Eveils*, in *Oeuvres*, VI, Gallimard, 1960, p. 492.

essays and a (relatively) reliable source of income. The art critic, André Lhote (1885-1962) and the music critic, Boris de Schloezer (1881-1969) both provided a steady stream of articles. For the intellectual history of the period, however, the most important *chroniques* were submitted by Alain, Albert Thibaudet, Ramon Fernandez and Julien Benda. They provided the backbone of the interwar *NRF*. Moreover, most important of all, Alain's *Propos*, Thibaudet's *Réflexions* and Benda's essays accounted for the identifiably *radicalist* orientation of the *NRF*.

## Alain

Contributions from the philosophy teacher Alain (Emile-Auguste Chartier, 1868-1951) began in April 1927, although the *NRF* had been attempting to secure his regular contribution since 1920.[55] Initially Alain's presence in the review met with tacit approval; indeed, in his sixtieth year, in January 1928 *Europe* produced a glowing tribute by *NRF* regulars, underlining the fact that the renowned 'philosopher of radicalism' was at home in the *NRF*. By 1930, however, Alain's *Propos* had begun to attract some rather more uncomplimentary remarks, particularly from Roger Martin du Gard and from Jean Grenier, who noticed perceptively that the motive for Alain's presence was to attract a large number of subscriptions from teachers: 'tu as besoin [d'Alain] pour ta clientèle des Ecoles Normales et E.P.S.'[56] Alain taught a whole generation of student-teachers who, during the interwar years, either perpetuated or questioned his mode of thinking and his moralism: these students included Raymond Aron and Jean-Paul Sartre, the latter representing a good example of a 'contre-élève'.[57] During 1936, Alain's monthly *Propos* ceased, although he still continued to submit material. From 1934 Alain lent his high-profile support to the Comité de vigilance des intellectuels antifascistes (CVIA) and wrote for the pacifist periodical *Vigilance*.[58]

---

[55]  On Alain, see A. Sernin, *Alain: un sage dans la cité*, Robert Laffont, 1985, and J.-F. Sirinelli, *Génération intellectuelle. Khâgneux et Normaliens dans l'entre-deux-guerres*, Fayard, 1988. The essays in the 'Hommage à Alain', *NRF*, September 1952, remain informative.

[56]  Grenier to JP, letter dated 4 October 1935 (AP).

[57]  The expression is Pierre Bost's; see 'Hommage à Alain', pp. 37-44.

[58]  N. Racine-Furlaud, 'Le Comité de vigilance des intellectuels antifascistes (1934-1939), antifascisme et pacifisme', *Mouvement social*, no. 101, 1977, pp. 87-113.

## Albert Thibaudet

A professor at the University of Geneva from 1924, Albert Thibaudet (1874-1936) was just as widely admired by teachers and students as Alain. He had begun to submit his contributions to the NRF as early as 1912.[59] Thibaudet's greatest influence was over the postwar generation of literary critics, including the NRF's own Ramon Fernandez. His lengthy studies of Bergsonism, Barrès and Maurras won him widespread respect in the early 1920s, and, as noted by the Swiss critic Léon Bopp, his style suited the NRF very well: '[Thibaudet a une] affection pour les contraires, [une] disponibilité aux divergences (qui fut l'une des marques d'un certain style NRF...)'.[60] The title of his rubric, Réflexions sur la littérature, was significantly shortened to Réflexions in early 1928, a change which, as we shall see, indicated an important shift of emphasis. This partial deflection away from literary matters did not please everyone at the review, notably Jean Prévost and André Gide[61]; however, Paulhan admired him deeply and praised several of the 'non-literary' essays, including the October 1930 'Appel au concile'. After Thibaudet's death in 1936 Paulhan was appointed his literary executor and prepared a homage in his honour.[62] At the NRF, such a prolific and assidious presence meant that it was difficult to replace him, although Paul Nizan and Jean Schlumberger were considered; in the event Marcel Arland broadened his own chronique into Essais critiques from 1937 onwards. Despite this, Thibaudet was profoundly missed at the heart of the NRF.

## Ramon Fernandez

Ramon Fernandez (1894-1944), introduced by Rivière in 1923[63], was a more controversial personality. Fernandez, the archetypal 'philosophical' critic whose profession of faith was ideally suited to that of the NRF,[64] had his first essay-length book review appear in October 1926. He took over the more regular Essais rubric, and by November 1933 he had submitted some thirty

---

59    J. C. Davies, 'Bibliographie des articles d'Albert Thibaudet', Revue des sciences humaines, April-June 1957, pp. 197-229, and L. Morino, La NRF dans l'histoire des lettres, 1908-1939, Gallimard, 1939, pp. 157-162.

60    'Hommage à Albert Thibaudet', NRF, July 1936, p. 15.

61    For instance, see Jean Prévost: 'J'aimerais bien parler de Clemenceau, dont Thibaudet n'a dir que des sottises, mais jugez vous-même (je regrette le bon temps où les Réflexions sur la littérature se spécialisaient dans la cuisine et Ubu-roi'; Prévost to JP [1930], (AP).

62    'Hommage à Albert Thibaudet', NRF, July 1936, pp. 5-176.

63    See W. Kidd, 'Un dialogue interrompu: Jacques Rivière et Ramon Fernandez', Bulletin des amis de Jacques Rivière et d'Alain-Fournier, no. 14, 1979, pp. 9-51.

64    'C'est dans les lettres qu'il faut chercher nos métaphysiques, et non pas dans la philosophie, qui se trouve, en France, un peu paralysée par la surveillance jalouse des savants'; in M. Rouzaud, Où va la critique?, Editions Saint-Michel, 1929, pp. 188-189.

essays, a tally which showed that Paulhan was responsive to Fernandez' self-confidence as a critic.[65] By 1931 he had established a solid reputation, gaining support in particular from Martin du Gard. During the 1930s Fernandez became increasingly tempted by political commitment, moving from 'apolitical' liberalism to support for and then involvement in the anti-fascist organisation Association des écrivains et artistes révolutionnaires (AEAR) after the shock of 6 February 1934; he even encouraged Gide during the crucial phase of his support for the Soviet cause. Shortly afterwards, however, having witnessed a bitter exchange between Louis Aragon and his friend Pierre Drieu La Rochelle, Fernandez veered across to the extreme Right. By 1938 he was writing regularly for Jacques Doriot's newspaper *Emancipation nationale*, where he freely attacked some of his former *NRF* colleagues. Later, during the Occupation, he regularly submitted material to the *NRF* (once it had been relaunched by Drieu La Rochelle), and continued his work for Doriot's Parti Populaire Français as an organizer for intellectual affairs.[66] However, during his most active period at the *NRF*, Fernandez was undoubtedly a great asset, since his intellectual rigour and powerful, clear argumentation found favour among many, both inside and outside the review.

### Julien Benda

The *chroniqueur* of the greatest importance for the *NRF* as a focus of intellectual debate was Julien Benda (1867-1956).[67] An early Dreyfusard, contributor to *La Revue blanche* and to Charles Péguy's *Cahiers de la quinzaine*, Benda was one of the most unswerving defenders of republican idealism. His presence unquestionably enriched the radicalist flavour of the *NRF*, particularly following the publication of his seminal essay *La Trahison des clercs* which, as part of a project to consolidate the success of the *NRF*, was serialised in late 1927. Ironically, as we shall examine in further detail below, the widespread repercussions of debates on intellectuals' responsibilities directly paved the way for the gradual, or partial, politicization of the *NRF* after 1932.

---

65    'Je puis, comme tous les auteurs, souhaiter voir mes écrits paraître, mais les sentiments que je nourris pour la Revue et pour son directeur sont beaucoup plus importants que mon impatience professionnelle. J'espère seulement qu'il sera possible d'assurer aux '*Essais*' une périodicité plus courte, mais seulement quand le mécanisme de la revue la permettra'; Fernandez to JP, letter dated 5 August 1928 (AP).

66    E.g. *Cahiers de l'Emancipation nationale*, Nov.-Dec. 1942, and Jan.-Feb. 1943.

67    See R. J. Niess, *Julien Benda*, Michigan: Ann Arbor, 1956, and L.-A. Revah, *Julien Benda*, Plon, 1991.

Benda was a prolific writer; he benefited from a regular *chronique* entitled *Scholies,* and contributed scores of book reviews and essays, in addition to the serialization of eight of his books. All this intense activity was the fulfilment of an ambition, for, in 1927, he confided to Louis Guilloux, then working at the publishing house, that 'Je voudrais bien devenir une éminence grise de la *NRF*'[68], an ambition which exerted a profound influence on a younger generation of intellectuals: 'Dans ces années proches encore de *La Trahison des clercs* [Benda] faisait figure d'éminence grise, presque du rédacteur en chef de la revue'.[69] This high profile could not have been sustained without considerable support, and Benda himself admitted that this came almost exclusively from Paulhan, whose admiration is well defined in a remark made in the company of Francis Ponge:

> Un jour, s'adressant à Julien Benda, Paulhan a déclaré: «il est un intellectualisme qui s'en tient à l'observation patiente et à l'expérience méthodique, tente de dégager quelques lois, évite les partis-pris, si séduisants soient-ils, et se garde le plus longtemps possible de conclure». Je voudrais que ce fût le mien.[70]

Benda reciprocated Paulhan's admiration and confirmed in his memoirs that his support was maintained in the face of much opposition from both within and outside the review:

> J'étais soutenu par le directeur, Jean Paulhan, qui publiait tous les écrits que je lui portais, évidemment parce qu'il savait ne nullement mener par là sa monture aux abîmes, et aussi, ai-je quelque raison de croire, par un goût qu'il avait pour eux, goût qui me touche d'autant plus que j'ai pu constater depuis, par les siens, qu'en de nombreux points il partageait l'esprit du lieu.[71]

Some within the *NRF* disliked Benda's constant presence, considering him to be a philosophical vulgarizer, if not a 'charlatan'. Most of the tensions caused by Benda's supposed preponderance at the *NRF* surfaced during the year following the Munich crisis in 1938, when his uncompromising anti-Germanism intensified: as a keen opponent of appeasement policy (as exemplified by the Munich accords), he was regarded as a warmonger and, being of Jewish extraction, he attracted a great deal of (sometimes vicious) anti-Semitic comment. By 1939 pressure was being exerted by some within

68   L. Guilloux, *Carnets 1921-1944,* Gallimard, 1978, p. 49.
69   A. Wurmser, *Conseils de révision,* Gallimard, 1972, p. 307. See also R. Etiemble, *Mes contrepoisons,* Gallimard, 1974, pp. 219-252.
70   Quoted in *Cahiers des saisons,* no. 10, April-May 1957, p. 274.
71   J. Benda, *Exercice d'un enterré vif,* Gallimard, 1968, p. 314. (Orig. ed. 1947.)

the review (especially Jean Schlumberger) to reduce his place in the *NRF*, but Benda defended himself vigorously:

> Voir moins fréquemment mon nom dans la *NRF* , être absent des *Airs du mois* sont des choses que j'accepte sans aucune peine. [...] J'aimerais que S[chlumberger] sût que je ne me suis jamais 'donné des gants' (n'ayant, d'ailleurs, aucun droit) 'd'être directeur de la revue'. Que de fois, sollicité par un jeune homme de faire passer un article dans la maison, j'ai répondu que je n'y avais aucun pouvoir, y étais un simple collaborateur. [...] Il est clair que si la direction veut ma peau, non pas seulement en raison de mon attitude dans la *NRF*, mais ailleurs, et en raison de la tendance politique générale, ma cause, notre cause, —puisque vous voulez bien me défendre—, *devient singulièrement menacée.*[72]

For all this, Benda was a valued regular contributor who, again, found favour among the review's radicalist teacher readership: it is certain that the *NRF* would have been very different without him.

### Andre Suarès

After repeated attempts, Paulhan finally managed to bring Andre Suarès back to the *NRF* in 1939 in order to resume his *Chroniques de Caërdal*. His distinctive polemical tone suited the review in January 1939: indeed, his texts led to problems with the censorship. If Suarès was widely regarded as eccentric, he was valued by Paulhan, for it was also recognised that Suarès detested the tendency for intellectuals to divide into factions with identifiable political allegiances; however, his abhorrence of Nazi racism ultimately outweighed his distate for Soviet totalitarianism, since he was of Jewish origin.

### The structure of the *NRF*

These *chroniques* were designed to satisfy readers' monthly expectations. Further components of the critical section which Paulhan organized to great effect were the book reviews—the *notes* or *notules*—and the important *Revue des revues*. His apprenticeship under Rivière had provided much experience in compiling and balancing the *notes*, some of which became longer review articles. Paulhan's correspondence abounds in instances of his commissioning *notes* from a wide range of contributors. Moreover, regarding the *notes* section, Paulhan relied on comments from critics such as

---

[72]    Benda to JP, letter dated 25 April 1939 (AP). Benda's italics.

Jean Grenier: timely warnings, such as the following from Martin du Gard, could alert him to the greatest danger, that of slipping into fatuity or banality:

> [...] Puis-je vous dire que, si le corps de la revue se maintient très riche, la partie *'notes'*, *'critique de livres'* et surtout de *romans* [...] s'affaiblit, me semble-t-il, de numéro en numéro. Et c'est fâcheux. La *NRF* renoncerait là, selon moi, à l'une de ses plus importantes missions, et à l'une de ses plus estimables traditions! Je ne crois pas être seul à l'avoir remarqué.[73]

Paulhan reinstituted the *notules*, a compendium of very short reviews, to deal with the less important part of an ever-increasing book production: this he conferred upon René Lalou in November 1925, who reviewed 176 titles in this manner until March 1927. To Lalou's distress, Paulhan decided to transform this rubric into the broader *Revue des livres* section in February 1928 because he wished to bring in more *NRF* regulars: a note in the issue for September 1929 explained this change to readers.[74] Paulhan himself delighted in these *exercices de style*, but Martin du Gard disliked them. They were, however, indispensable, and later, under his pseudonym Jean Guérin, they were incorporated into the *Bulletin* rubric.

The *Revue des revues* was another essential section which conformed to the accepted and widely used practice of reprinting and commenting on extracts from significant articles in competing or opposing reviews. Thus *NRF* authors appearing elsewhere could be quoted, as well as material from reviews which Paulhan supported or wished to promote, particularly those close to the *NRF*, like *Commerce*, *Mesures*, *Bifur*, *Le Grand Jeu* or *Le Minotaure*. Also, mention could be made of writers who otherwise would never (or very rarely) appear in the *NRF*, such as Henri Massis or Charles Maurras. Extracts from periodicals such as *Action française* or *Candide* could be inserted as documentation to supplement debates engaged in the *NRF*, like the one following the publication of *La Trahison des clercs*, or the debate surrounding Gide's declarations of support for the Soviet Union. Paulhan, for whom this rubric was a particular pleasure, provided most of the material and again, later, incorporated the section into the *Bulletin*.

These rubrics provided the basic structure or framework for organizing the monthly contributions to the review: regardless of their presentation,

---

73  Martin du Gard to JP, letter dated 29 April 1930 (AP).
74  'Une revue ne peut s'étendre hors de son programme, ni commenter ce qui est clair, ni discuter ce qu'elle approuve, ni répéter (même à propos d'un bon livre) ce qu'elle a dit ailleurs. Pour ne pas omettre ainsi des oevres excellentes ou importantes, nous proposons certains jugements sous la forme la plus resserrée'; *NRF*, September 1929, p. 431.

they were a constant feature. Given the nature of historical developments during the 1930s, however, from time to time the review needed to be rethought or refreshed.

### Consolidation, change and expansion

Barely two years after his appointment as editor, during 1927 Martin du Gard (and Gide) praised Paulhan for the positive impetus he had given the review:

> Je soupçonne ce qu'est votre double vie de travail, la fièvreuse besogne qui fait que la NRF ne cesse de croître entre vos mains. [...] J'éprouve un sentiment de réconfort à voir peu à peu la consécration de ce long effort silencieux ou presque, qui vous vaut, depuis longtemps, l'estime des meilleurs.[75]

In March 1927 a letter to subscribers was inserted in the leading publicity brochure. It confidently announced that the NRF had enjoyed a 'succès rapide, inattendu, qui a fait en trieze années de la NRF la première revue litteraire en France'. Promises were made to expand the critical section and in August the pagination duly increased from 128 to 144 pages: Paulhan's plans for the renewal of the review could be implemented. Alain's *Propos* began in April 1927, 'Jean Guérin' began the expanded *Revue des revues* section in July, and the critical pages were augmented and consolidated after August. Gallimard's choice had been vindicated: under Paulhan, advised as he was by Gide, Martin du Gard, Schlumberger and Grenier, the NRF had entered its most successful phase. The figures given above for increases in subscription levels provide a convincing measure of Paulhan's success.

The consolidation and expansion of the NRF in 1927 represent a turning point in its fortunes which coincided with the extension of Gaston Gallimard's publishing empire: by 1928, Gallimard had added the high circulation periodical *Détective* and the quality review *Du Cinema* to his domains under the umbrella company ZED publications.[76] In 1932 Gallimard entered the market of high circulation political weeklies with *Marianne*, edited by Emmanuel Berl. '*Marianne* est de gauche—comme fut l'Encyclopédie', boasted a publicity brochure in the NRF. Politically, Berl's proximity to the Radical Party leader Edouard Herriot and the *quai d'Orsay*

---

[75] Martin du Gard to JP, letter dated 31 March 1927 (AP).
[76] On *Détective*, see P. Assouline, *Gaston Gallimard*, pp. 207-214. Brice Parain was the *gérant* of this money-spinning weekly which quickly built up a circulation of 350,000. *Du Cinéma*, founded by Corti in December 1928, was transformed into the *Revue du cinéma* in October 1929, with the Gallimard imprint appearing in May that year. See especially 'Sous la bannière de la *NRF*', in *Revue du cinéma*, [reprint in 5 vols] published by Pierre Lherminier éditeur, 1979, pp. xxiii-xxxii.

placed *Marianne* close to governing circles; although sympathetic to the *Front populaire*, it was never fanatical. It faced competition from *Vendredi* in 1935, and after suffering falls in circulation in 1937, Gallimard sold it to radical politician Raymond Patenôtre. Yet the founding of *Marianne*, the commercialization of Gallimard's, and political pressures all caused tensions between Paulhan and the publisher:

> Je serais gêné d'avoir à demander [...] quelque chose à Gaston. Il a changé avec moi, deuis quelques années, et même il ne cesse pas de changer. Comme les reproches qu'il me fait ouvertement sont absurdes, et qu'il n'y pqut pas trop croire lui-même: par exemple, que la revue ne parle pas assez souvent ni avec assez d'éloges de Maurois ou de Morand, ou bien que «la NRF n'a pas assez de retentissement», qu'«il n'y a pas assez de collaborateurs "jeunes"», que «*Marianne* est mille fois plus vivante», etc. Je pense que simplement il n'a plus de sympathie pour moi, comme d'ailleurs il s'efforce à demeurer "gentil" dans nos relations, je ne parviendrais pas à lui demander quoi que ce soit.[77]

Indeed, as we shall see, towards the mid- to late-1930s, in particular just prior to the Popular Front victory of June 1936, internal pressures to politicize the NRF itself built up. Paulhan confided that 'ils ne peuvent pas souffrir, dans la *NRF*, qu'elle soit si peu politique... je me sens assez seul, dans cette maison'.[78] Accompanying these pressures were suggestions that Gallimard should either take over the rival *Europe* or set up a new political review under Jean Guéhenno, removed recently from it; in the event, neither of these moves was made.[79]

In 1938 the Librairie Gallimard took over the fortnightly review *Les Nouveaux Cahiers*—Paulhan himself contributed articles to the *Analyse des mots* section.[80] A further development came in 1938, when Gallimard expanded into the burgeoning medium of radio by arranging for major NRF authors to give talks on their work. Although presentations by Paulhan, Gide, Suarès and Claudel were either scheduled or envisaged, the *Quart*

---

77  JP to Jouhandeau [1932-3] (BD).
78  JP to Jouhandeau [March 1936] (BD).
79  'Je crois que Gallimard va reprendre *Europe* (ou plutôt donne à Guéhenno la direction d'une nouvelle revue)'; JP to Grenier, letter dated 10 February 1936 (AP).
80  Founded by a group of 'technocrats' of various political affiliations, inspired by Péguy's *Cahiers de la quinzaine*, and edited by Paulhan's friend Guillaume de Tarde, the intention of *Les Nouveaux Cahiers* was to 'libérer la pensée de l'asservissement auquel la soumettent les intérêt particuliers, l'esprit de parti et l'esprit de classe'. See G. de Tarde, 'Sur les *Nouvelles Cahiers*', *Les Nouveaux Cahiers*, no. 20, 1 March 1938, pp. 13-18.

34

*d'heure de la NRF*, broadcast by *Radio-37*, was doomed to failure when a talk on Claudel's poetry overran by two minutes and was cut off by a concert. Early in 1939, the experiment came to an end by mutual consent.[81]

### Editorial policy and political questions

Such commercialism helped to consolidate the review's success. There was no guarantee, however, that the review could adhere to the same formula and succeed indefinitely; from time to time certain risks had to be taken to infuse new strength which influenced two important areas, content (and editorial policy) and the format of the review itself. Two of the most persistent critics from within were Gide and Martin du Gard. Partly due to Martin du Gard's interests in Franco-German relations, and to Gide's support for the Soviet cause, the year 1932 saw pressures being brought to bear, pressures which eventually would lead to the instigation of new priorities in policy, as well as to changes in the aspect of the *NRF* itself. At this time Gide was very distracted from 'literary' concerns: he confessed to Louis Martin-Chauffier that 'je pense tout le temps que des événements si importants se préparent qu'on a presque honte de s'occuper de la littérature'.[82] One direct result of these preoccupations was that Gide decided to publish extracts from his *Journal* in the *NRF*. He told Paulhan that this publication was of great importance; plans were even discussed for a new rubric called *Discussions et controverses*, and later, although this idea was not adopted more permanently, in January 1933 a selection of documents on Russian youth appeared.[83] When Gide's pro-Soviet statements appeared in June and July, the reaction, not surprisingly, was widespread and sometimes polemical. Among others François Mauriac went on to the offensive, and Gide agreed that Paulhan should insert extracts from Mauriac's article ('Les esthètes fascinés', *L'Echo de Paris*) in the *Revue des revues*. Gide's remarks to his editor are valuable because they show that he was fully conscious of the risks he was taking in publishing such potentially explosive material in a literary review like the *NRF*; he considered *balance* to be the paramount consideration:

---

[81] The memoirs of Fernand Pouey, an administrator of *Radio-37*, show that this venture was not the success implied by Pierre Assouline (who does not refer to Pouey): 'ce fut la catastrophe. [...] Ces meurtrissures ne m'eussent guère affecté si le coup du crochet dont avait souffert [Claudel] n'avait blessé, par ricochet, Jean Paulhan. Nous la supprimâmes d'un commun accord'; F. Pouey, *Un Ingénu à la radio*, Domat, 1949, p. 167.

[82] M. Van Rhysselberghe, 'Les Cahiers de la Petite Dame', 2, 1929-1937, in *Cahiers André Gide* 5, 1973, p. 146 (28 May 1931), and p. 165 (14 October 1931). Referred to as *CAG* 5.

[83] 'La jeunesse russe', *NRF*, January 1933; see below, chapter 5.

> Il importe que la *NRF* se maintienne le plus possible non-tendancieuse et arbitrale. Je ne me fais point d'illusion sur le péril que mes pages du *Journal* lui font courir. Il importe aussi que vous la préserviez de tomber tout dans un sens, de verser de côté. Roger Martin du Gard me communique à ce sujet vos réflexions, qui sont parfaites. Vous me connaissez assez pour bien penser que tout cela se livre de terribles débats et combats dans ma cervelle, où j'ai souvent grand mal d'y voir clair.[84]

Gide appeared to be genuinely troubled by the impact of his political stance on the *NRF*, especially since it began to receive a number of cancelled subscriptions. This concern was translated by the fact that he was very keen to maintain the demarcation between his own *engagement*, and the *raison d'être* of the review: in spite of his political declarations, he insisted that the *NRF* should remain independent. Yet if this subtle distinction was made clear to Paulhan and others within the *NRF* circle, outside it was an entirely different matter. Indeed both Schlumberger and Martin du Gard expressed increasingly forceful reservations about the public effect of Gide's political stance, and how it was steering the *NRF* into danger. This question is crucial in any explanation of the policy underlying the success of the *NRF*, and it remained central in editorial policy at any period in the history of the review in the interwar years.

Here we should consider Paulhan's own political position. If Jacques Debû-Bridel, remembering his friend during the 1960s, is right to assert that 'Jean Paulhan échappe au clivage classique mais facile de notre terminologie politique: il ne s'est laissé accaparer par aucun clan',[85] for others, such as Paul Léautaud or Jean-Paul Sartre, writing during the 1930s, he was a man of the Left, even a socialist, or at least a sympathizer with (if not a supporter of) the Popular Front. Others still have since called him a 'man of the Right.'[86] With the benefit of hindsight, Paulhan's politics in the 1930s were clearly quite different from what they became in the years after the Liberation, when the purges of compromised writers, some of whom were his close friends, and communist dominance over the literary scene, determined his choice to move further over to the political Right. The perception of Paulhan as a socialist probably derived from his selection as municipal councillor in the

---

84    Gide to JP, letter dated 21 July 1932 (AP).
85    'Jean Paulhan, citoyen', in Paulhan, *Oeuvres*, V, pp. 483-492 (p. 492).
86    For Léautaud's judgement see his *Journal*, XII, p. 212, and for Sartre's, see *Lettres au Castor*, I, p. 201. The right-wing judgement is Jean Louis Ferrier's, *L'Express*, 7 June 1970. Pierre Boutang rightly detects Maurrassian influences in Paulhan, 'comme l'union d'une sorte d'anarchisme et d'un monarchisme nullement dissimilé chez [lui]'; in *Maurras– la destinée et l'oeuvre*, Plon, 1984 (p. 663).

Paris suburb of Châtenay-Malabry in May 1935, on Jean Longuet's list of socialist candidates: 'Imaginez que je suis candidat au conseil municipal, Longuet m'ayant porté sur la liste', he wrote to Martin du Gard. He added, modestly, that 'la confiance des gens dépasse les bornes raisonnables'.[87] Privately, and with a typical dose of irony, Paulhan was willing to admit to Martin du Gard that 'je n'aime ni les révolutions, ni les révolutionnaires et je me sens tout près, pour bien marquer la confiance que je porte à la société actuelle [...] d'adhérer au parti SFIO ou communiste'.[88]

What is clear is that as editor of the NRF Paulhan's authority grew after 1935: he followed his own course, and his political writings in 1939-1940 bore his own name, emphasizing that the views he expressed were his own and not necessarily the review's. As far as the NRF was concerned, Paulhan saw its politics as kaleidoscopic in nature. In harmony with its image as a *revue radicalisante*, he liked to quote Alain's opinion of the NRF:

> Alain [disait] que c'était une revue «toujours modérée et toujours hardie». Eh bien, peut-être tenons-nous maintenant la raison de cette modération et de cette hardiesse: c'est que la NRF ressemble à toutes les revues et à tous les livres, et à tous les hommes.[89]

'Moderation' and 'boldness' were the same contradictory qualities exalted in Alain's exposition of radical 'doctrine', *Le Citoyen contre les pouvoirs*; they were also fundamental to the nature and policy of Paulhan's NRF. A close reading of the NRF shows that these comments were in fact originally made by Paulhan (using his own name, *not* his pseudonym Jean Guérin) in July 1938. Referring to a critique by Robert Brasillach of a volume by Thibaudet, and having indicated the inaccuracies of the account, Paulhan conceded that Brasillach had a point when he stated that Thibaudet had been well suited to the review, for 'on reconnaît bien là *l'esprit scolaire et anarchique* à la fois de la NRF.'[90] Paulhan concluded:

---

87    JP to Martin du Gard, Fonds RMG, vol. 118, letter dated 7 May 1935. On his election Paulhan told Jouhandeau that 'je me trouvais sur beaucoup de listes «modérées», ajouté à la place d'un nom que l'on avait rayé. Si ni les uns ni les autres ne me connaissent, c'est peut-être le nom qui plaît ou déplait. [...] Je m'intéresse mieux à Châtenay, et il vient aux réunions de vieux hommes de métier, compagnons de Tour de France et socialistes depuis Proudhon que j'aime bien'; letter dated 20 May 1935 (BD).
      Longuet, grandson of Karl Marx, was a SFIO *minoritaire* socialist; see J. Lacouture, *Léon Blum*, Seuil, 1977, p. 136, and NRF, *Bulletin*, October 1938, p. 701, on Longuet's death.
88    Fonds RMG, vol. 118, letter dated 7 May 1935.
89    'La méthode critique de la NRF', in NRF, May 1969, p. 987.
90    NRF, July 1938, pp. 154-5, *Les Revues* (my emphasis). Brasillach's article appeared in the *Revue universelle*, 15 June 1938.

Il faut avouer que [Brasillach] a gardé un sens admirable de la formule, et du raccourci. Anarchique et scolaire, pouvait-on mieux dire? *C'est à la fois l'extrême indépendance, l'extrême discipline; la hardiesse, mais la modération; la liberté, mais l'obéissance.* Si la *NRF* n'est pas encore digne d'un tel éloge, elle s'efforcera de le mériter.[91]

At around the same time, Paulhan explained over the airwaves that such liberal even-handedness was the principal ingredient in the editorial policy of his review, and that it extended into the political domain:

La *NRF*, c'est une revue littéraire [...]. Il lui arrive de parler politique, mais c'est, en général, en des sens contradictoires. Et le lecteur qui la suivrait fidèlement devrait se résigner à être réactionnaire un mois, et révolutionnaire le mois suivant; fasciste en janvier et antifasciste en mars.[92]

The editorial policy of the *NRF* was self-conscious and self-regenerating to the extent that the review's *status quo*, or to use Paulhan's word, *orthodoxie*, was constantly tested by newer, 'non-conformist', elements or forces to which it gave birth and nurtured. In a sense this 'policy' was an extension of the care applied to balancing the review, whether in the presentation of the first section, or in counter-balancing different political views. Here Paulhan attempted to place the *NRF* at the centre of an oscillation between what he called the 'saugrenu' — in other words, texts (not necessarily literary) which challenged the *status quo* — and the 'orthodoxe'. This may be illustrated by an example from 1935. Jean Grenier reported to Paulhan that a text by Raymond Roussel, and a piece by Michel Leiris accompanying it, had 'épaté tous les bourgeois qui lisent la *NRF*.'[93] He perhaps did not know that he was referring to an issue which would preoccupy the new director of the *NRF* for some time to come in a defence of his policy aimed primarily at Jean Schlumberger. In two long letters of July 1935, Paulhan vigorously defended his approach. His initial remarks were predominantly literary in scope and content, and were directed towards criticisms of the *NRF* which, he reminded Schlumberger, were by no means new:

---

91     Ibid.
92     'Présentation de la *NRF* à *Radio-37*', *Oeuvres*, IV, p. 364.
93     Grenier to JP, letter dated 9 April 1935 (AP). The texts referred to are Michel Leiris' 'Raymond Roussel', and the latter's 'Comment j'ai écrit mes livres', in *NRF*, April 1935, pp. 575-595.

[...] Bien entendu, il y a des lecteurs qui trouvent dans la *NRF* un peu trop de saugrenu. Mais enfin est-ce qu'il n'y en a pas eu de tout temps? Et est-ce que de tout temps ce n'est pas eux qui ont eu tort? C'étaient ceux qui se désabonnaient en 1911 pour Léger [i.e., the poet Saint-Jean-Perse], en 1912 pour Fargue, en 1921 pour Breton. Mais Léger, Fargue et Breton ont tenu le coup, tandis que l'on oubliait pas mal de gens raisonnables: de 1911, Ducôte, de 1912, Llona ou Ruyters; de 1921, Gil Robin ou Nicole Stiebel. Après tout il y a eu dès l'origine une orthodoxie de la *NRF* qui n'allait pas sans une pointe de saugrenu (songez que le saugrenu a été longtemps ce que l'opinion publique reprochait à Claudel'.[94]

Most importantly his defence is applicable to the motivating principle underlying a broader conception of the *NRF*, a conception that also embraces the political domain:

Cette orthodoxie, songez aux dangers contre lesquels il a fallu la défendre: après tout, la *NRF* a infiniment risqué de devenir trop moralisante à la suite de Pontigny, trop communisante à la suite de Gide, trop métaphysicienne à la suite de Benda; elle aurait pu glisser avec Maurois et Morand vers un conformisme assez plat; avec Kessel vers un romanesque assez vulgaire et tapageur. Et je ne dis pas qu'elle soit parfaite: du moins a-t-elle conservé, à la faveur justement du saugrenu et de l'experience littéraire, une ouverture vers les jeunes gens et cette sorte de faculté de renouvellement continu qui fait que lorsqu'il se fonde, aujourd'hui encore, un pamphlet ou un journal des jeunes—*La Bête Noire* ou *Le Minotaure*— c'est à des collaborateurs de la *NRF* que l'on fait appel. Lisez les derniers numéros de ces deux revues (*Le Minotaure*, notamment, admirable). J'ai fait le compte: plus de la moitié du texte y est donné par des écrivains de la *NRF*. C'est la preuve, il me semble, que l'orthodoxie—que vous aviez du premier coup formée—n'a pas cessé de demeurer valable. Avouez qu'elle implique aussi nécessairement aujourd'hui Roussel (étant donné surtout l'admiration que Gide éprouve pour son oeuvre) et Audiberti, qu'en 1912 Léger et Fargue.[95]

One of the keys to understanding the success of Paulhan's *NRF* is contained in the following sentence: 'Du moins a-t-elle conservé [...] une ouverture vers les jeunes gens et cette sorte de faculté de renouvellement continu'. The 'pointe de saugrenu', or deliberate, self-conscious element of

---

[94] JP to Schlumberger, letter dated 1 July 1935 (BD). See also Paulhan's defence against criticism of the 'vieillissement de la *NRF*' in *CJP* 1, pp. 157, 159.

[95] JP to Schlumberger, letter dated 1 July 1935 (BD).

non-conformism which was implanted into the longstanding 'orthodoxy' of the *NRF*, held the fertile kernel of renewal or rejuvenation. Unlike other more unadventurous reviews, the *NRF* was not afraid to offer material which displeased its readers, or, in Grenier's words, material which could 'épater le bourgeois'. His reply illustrates how difficult it had become for Schlumberger to reconcile his own conception of the *NRF* with Paulhan's, even though he admired the new director's 'balancing act'. In other words, and in generational terms, their differences amounted to a sort of *querelle des anciens et des modernes* in which the conservative Schlumberger preferred the classicist's conception of the *NRF*, whereas Paulhan conceived of the review in terms of invention and rejuvenation:

> Bien sûr, mon cher Jean, vous avez raison, et tout vaut mieux que de tomber dans une morne sagesse. Il eût été bien difficile de concevoir une influence de Gide sans un considérable apport de singularités et de cocasseries. Mon infirmité de ce côté-là peut m'entraîner à des moments d'humeur, une méconnaissance de ce qui fait la force de la *NRF*. Son prestige dans le monde tient à ce qu'elle représente, mieux qu'aucune autre publication, les intérêts de la technique littéraire, et nous ne pouvons faire que la technique de l'après-guerre n'ait poussé ses points vers le saugrenu. J'y vois un symptôme de sénilité nationale plus que de vitalité; et l'on pourrait soutenir que sans la *NRF*, sans la bénédiction qui lui ont donné Valéry et Gide, le mouvement surréaliste aurait avorté; mais vous me répondriez que c'eût été grand dommage.
>      Et vous auriez sans doute raison, car on ne doit pas combattre ces sortes de folies en les étouffant, mais en leur opposant une production plus solide. S'il m'arrive de pester, soyez sûr, cher Jean, q'il m'arrive bien plus souvent d'admirer le tact avec lequel vous parvenez à maintenir un difficile équilibre. Rivière avait tendance à faire de la revue l'expression de ses préoccupations personnelles, qui étaient unilatérales et évoluaient rapidement. Votre angle de vision est autrement large. Si j'étais directeur, je ne saurais pas faire place à toute une ménagerie curieuse...[96]

In short, within the range of literary periodicals the *NRF* could bend both ways, whereas a review like the *Revue des Deux Mondes*, for instance, was produced by Academicians for a conservative audience which expected it to publish 'conservative' texts. It would never seriously have contemplated publishing texts which might have threatened established, even

---

[96]    Schlumberger to JP, letter dated 13 July 1935 (AP). Cf. also the two epigraphs to this chapter.

institutionalized, norms of literary or intellectual acceptability. Of course the obverse of the same coin is important because readership expectations and tolerance had to be considered: the *NRF*'s own 'orthodoxy' was strong enough to enable it to publish Artaud, Roussel and Audiberti (or even Léautaud from the older generation) with negligible risk to its survival. If some subscriptions were lost, then others might be gained from different quarters.

This explains why Paulhan nurtured his connections with *avant-garde* reviews, some of which were certainly ephemeral, but, as he rightly pointed out, they were often founded by former or future contributors to the *NRF*. Paulhan's astuteness as editor and literary impresario resided, in large part, in exploiting his networks and contacts, from the Académie Française (through Daniel Halévy as intermediary) to the surrealists and communists (through either André Rolland de Renéville or Aragon), with the radical-socialist (*radicalisant*) sector of the teaching profession occupying the middle ground. This policy enabled the *NRF* to include enough non-controversial material to appeal to its liberal audience, but it did not exclude texts which might only have a limited appeal. Paulhan knew that some would cause a stir and would take some time to be recuperated into the broader spectrum of literary taste, for, after all, as noted by commentators since, publication in the *NRF* conferred a sort of literary apotheosis.

The controversy on the motivating principles of the *NRF* wore on: in April 1937, Gide and Schlumberger were still discussing Paulhan's predilection for the 'genre du saugrenu', as Gide put it, a 'genre' which Gide himself claimed to have revived.[97] As for Paulhan himself, he continued to defend his conception of the *NRF* in various texts[98], even until eight years before his death, when, in a letter to Bernard Garniez, he talked again of the review's peculiar 'orthodoxy':

> Si je tentais de résumer la conduite de la *NRF* entre '20 et '40, voici à peu près ce que je dirais: c'est qu'elle s'est consacrée [...] à la défense et à l'illustration de la littérature: bref, à une certaine *orthodoxie* littéraire. Il est toujours facile d'être un moderniste, il est facile d'être un snob, il est facile d'être un fou. Il n'y a rien de plus facile que d'être un dada ou un surréaliste. Il est toujours facile de tomber. Mais la *NRF*, tout en se gardant d'accueillir de

---

[97] 'Ils parlent de Paulhan, de son goût exagéré parce que quasi exclusif pour le saugrenu, genre [sic] particulièrement contraire à Jean [Schlumberger], qui annonce l'intention de faire un prochain article sur le sujet [...]. Nous tombons d'accord que le saugrenu de Malraux, qu'il a baptisé farfelu, est pour nous complètement sans saveur, inexistent'; *CAG* 6, pp. 8-9, entry dated 6 April 1937.

[98] For example, see the section 'Présentations de la *NRF*', in J. Paulhan, *Oeuvres*, IV, pp. 361-77, especially the *Radio-37* texts of late 1938, pp. 361-365.

> surréaliste ou le néo-classique, a inventé et maintenu une place
> pure, où la littérature pût se tenir debout, sans concessions et
> sans facilités. Où, tout en demeurant prête à accueillir les
> hérétiques, elle refusât les hérésies.[99]

Of course there were widely differing views on the direction taken by the
*NRF*, but Paulhan certainly had his defenders. In 1936 Martin du Gard
praised the *unique* position that the review occupied in the world of
literature and culture:

> La *NRF* est d'une qualité si particulière, elle occupe aujourd'hui
> parmi les revues une place si isolée, si "différente", que je n'ai eu
> aucune difficulté à trouver de quoi satisfaire, à peu près, *Europe*,
> *Commune*, *Vendredi* et *tutti quanti*.[100]

**Refreshing the *NRF***

We have seen how in 1927 the *NRF* embarked on a programme of expansion
and renewal. These efforts to refresh the review, to make it more responsive
to events, were repeated from time to time during the 1930s. In the face of
political and other pressures from such as Gide, Paulhan was pursuaded that
the review was too restricted, too inflexible. He confessed in 1933 to Franz
Hellens that he was thinking of 'une refonte totale de la partie *notes* de la
*NRF*: quelque chose de plus complet et de bien plus bref (aussi, peut-être des
notes politiques—mais les faire intelligentes et sans parti, c'est terriblement
difficile)'.[101] After much deliberation, Paulhan finally developed the formula
he had been seeking to enlarge the scope of the review. In November 1933, he
shared his idea with, among others, Jean Grenier and Francis Ponge:

> Je voudrais donner chaque mois dans la *NRF* une rubrique
> d'Actualité (si l'on peut dire). [...] Le tout traité en notes brèves,
> d'une demi-page chacune. Je t'en prie, songes-y sérieusement et
> donne-moi avant dix jours deux ou trois notes. Après tout,
> pourquoi ne parlerions-nous pas de ce qui «se passe» aussi bien
> que n'importe quelle *Marianne* ou *1933*?[102]

In December 1933 appeared the first *Airs du mois* section covering seventeen
pages at the end of the review; the longest of the contributions covered one
and a half pages, and the shortest four lines. Twenty four short texts were

---

[99]    Letter in B. Garniez, *La Nouvelle Revue Française pendant la période de l'entre-deux-guerres*, unpublished Ph.D. dissertation, New York University, 1960, p. 39.
[100]  Martin du Gard to JP, letter dated 6 September 1936 (AP).
[101]  JP to Hellens [1933] (BD).
[102]  JP to Grenier, letter dated 7 November 1993 (AP), and *JPC* 1, pp. 307-308.

included, by authors as diverse as Drieu La Rochelle, René Daumal and Eugène Dabit. Thereafter this format changed little. The intention, as the name suggests, was to introduce 'fresh air' into each issue. Reactions to the innovation were swift, but by no means were they all favourable: Martin du Gard, Schlumberger and Grenier all expressed reservations about the 'journalistic' nature of the material. After the riots of 6 February 1934, the new section came into its own, however, allowing Paulhan to commission a variety of short texts in time for the issue appearing on 1 March.

By 1937 the director of the *NRF* began to find that there was a growing demand for comment on recent developments, as well as for indications of forthcoming events. He told Grenier:

> Nous allons publier dans chaque numéro (à la demande générale) quatre pages destinées à mettre le lecteur au courant de *tout*: événements littéraires, livres, théâtre, cinéma, etc. Je t'en prie, envoie-moi huit ou dix notes de 2 à 3 lignes sur ce que tu voudras (surtout des livres).[103]

Thus the *Bulletin* was inaugurated in March 1937 as a complement to the *Airs du mois*. It later assumed a place of its own and incorporated brief notes on *Evénements-Les Livres-Spectacles*. From February 1938 Paulhan himself prepared the *Bulletin*, using his pseudonym Jean Guérin; here, influenced by the work of Félix Fénéon, he often achieved an ironical, even controversial, effect in juxtapositions and elliptical notations. From October 1939, the *événements* disappeared; it seemed to be no longer appropriate to continue this commentary in view of the gravity of the international situation.

From early 1938, partly as the price paid for his growing independence as director, Paulhan became embattled at the review. Most worrying of all were signs of a decline in the quality of the *NRF*, because attempts made during 1937 to inject new life had not been overwhelmingly successful. A number of factors led Paulhan to dispatch a circular letter to several writers on 31 March 1938, in which he solicited their opinion on the *NRF*, and ways in which they thought its performance might be improved. The circular letter began:

> Jamais on n'a reproché la *NRF* d'être glaciale et morne avec plus de violence que depuis quelques semaines. Brasillach (entre

---

[103]  JP to Grenier, letter dated 8 February 1937 (AP).

autres) nous appelle des diplodocus; et Jean Marteau, des pédants.[104]

The *notes* were felt to be most at fault: 'Elles vont un peu dans tous les sens', Paulhan wrote; somehow the 'moving spirit' of the review had faded, or was no longer tangible, at least not in the sense that it was present in *Esprit* or *Europe*, in spite of the fact that these two periodicals were subordinated to 'un catéchisme politique ou moral'.[105] For all this he believed that the unity of the *NRF* group still thrived: it should, however, be more prominently exposed in the review itself. At the same time, once again Gide was ruminating to Martin du Gard that he too regretted that the *NRF* was not more open to contemporary preoccupations.[106] Jean Grenier, one of the recipients of the circular, wrote back to give Paulhan some encouragement:

> La *NRF* n'a jamais été plus vivante ni plus suggestive. Le numéro d'Avril [1938] est un chef d'oeuvre à ce point de vue. *Esprit* et *Europe* sont des revues qui ont besoin d'une unité formelle. Mais c'est très bien que la *NRF* garde sa pluralité qui est une richesse et qui cache une unité d'esprit. Si tu demandes à tes collaborateurs de juger les notes d'autrui, tu risques de laisser entamer ton autorité (on voit où cela mène la France!). [...] Peut-être pourrait-on en revenir aux chroniques: une série déterminée de livres critiquée par la même personne (comme faisaient très bien Arland et Thibaudet). Ou confier toutes les notes un mois à l'un, un mois à l'autre. Si tu adhérais complètement à un système (de manière à avoir un panorama très partiel—philosophie, politique ou religion) la chose serait évidemment simplifiée.[107]

This was the sort of constructive criticism on which Paulhan came to rely. Comments such as these, from his friends and regular contributors, provide evidence of one of the most effective (if unapparent) ways in which Paulhan maintained the review's high quality.

---

104 This letter was sent to several contributors: see for example J. Kohn-Etiemble, *226 lettres inédites de Jean Paulhan. Contribution à l'étude du mouvement littéraire en France, 1933-1967*, Klincksieck, 1975, pp. 155-156, and *JPC* 2, p. 48 (letter to René Daumal dated 11 April 1938).
105 Quoted in *NRF*, May 1969, p. 1010.
106 Gide to Martin du Gard, letter dated 1 April 1938, quoted in Gide-Martin du Gard, *Correspondance*, vol. 2, *1935-1951*, Gallimard, 1968, p. 129.
107 Grenier to JP, letter dated 10 April 1938 (AP).

44

**The intrusion of history**

By late summer 1938 Paulhan felt uneasy about the critical section of the review and (as he had done several times during the 1930s) invited Jean Grenier to contribute a regular *chronique* and *notes* for the forthcoming year. This time, however, as we shall discover in detail in chapter seven, contemporary events would provided the revitalization he was looking for: the Munich crisis of late September led directly to the *NRF* adopting a partisan, anti-appeasement stance with its November issue.

A year later, at the time of the declaration of war in September 1939, many *NRF* writers were mobilized and sent to the front: Marcel Arland, Jean-Paul Sartre and Armand Petitjean, among the regulars of the review's critical section, could no longer be relied upon to submit copy. René Etiemble and Roger Caillois were away in the Americas. Paulhan had to seek elsewhere for material. In September 1939 he wrote that 'il me semble qu'il faut à la guerre une revue un peu élargie (et d'autant plus je vais avoir moins de notes et d'*Airs du mois*)'.[108] In the event he resorted to some 'general interest' texts and complemented them with some short, unpublished material.

Before long however, Paulhan's worries as editor were overshadowed by the realities of war. Indeed the outbreak of hostilities literally displaced the *NRF*: in September 1939 the whole operation was moved from Paris to Gallimard's property 'Mirande', near Sartilly in the Manche department. Finally, in June 1940, Paulhan and his review were overtaken by events: as the Nazi invaders swept across France it proved impossible to bring out the issue for July.

Although he did not invariably meet with success, Paulhan consolidated the reputation of the *NRF*, which, to some extent, had already been established by the time he took over as editor in 1925. Supported by a number of correspondents and advisors, he maintained and even augmented the vitality and status of the review, and changed the emphases of his editorial policy to suit the exigencies of the moment. What is more, he did not shy away from altering its aspect and structure if, as a result, it could be refreshed. And, most importantly for what follows, despite his reservations and his principles, Paulhan found that to ignore the preoccupations of the day would have made the *NRF* less arresting as an intellectual venture.

The treatment of such questions followed in the wake of a prolonged debate conducted both inside and outside the *NRF* on the nature and rôle of

---

[108]  JP to Schlumberger [September 1939] (BD).

the intellectual and his responsibilities within society: this debate found its catalyst, if not its very centre of gravity, in a work published by Paulhan in the *NRF*. This work, Julien Benda's *La Trahison des clercs*, marked the beginning of a phase whereby French intellectuals in general—not merely those circulating at the *NRF*—defined their stance relative to Benda's own apparently haughty position. It is highly significant that a supposedly exclusive literary review should open itself as a forum to discuss topical and social issues, even if the periodical did not harbour writers of any one, predominant or identifiable political persuasion, or even if many of these same writers declined to descend into the public arena. Furthermore, Benda's text not only contained references to issues relevant since the Dreyfus Affair and even before, it also presaged those questions which, during the 1930s, would become paramount. It is to this debate that we should now turn.

# Chapter 2

## Catalyst for intellectual *engagement*:
## the serialization of *La Trahison des clercs*

*Peu d'articles de la* NRF *ont soulevé plus d'émotion, de l'enthousiasme de Gide à l'horreur de Marsan, que* La Trahison des clercs. *Il va y avoir des ripostes assez dures.*[1]

In 1920 Albert Thibaudet, with remarkable foresight, in an essay for *The London Mercury* on 'The Young Reviews' in France, accurately identified what would continue to be the major characteristic of intellectual life in France for the next twenty years:

> It is almost impossible in France, for artists today, to divest themselves of political preoccupations. [...] The young French reviews today are preoccupied with ideas first and art second. It is difficult for them, even when they are willing, to avoid a definite orientation towards politics. They are the natural voices of a generation which is prevented by actual events from indulging in detached speculation.[2]

No one now would dispute that the intrusion of contemporary politics into French intellectual life is the overriding characteristic of the interwar period. The uncertainties engendered by the First World War gave rise to long and intense debate, much of which was conducted in the pages of the reviews of the period. The question of whether, and under what circumstances, intellectuals should become politically committed found its focal point in the appearance in 1927 of Julien Benda's *La Trahison des clercs*, a work whose

---

1     JP to Schlumberger [November 1927] (BD).
2     *The London Mercury*, vol. 1,1919-1920, pp. 622-624.

importance and posterity have attracted a great deal of critical attention.[3] It has also been considered as a precursor text for later 'intellectual resistance', and has inspired a new generation of French intellectuals in their polemical endeavours.[4] It is not remembered often enough, however, that this work appeared first in the pages of the *NRF*. In fact Thibaudet's assessment quoted above may be applied forcefully to the *NRF*, especially when it is remembered that Régis Debray identified the *NRF* as the major vector of 'le pouvoir intellectuel en France' during the interwar period.[5] Benda's work made such an impact that the debates to which it gave rise, both within and outside the *NRF*, prepared the way for the public political commitment of many intellectuals, whether they were closely associated with the *NRF* or not. Furthermore, its catalysing effect revealed important differences of opinion between generations of intellectuals.[6] This chapter retraces the steps of this process, from the outwardly idealistic but essentially sterile position of Benda's *La Trahison des clercs*, through the intervening confrontations and shifts of intellectual opinion, to examine finally the publicly expressed stances which came later in 1932, as exemplified particularly by André Gide and others' support for the Amsterdam-Pleyel peace movement.

### Julien Benda and *La Trahison des clercs*

Under the editorship of Jacques Rivière, Julien Benda had been kept at a distance from the *NRF*. Jean Paulhan, however, had a deep admiration for the resolute defender of republican ideals, and introduced him to the review, giving him much support during his long association there. Benda's constant presence in the pages of the *NRF*, alongside other stalwart figures like Alain and Albert Thibaudet, reinforces the view that it was a *revue radicalisante*. It certainly may be seen as such in Rivière's profession of faith dating from 1919, when the *NRF* restarted after the war. In the opening text of the first number to appear after the hostilities, Rivière wrote:

---

3     D. L. Schalk, in *The Spectrum of Political Engagement*, Princeton: Princeton U.P., 1979, pp. 26-40, discusses the posterity of Benda's book. See also H. S. Hughes, *Consciousness and Society*, New York: Knopf, 1958; R. Debray, *Le Scribe*, Livre de poche, 1980, pp. 87-101; and .

4     See J. D. Wilkinson, *Origins of Intellectual Resistance in Europe*, Cambridge, Mass.: Harvard University Press, 1981, and A. Finkielkraut, *La Défaite de la pensée*, Gallimard, 1987.

5     R. Debray, *Le Pouvoir intellectuel en France*, Ramsay, 1989, pp. 73-94.

6     On the question of intellectual 'generations', see J.-F. Sirinelli (ed.), 'Générations intellectuelles', *Cahiers de l'Institut d'histoire du temps présent*, no. 6, novembre 1987, and the special issue of *Vingtième siècle—revue d'histoire*, no. 22, avril-juin 1989, 'Les générations'.

> Ce ne seront jamais tout à fait des professions de foi politiques:
> plutôt une sorte de critique et d'interprétation de l'histoire
> contemporaine, mais à travers lesquelles forcément s'entreverra
> une couleur politique.[7]

The very ambivalence of this statement bears witness to how the *NRF* was steeped in the prevailing cultural atmosphere of the postwar Third Republic. Although it might not have promoted 'political professions of faith', because of the constituency of the intellectuals to whom it gave a voice, the political 'colour' of the *NRF* was inescapably radicalist. And Paulhan followed the same course: by publishing *La Trahison des clercs* the *NRF* would appear to remain aloof from the factionalism of which so many of the intellectuals accused by Benda—Barrès, Nietzsche, Sorel, Maurras, or even Péguy—were guilty.

The first two parts of the serialization examined the 'perfectionnement moderne des passions politiques', and outlined the definitions of these passions; the third part, 'Les Clercs', contained the main polemical thrust of the work, and exposed the so-called 'treason of the intellectuals' in the light of these political passions. Benda's thesis was that the *clercs* (or intellectuals, writers and philosophers) had betrayed their secular calling by preaching action. The force of the argument derived partly from the abundance of examples Benda adduced to illustrate his case, however contestable some of them might appear. The treason was attributable to three main factors: firstly, 'les clercs adoptent les passions politiques'.[8] Instead of restraining factionalism, the intellectuals he identified were now the agents of its spread. Most of all, 'la passion nationale', or nationalism, had superceded commitment to universal values. Benda was enough of a Dreyfusard, however, to allow intellectuals' intervention in the public or political arena so long as they did so in the name of universal values such as Truth and Justice, as in the case of Zola's defence of Dreyfus. Secondly, he argued that nationalistic fervour had been fully absorbed into intellectuals' works: 'les clercs font le jeu des passions politiques par leurs doctrines'.[9] By exalting the Nation, the *clercs* had betrayed humanism; and indeed the concept of humanism was the first major issue to receive detailed and considered treatment in the debate to follow. In the great betrayal, humanism was good only in so far as it promoted or protected the interests of either Nation or Class. For Benda, modern intellectuals only used culture to exalt the national

---

7     *NRF*, June 1919, p. 11.
8     *NRF*, August 1927, p. 129.
9     *NRF*, September 1927, p. 325 .

good: the Parti de l'Intelligence was a case in point.[10]  Thirdly, when national fervour infused the writing of history, the treason reached its most dangerous state.  Right-wing historiography, in particular as practised by those intellectuals circulating around the Action Française movement, and the controversy surrounding responsibility for the First World War, were further subjects for debate in the months to follow.

The November 1927 issue carried the remainder of the book's third part, 'Les Causes'.  Here Benda argued that modern social conditions had rendered the *clerc*'s predicament even more difficult: paradoxically, secularized republican institutions and the 1905 Separation of Church and State had simply rendered it impossible to maintain 'une classe d'hommes exempts des devoirs civiques'.[11]  In short, the Third Republic had politicized its institutions and intellectual class.  This led Benda, over a decade in advance of Sartre, to excoriate the subservience of what he termed the 'écrivain pratique' to the bourgeoisie, 'laquelle fait les renommées et dispense les honneurs'.[12]  In Benda's mind the modern writer did little more than uphold and perpetuate the bourgeois order, a point of view which, again, would attract much discussion from a younger generation of writers.  This last instalment ended with the 'Vue d'ensemble—Pronostics'.  Benda's tone changed considerably here: he raised the spectre of war, both the 1914-1918 conflict and the coming apocalypse.  His central concern was the following:

> Si, en effet, on se demande où va l'humanité dont chaque groupe s'enfonce plus âprement que jamais dans la conscience de son intérêt particulier et se fait dire par ses moralistes qu'il est sublime dans la mesure où il ne connaît pas d'autre loi que cet intérêt, un enfant trouverait la réponse: *elle va à la guerre la plus totale et la plus parfaite que le monde aura vue, soit qu'elle ait lieu entre nations, soit entre classes.*[13]

Peace, like Justice and Reason, should be a universal principle: 'la paix, si jamais elle existe, ne se reposera pas sur la crainte de la guerre mais sur l'amour de la paix; *elle sera l'avènement d'un état d'âme'.*[14]  This important statement represents, in embryo, an expression of the politically committed state of mind which was to underpin the adherence of intellectuals to the international peace movement in 1932.  However much *La Trahison des*

---

10   J. David, *Le Procès de l'intelligence, 1919-1927*, Nizet, 1966.
11   *NRF*, November 1927, p. 591.
12   Ibid., p. 594.
13   Ibid., p. 605 (my emphasis).
14   Ibid., p. 606 (my emphasis).

*clercs* bears witness to Benda's idealism and to his calls for the maintenance of universal values, the clear implication of the book was that it had become impossible for intellectuals to ignore the forces of history.

Within the *NRF* Gide and Paulhan acclaimed *La Trahison des clercs*.[15] In the December issue reactions began to appear: Paulhan had at least expected them if not encouraged them. Albert Thibaudet, in his *Réflexions* rubric, welcomed Benda's ideas in the context of the review's internal tradition, adding the proviso that '[ces pages] appellent en effet la discussion et les réserves comme une terre sèche appelle la pluie'.[16] The overriding criticism was that Benda tended to be a victim of his own prejudices. For instance, his anti-Bergsonism led him to dismiss all pragmatism. 'Il pense sous la catégorie du "Non!"', stressed the Bergsonist Thibaudet.[17] Feeling that Benda's method was too inflexible, Thibaudet went right to the crux of the matter:

> Je pense bien que, pour M. Benda comme pour nous, tout le mal, si mal il y a , réside dans le suffixe: *isme*, car les nationalités ont fait la richesse, la variété, la complexité de l'Europe moderne. [...] Je suis extrêmement sensible [...] au grand style intérieur du désespoir de M. Benda. [...] Ma pensée, ou ma nature, se refusent à en partager la substance.[18]

Thibaudet found that Benda was essentially 'en lutte contre son temps.'[19] The philosopher Gabriel Marcel and the *NRF*'s own critic Ramon Fernandez concurred: on the grounds of metaphysics Benda had misunderstood the vital point that far from operating in a vacuum, the modern thinker functioned in direct and unavoidable relation to reality. While Marcel was dismissive, concluding that metaphysics was utterly sterile unless applied to reality, Fernandez felt that with his multiple perspectives, Benda had at least produced a new outlook on the problems facing intellectuals. He had some criticisms which he expressed to Paulhan[20], however, and went on to agree

---

15    On 2 August 1927 Gide wrote enthusiastically to Paulhan (AP), who also told Jean Schlumberger that 'la fin du Benda est *très bien*'; JP to Schlumberger [October 1927] (BD).
16    'La Question des clercs', *NRF*, December 1927, p. 810.
17    Ibid., p. 811.
18    Ibid., p. 819.
19    Ibid., p. 810-811.
20    'Le Benda vaut par les principes ou les questions soulevées, mais pèche par les exemples et l'esprit de la dialectique. Il ne marque aucune distinction entre, et donc confond perpétuellement, les idées qui ressemblent à l'intelligence, et qui peuvent ne pas lui ressembler. Que diriez-vous d'une chronique lui répondant dans ce sens?' Fernandez to JP [late 1927] (AP).

with Marcel by affirming that 'ces idées n'ont d'existence, *en tant qu'idées*, que si elles se déterminent et se justifient dans l'expérience'.[21]   In a striking formulation full of resonances for the decade to come, Fernandez ended by urging Benda's *clerc* away from asceticism towards some form of *engagement*:

> Julien Benda est le philosophe aristocrate, *le philosophe aux mains propres. Je crois qu'il faut se salir un peu, et même beaucoup,* pour sauver ce qu'il révère avec une intransigeance qui lui fait honneur.[22]

On 26 January 1928 the Union pour la Vérité, Paul Desjardin's organization responsible for the famous 'décades' held at Pontigny and closely associated with the *NRF*, held a conference entitled 'Autour de *La Trahison des clercs'*. In front of an audience of well known intellectuals, Benda made the first public reiteration of his important concession that the *clerc* could defend a cause so long as he did so in the name of universal values. His minuted intervention states forcefully that

> le clerc peut, et je l'ai dit, descendre sur la place publique sans cesser d'exercer sa fonction. Mais il a une manière meilleure de l'exercer, c'est d'être par sa vie même une constante protestation. C'est ainsi qu'il sera, en réalité, le plus actif.[23]

This opening meeting, and the continuing wave of reactions from the nationalist press, some examples of which Paulhan reproduced in the *NRF* for March 1928, gave Benda the chance to assemble materials for the sequel to *La Trahison des clercs* which was due to appear in the review from August to October that year as *La Fin de l'éternel*.

In June 1928, Thibaudet again devoted his *Réflexion* to 'Les archives de *La Trahison des clercs'*.  Unable to avoid almost daily reference to and discussion of Benda's book, he declared that 'le livre a prouvé son contenu par son succès: pour passionner les hommes il faut un aliment pur. Ils exigent des essences, un absolu, un aliment qui soit un élément. Benda apporte l'idée de clerc pur'.[24]  In spite of their forcefulness and their 'purity', Thibaudet voiced the conviction of many that, reduced to their basic thesis, Benda's ideas were suitable only for ascetics.  Thibaudet pared down the conception of 'le clerc pur' to its most sterile form:

---

21      *NRF*, January 1928, p.104.
22      Ibid., p. 107 (my emphasis).
23      *Bulletin de l'Union pour la vérité*, 36e série, January-February 1928, p. 8ff.
24      *NRF*, June 1928, p. 825.

> Le clerc trahit dans la mesure où il sort de la représentation pure. Mais le monde est représentation et volonté. Donc le clerc trahit en tant qu'il ne dit pas non à la volonté, c'est-à-dire au monde, à la durée. Le clerc trahit en existant, et l'existence est injustice. Conclusion: le bouddhisme.[25]

And this was not the last time that Thibaudet would take issue with Benda: the opportunity arose again during the publication of *La Fin de l'éternel*. The first part assembled Benda's objections to the 'Réaction du clerc de «droite»'. Here he did little more than refute the idea that 'il n'y avait là nulle trahison de leur part, mais entière fidélité à leur essence et que tout mon procès contre eux portait à faux'.[26] In short, Benda showed that their objections to his attacks on nationalism merely proved the points he had made in *La Trahison des clercs*.

The second part of *La Fin de l'éternel* took a new turn in its treatment of the left-wing intellectual. Benda repeated his conviction that 'la passion de la justice, plus encore celle de la vérité, *ne sont point des passions politiques* et que ceux qui descendent au forum mus par elles ne me paraissent trahir aucune noble fonction'.[27] Here Benda considered critically the notion that was held by both left- and right-leaning intellectuals that in the modern world it had somehow become worthless to remain a 'clerc contemplatif': indeed, contemporary intellectuals were insisting that 'la suprême fonction du clerc est d'agir, et le cultivateur solitaire de l'esprit est un clerc inférieur'.[28] In turn, these intellectuals were aggravated by Benda's insistence on separating thought and action: for them, thought was deemed worthless unless it led directly to action, or had practical results. For so many of Benda's adversaries, including Fernandez within the *NRF*, this line of thinking had almost become a profession of faith: thinking 'in the void' was no longer a creditable option for intellectuals. Benda's commentaries on these objections shows clearly how intellectuals on all sides were evolving at this time.

The next series of objections concerned the question of responsibilities for the First World War. For Benda, the shrill reaction of some left-wing intellectuals to his refusal jointly to condemn both German and French

---

25    Ibid., p. 830.
26    *NRF*, August 1928, p. 162.
27    *NRF*, September 1928, p. 336. Benda took care to confirm to his editor that this second instalment 'dit vraiment des choses nouvelles par rapport à *La Trahison des clercs* et propres à frapper le lecteur notamment dans la défense que j'ai faite de ma position quant à la question de la responsabilité de la guerre'; Benda to JP, letter dated 6 May 1928 (AP).
28    *NRF*, September 1928, p. 342.

responsibilities for the war was highly illuminating, and indicated the basis of a leftist 'betrayal' whereby pacifism was interpreted as a new type of intellectual 'terrorism'. Benda's riposte was based on considering not only the will of national governments, but also the 'will of the people' of each nation concerned. Benda displayed his own deeply felt anti-Germanism when he argued that the Germans' national psychology had been in a bellicose state in the fifty years preceding the outbreak of war: the actions of the German government had only reflected the will of their people.[29] The German nation, he continued, across all barriers of class, had wanted war with France and had welcomed acts of provocation, whereas belligerence on the part of the French government had *not* been welcomed by the people.[30] Ironically enough, Benda's anti-Germanism and the preconceived ideas upon which it was based aligned him with nationalists and Maurrassians on this issue. Benda's stance also provided the opportunity for Paulhan to use his work as a counterbalance to what the editor of the *NRF* considered to be dangerous forays into the domain of Franco-German relations.[31]

The final part of *La Fin de l'éternel* dealt with what was for Benda the most important aspect of the whole controversy. Referring to the articles by Thibaudet, Gabriel Marcel and Fernandez which had appeared in the *NRF* over successive months,[32] he reiterated his stance against putting philosophy at the service of particular interests, and against the exaltation of irrationalism.[33] For Benda, the worst betrayal of all was the rejection of the Eternal, the repudiation of a fixed Ideal. Willing to admit that the modern thinker could not exist outside his own time, he should, however, respect the desire of those who wished only to contemplate the universal: 'le clerc moderne proclame une fois de plus qu'il ne se veut pas homme de pensée et refuse d'honorer celui qui le demeure'.[34]

The scale of the reactions to Benda's works, considering only those which appeared in the pages of the *NRF*, reflects a lively interest in the problems it raised. However, as the months went by, discussion of these abstract concepts seemed to involve increasingly minute readjustments which amounted to little more than fine tuning: *La Trahison des clercs* had

---

29      Ibid., pp. 353-354.
30      Ibid., pp. 355-356.
31      On the *NRF* and attitudes to the German question, see chapter 4 below.
32      Thibaudet, 'Pour les archives de *La Trahison des clercs* (suite)', *NRF* , September 1929, pp. 404-409. Cf., in its turn, Fernandez' rejoinder 'Remarques sur *La Fin de l'éternel*', *NRF* , July 1929, pp. 104-110.
33      *NRF* , October 1928, pp. 525ff, 536f, 551.
34      Ibid., p. 552.

served its purpose by galvanizing intellectual opinion.[35] Plainly the time had come to move on and to reorientate the debate in order to confront directly the problems thrown up by Benda, in short, to transform his critique into a more positive impetus. Paulhan turned the focus of the *NRF* on to the question of culture and humanism.

## Culture and humanism

In November 1928 Paulhan printed Jean Guéhenno's essay 'L'Humanité et les humanités'. This was a shrewd choice indeed, because Guéhenno's essay and the discussion it provoked provided the spur for much of the subsequent debate about culture and humanism in the coming decade.[36] The burning question for Guéhenno was 'how can culture help *all* humanity?' His premiss, given that the people ['le peuple'] had come of age in the mass political culture of the twentieth century, was that the long work of the eighteenth century ideologues was no longer necessary. 'Le peuple se méfie de la culture', claimed Guéhenno.[37] He went on to examine the problem of how culture should be defined in the light of a phenomenon which Benda had only hinted at: in other words, revolutionary communism. Seen from the Leninist perspective, culture was worthy of deep suspicion, and could be used as an instrument of domination in the hands of inhumane masters. Thus the nature of culture and its disseminators, the intellectuals, needed reassessment in the light of the new (Bolshevik) revolution and, in parallel with Benda, Guéhenno contended that after the hopes in the legacy of the French Revolution had faded, the majority of modern intellectuals had turned towards the political Right. With the advent of world conflict and its universal barbarism, the central challenge was clear:

---

35     Thibaudet, in spite of his own grave reservations, returned to assess rather more favourably the contribution of *La Trahison des clercs* and its sequel in his 'Réflexion' 'Histoire de vingt-cinq ans', *NRF*, May 1929, pp. 708-719. Here Thibaudet evaluated Benda's work in the context of the intellectual history of the preceding twenty five years by referring to it and Charles Maurras' *L'Avenir de l'intelligence* (1905) as 'les deux formes les plus philosophiques du dialogue français autour du procès Dreyfus' (ibid., p. 708). Although the tone of this article is more sympathetic, Thibaudet admits that 'ce qui me gêne un peu, c'est de trouver, chez ce doctrinaire, si peu de doctrine' (ibid., p. 709).

36     *NRF*, November 1928, pp. 629-642. This essay is reproduced in *Conversion à l'humain*, itself appended to *Caliban parle*, Grasset, 1928, republished in 1962. Correspondence shows that the essay had originally been destined for the *Revue hebdomadaire*, and that Paulhan delayed its publication to coincide with the appearance of the volume (AP).

37     *NRF*, November 1928, p. 630.

> Comment l'humanité n'eût-elle pas désespéré de la culture, des 'humanités', si la culture ne menait plus qu'à de telles catastrophes et en prenait même avec une sorte de fierté la responsabilité? [38]

The humanities, once treated as the fountain-head of wisdom and education, had now become debased, for their acquisition helped to bolster class interests:

> Benda nous parlait de la trahison des clercs; ce n'est pas assez dire peut-être. Peut-être faut-il parler d'une trahison de la culture elle-même, d'une trahison des Humanités.[39]

Guéhenno called for the introduction of a new spirit of education; because humanity had moved on, culture should no longer be solely the domain of the privileged—'jamais encore on n'a enseigné le peuple au peuple'.[40] These were strong words indeed to appear in the hallowed pages of the *NRF*, a review that prided itself as the foremost disseminator of French culture. If Paulhan had expected them to provoke comment, he was not to be disappointed, for they sparked reactions both within and outside the review. Guéhenno at this time was editor of the *NRF*'s rival *Europe*. His mentor there, Romain Rolland, criticized his own *protégé* by arguing that precisely *because* he had published his work in the *NRF* he risked devaluing the sentiments he expressed:

> Puisque vous écrivez à la *NRF*, vous devez vous rendre compte que, malgré sa haute tenue de pensée "intellectuelle", les "humanités" l'emportent chez elle sur l'humanité, et il y a plus de chances pour celle-ci de vivre encore à *Europe* que partout ailleurs.[41]

Within the review it was Ramon Fernandez who responded to the challenge thrown down by Guéhenno, because he had already been involved elsewhere in discussions on new approaches to culture and humanism.[42] Having told Paulhan that he felt Guéhenno's article was 'highly unsatisfactory',[43] he made

---

[38]  Ibid., p. 635.

[39]  Ibid., p. 640.

[40]  Ibid., p. 641.

[41]  *L'Indépendance de l'esprit. Correspondance entre Jean Guéhenno et Romain Rolland, 1919-1944*, Albin Michel,1975, p. 37. On the acrimonious relations between Rolland and the *NRF*, see *Romain Rolland et la NRF*, Albin Michel, 1989, *passim*.

[42]  Fernandez had had the chance to rehearse this debate in the short-lived venture he founded with Emmanuel Berl and Pierre Drieu La Rochelle, *Les Derniers Jours*. See the facsimile reprint (J. Place, 1979), in particular the exchanges with Berl in the issues for 20 March 1927, 10 April 1927 and 15 May 1928.

[43]  Fernandez to JP, letter dated 4 November 1928 (AP).

his views clear in a long book review on *Caliban parle*. This is how Fernandez summarized the problem:

> Il n'a visé qu'à nous rappeler la réalité, l'importance, la valeur de cette masse humaine dont les politiciens se servent avant de lui interdire l'entrée des palais qu'elle leur livre'.[44]

Fernandez criticized Guéhenno for not thinking more seriously about the implications of communism for the intellectuals, and he applied Benda's recommendations in order to broaden the scope of the problem:

> Tout ce qu'on demandera à l'intellectuel sorti du peuple c'est de choisir, après avoir fait son examen de conscience, d'être un serviteur de sa classe ou d'être un serviteur désintéressé de l'esprit.[45]

Fernandez saw no reason why the 'intellectuel sorti du peuple' should have to serve the interests of a class to which he did not belong. The significance of this standpoint is that where Benda in his writings allowed no such choice, Fernandez, although critical of certain weaknesses in Guéhenno's view of the role of culture, positively encouraged the choice.

Next month Paulhan, writing under his pseudonym of Jean Guérin, reported with heavy irony on the discussion of *Caliban parle* at the Union pour la vérité. 'M. Guéhenno, fils de prolétaire, a le physique laforguien, le regard et la moustache tristes', he wrote.[46] He characterized the book as 'une plainte timide, [...] une suite de cris de coeur touchants'. According to Paulhan's report, instead of the expected reaction from right-wing quarters, Guéhenno's position was attacked by 'trois révolutionnaires':

> M. Emmanuel Berl, qui s'est fait récemment pamphlétaire après quelques tentatives dans l'ordre de la métaphysique et du roman: M. Brice Parain, plus subtil [...] enfin, M. André Malraux, courtois et méphistophélique.[47]

Paulhan's account is important because it shows how aware he was that there was a generation of younger writers willing to take the arguments about culture and humanism much further than Benda and Guéhenno. In a point noticed by Paulhan, Berl, Parain and Malraux wanted to counter Guéhenno

---

44  *NRF*, February 1929, p. 259.
45  Ibid, p. 261.
46  *NRF*, March 1929, p. 427.
47  Ibid. The 'pamphlet' by Berl referred to here is *Mort de la pensée bourgeoise* which was being serialized by *Europe* at this time from January to March 1929.

by insisting that 'nous voulons une culture prolétarienne sans accointance avec la culture bourgeoise'. If, in his commentary, Paulhan had wanted to deflate the seriousness of this debate,[48] the exchanges engendered by Guéhenno's article showed that there was a real momentum building up within the *NRF* to continue to address the crisis in humanism.

## Bourgeois thought

No-one was more attuned to this problem than André Gide who, although regarded as the founding spirit of the *NRF* and therefore as belonging to an older generation of writers, was living through a period of confusion and self-doubt at this time about the nature of his own role.[49] Evidently the exchanges in the *NRF* had been fuelling Gide's uncertainty, but by July 1929 the review article of Berl's essay *Mort de la pensée bourgeoise* helped Gide to define and focus his own position.

Like Guéhenno's book, *Mort de la pensée bourgeoise* was another 'cri de coeur': Berl, however, mounted a much more ferocious attack on conformist ideas. Dedicating his text to Malraux's central character in *Les Conquérants*, Garine, Berl accused all other modern writers of conformism and of shying away from the lessons of the new Revolution.[50] Where Benda had argued that writers and intellectuals were subservient to and cowed by a dominant — and bourgeois — cultural system, Berl went on to develop the argument in the full light of an awareness of the potential afforded by the Revolution. Effectively Berl stood Benda on his head and posited that the *clerc* committed treason by not acting; this fear of action had to be overcome. Thought and action, as for Garine in *Les Conquérants*, had to be coterminous. By the same token, Berl accused Benda of dilettantism: his 'nostalgie du cloître' was artificial and sterile in the post-revolutionary context. The basic thrust of Berl's argument was that despite efforts to conceal the fact (through conformism, through dilettantism), 'la pensée est révolutionnaire ou n'est pas'.[51] Even more than for Guéhenno, the figure of the intellectual in the modern world was tragic, the tension deriving from the fact that the

---

48    Paulhan's ironies misfired in that they produced correspondence from a participant at the conference who alleged that his intervention had been misrepresented by Paulhan; see 'Divers', *NRF*, April 1929, p. 592, and a further letter from Berl reproduced in *NRF*, May 1929, p. 744.

49    Maria Van Rhysselberghe reported Gide's presence at a lively discussion on these problems with Berl and Malraux; see *CAG* 4, p. 402.

50    *Mort de la pensée bourgeoise*, Grasset, 'Les Ecrits', 1929, pp. 12ff.

51    Ibid., p. 128.

intellectual was a product of capitalism who, at the same time, found it anathema to adhere to a doctrinaire communist programme.

Reviewing the book for the July issue, Jean Prévost considered that Berl's book was worth studying if only for its faults: in this way it worked as a catalyst like *La Trahison des clercs*. Prévost believed that there was no bourgeois thought because 'toute la bourgeoisie est puissance, acquisition, manoeuvre; pouvoir tout temporel, et même pouvoir caché'.[52] Prévost thought the allusion to *Les Conquérants* was inappropriate since French political culture would not produce the conditions to sustain a revolution like the Bolshevik one of 1917. Prévost was much more pragmatic: 'one should only aspire to what one can achieve', was his watchword. In fact the review article was scathing about Berl: 'cette légèreté d'informations, cette lourdeur de style, cette confusion d'esprit semblent passées en habitude, et presque autorisées par les moeurs'.[53] Not surprisingly Berl wrote complaining to the NRF: because Malraux was in the process of helping Berl transfer from Grasset to Gallimard, it was all the more mystifying that a potential Gallimard author should be attacked so viciously in the 'house' review.[54] Correspondence reveals that Paulhan harboured an intense dislike for Berl, in one sense seeing him as a competitor for the attentions of Gaston Gallimard; Paulhan certainly supported Prévost's view in this affair. Of prime importance here, however, is the fact that Gide felt prompted to intervene; having read the page-proofs of his article, Gide wrote direct to Prévost to express his objections:

> J'ai lu avec intérêt votre article. Vous éclairez fort bien certains points de la thèse de Berl sur lesquels mon incompétence parfaite me laissait me méprendre. [...] Vous m'étonnez un peu en parlant de 'lourdeur de style' [...]. Malgré tous ses défauts, *Berl nous entraîne et nous force à le suivre, fût-ce pour le combattre*.[55]

Gide stressed that in spite of its stylistic infelicities, Berl's assertions had caught the attention of many, including those who were ill-disposed towards Berl himself. Gide added that his own close interlocutor and *confidant* Roger Martin du Gard was even more attracted to Berl's thesis.[56] Julien Benda

---

52    *NRF*, July 1929, p. 120.
53    Ibid., p. 123.
54    See Berl's letter in *NRF*, August 1929, pp. 291-292, and Emmanuel Berl with Patrick Modiano, *Interrogatoire*, Gallimard, 1976, p. 49.
55    Letter dated 14 June 1929, reproduced in Gide-Martin du Gard, *Correspondance*, vol. 1 *(1913-1934)*, Gallimard, 1968, p. 692 (my emphasis).
56    Martin du Gard agreed that 'ce livre n'est pas rien'; ibid., p. 369.

contributed too to the discussion. In his *Scholies* rubric entitled 'Sur la pensée bourgeoise' for the *rentrée* issue that year, he reported that his reading of Berl had allowed him to refine his own critique of bourgeois hegemony over culture which he had outlined in *La Trahison des clercs*:

> C'est la pensée qui est décidée à l'avance à respecter, et au besoin à fortifier, les idées sur lesquelles repose l'ordre social qui profite à la bourgeoisie. Ces idées reviennent au fond à une seule, à savoir que la direction politique de la société doit appartenir à la classe bourgeoise.[57]

In a characteristic gymnastic inversion, Benda reformulated his stance by positing the following equation: '1. La pensée bourgeoise est de pensée morte; 2. Cette mort, en France du moins, n'a jamais été plus vivante'.[58]

Thus an important turning point had been reached: thanks to the catalysing effect of *La Trahison des clercs* and its sequel, the exchanges they produced had brought into the *NRF* an ever-increasing awareness of the historical fact of revolution. This was all the more surprising since the *NRF* was supposedly a bastion of the French literary establishment. The process had begun whereby intellectuals would embark on publicly expressed political commitment during the 1930s.

### 1930: a turning point

These debates were being conducted against a background of political turmoil both in France and abroad. Although the effects of the Wall Street Crash of October 1929 would not be felt in France until 1931, this capitalist crisis caused great anxiety; and in French domestic politics governmental instability seemed to have become the rule, because in the short space between November 1929 and March 1930 there followed a succession of three goverments. The fact that a turning point had been reached was marked in the pages of the *NRF* by Paulhan's insertion of an important essay by Marcel Arland which furthered the debate about intellectual *engagement*. Arland opened his essay 'Episodes'[59] by contrasting the intellectual climate he had described in an earlier piece with the contemporary mood[60]. A few years

---

57    *NRF*, September 1929, p. 393.
58    Ibid., p. 399.
59    *NRF*, July 1930, pp. 104-111. Reproduced in Marcel Arland, *Essais critiques* Gallimard, 1952, pp. 29-37.
60    Cf. the influential essay 'Nouveau mal du siècle', in *NRF*, February 1924, pp. 149-158; this earlier mood is discussed by Nicholas Hewitt in *'Les Maladies du Siècle': The*

previously intellectuals' preoccupations had been influenced heavily by this new 'mal du siècle' (or *'inquiétude'*); now the influence was politics. Arland explained himself:

> Les attaques de M. Benda n'y ont rien changé. *Un écrivain, qu'il le veuille ou non, est contraint de compter aujourd'hui avec les partis politiques.* Il ne peut écrire un livre qui ne soit aussitôt jugé de droite ou de gauche. Ce sont les partis de gauche qui ont assuré le succès de *La Trahison des clercs*; ces mêmes partis, comme M. Benda répondait insuffisamment à leurs avances, se tiennent aujourd'hui sur la réserve.[61]

An intense interest for politics among young writers of his generation was perfectly comprehensible to Arland, the reason being that 'ils y trouvent un moyen d'action immédiate'. He observed that now 'le public réclame [...] une formule, une étiquette, nette, frappante, sonore', and concluded with a striking 'formula' of his own: 'c'est l'heure où ceux qui ne croient pas s'être trahis prennent envers eux-mêmes un nouvel engagement'.[62]  In another long and complex essay on 'La Pensée et la Révolution', Ramon Fernandez pleaded for a complete reassessment of the role of the individual in the face of both Marxist and right-wing thought, especially because 'nous constatons, dans beaucoup de milieux différents, la faillite des croyances dont les deux siècles précédents ont vécu'.[63]  The effect of such uncertainties was compounded further by anxieties regarding the perceived failure of the peace treaty concluded at Versailles to guarantee France's security. The Young Plan, which renegotiated reparations in Germany's favour, had been ratified on 29 March 1930.  Moreover, the feeling that the 1918 victory over Germany had been squandered was epitomized in Georges Clemenceau's bitter, posthumous, work *Grandeurs et misères d'une victoire*.[64]  This explains why Fernandez could write: 'La paix actuelle [...] n'est qu'une guerre délayée dans l'eau saumâtre des parlottes diplomatiques, [une] guerre latente qui couve sous les traités'.[65]  Fernandez felt that in the confusion something needed to be done: in his concluding paragraphs he called for a 'philosophie virile' which would save France from decline, and exhorted intellectuals to fulfil

---

*Image of Malaise in French Fiction and Thought in the Inter-War Years*, Hull: Hull University Press, 1988, especially pp. 5-21.
[61]    *NRF*, July 1930, p. 106.
[62]    Ibid., pp. 107, 110-111.
[63]    'La pensée et la Révolution', *NRF*, September 1930, p. 307.
[64]    Published in 1930 by Plon.
[65]    *NRF*, September 1930, p. 311.

their duty: 'est-il besoin d'ajouter que la défense de l'individu [...] est pour l'intellectuel non seulement un devoir, mais une nécessité inéluctable?'[66],

The fact that a change had taken place was soon noted in one of the more popular literary newspapers: Louis Martin-Chauffier, close to Gide and Malraux at the *NRF*, averred that 'depuis un peu de temps, on constate une grande nouveauté: la descente des clercs sur le pré'. The cause of this new turn of events was, precisely, the peace issue. According to Martin-Chauffier, 'les clercs voient la paix instable et menacée': this time, it was a life or death question, and if no action were taken civilization would soon collapse into a new war.[67] It was necessary for intellectuals to become involved because politicians were ineffectual and acting without due regard for future consequences. Martin-Chauffier voiced the conviction of many at the time that intellectuals, by reflecting and commenting upon events, would help stabilize the situation by exerting their considerable influence on those in authority. The opportunity for the intellectuals to make public their concerns was afforded three weeks later. In an issue of *Notre Temps,* a manifesto appeared entitled 'Contre les excès du nationalisme, pour l'Europe et pour l'entente franco-allemande'. Signed at first by 186 writers and artists, the most significant names were closely associated with both the *NRF* and *Europe*. The only notable absence from this very impressive roll-call was Gide; even Paulhan and Benda had signed.[68] The author of *La Trahison des clercs* had evidently felt that he could sign, because of the insistence of the text on civilization rather than nationalism. It was, in addition, the *international* flavour of the manifesto which appealed:

> [Les intellectuels] n'ignorent tout ce qui menace la paix en d'autres pays et ils comptent que les intellectuels étrangers sauront mener contre les excès de leurs nationalismes l'action qu'eux-mêmes sont résolus à soutenir contre ceux du nationalisme français. Ils affirment que le vrai visage de la

66  Ibid., p. 328. In a telling footnote Fernandez displayed his conviction that 'nous retombons en enfance si une philosophie virile ne vient pas nous sauver à temps'. (*NRF,* September 1930, p. 324). Later in the 1930s, it should be recalled, Fernandez veered to the extreme right and militated in Doriot's Parti Populaire Français.

67  See 'Les clercs sur le pré', *Les Nouvelles littéraires,* 20 December 1930.

68  'Contre les excès du nationalisme, pour l'Europe et pour l'entente franco-allemande', *Notre Temps,* 18 January 1931, pp. 83-84. The best known of the signatories were: Julien Benda, Emmanuel Berl, Jean-Richard Bloch, Jacques Chardonne, Pierre Drieu La Rochelle, Ramon Fernandez, Jean Guéhenno, Jean Giono, Gabriel Marcel, Louis Martin-Chauffier, Roger Martin du Gard, Paul Morand, Jean Paulhan, Jean Schlumberger. On p. 137 Marcel Arland was included among later signatories.

France n'est pas de haine et de guerre, mais de justice et de paix.[69]

As the weeks and months of 1931 went by, a variety of texts and surveys reflected the fact that French intellectuals, both right- and left-wing, had absorbed the lessons of the debates of the previous four years, and that the *'fin de l'après-guerre'* had been reached.[70]

At the same time, the activities of the pacifist groups were infuriating militant sections of the political Right and extreme-Right. The Camelots du Roi, closely affiliated to the Action Française, had taken increasingly to direct action. On 27 November 1931, the pacifists' meeting at the Trocadéro, presided by Edouard Herriot, was broken up by the Action Française.[71] This brawl set off a chain of events which, once and for all, changed the direction of the *NRF*, against Paulhan's deepest wishes. On 1 December Gide met André Chamson who, close to important figures in Herriot's Radical Party, felt that some form of protest was necessary against the Action Française in order to attenuate what Gide felt to be 'le déplorable effet que cela peut avoir en Allemagne'.[72] Chamson persuaded Gide that a group of intellectuals should head the protest, *not* in *Europe*, characterized as 'une revue trop colorée', but in the *NRF*, precisely because it was renowned as a predominantly literary review with no clearly defined political affiliation. 'La Petite Dame' reported that Gide thought of persuading Jean Schlumberger, one of the founders of the review, to write this protest. Schlumberger should 'prendre la parole dans un article que *tous pourraient signer* du reste, mais [Gide] est un peu incertain sur l'opportunité de cette manifestation'.[73] This episode is very important in that it shows how Gide, although still unsure of his own stance, was willing, eventually, to exercise his powerful influence over the policy of the *NRF*. In the event, Schlumberger argued that the copy deadlines of the review would prevent the inclusion of such an article because the delay of three weeks until the next issue would mean that instead of being an 'objective' article it would appear as a 'protestation de principe'.[74]

---

69    *Notre Temps*, 18 January 1931, p. 83.
70    A long catalogue of items could be given to illustrate this point. Among the articles in the *NRF*, Benjamin Crémieux's 'Inquiétude et reconstruction' (May 1931, pp. 671-690) is the most important. See also the interesting survey in *Candide*, 'La fin de l'après-guerre', with replies in issues for 27 August, and 3, 10, 17 and 24 September 1931. Robert Brasillach interviewed Jean Paulhan in the issue for 3 September.
71    Cf. E. Weber, *L'Action Française*, Stanford University Press, 1962, chapter 16.
72    Reported in *CAG* 5, p. 207.
73    Ibid., pp. 207-208 (my emphasis).
74    Ibid., p. 208.

Paulhan too felt that such a move would be very ill-advised, as he told Jean
Grenier:

> Gide voudrait que nous protestions dans la *NRF* contre les
> incidents du Trocadéro [...] et Marcel contre la carence du
> gouvernement [...]. Il y aurait beaucoup à dire sur ce besoin
> d'être ridicule, qui est commun à tant d'intellectuels. Je crois que
> je les apaiserai.[75]

This time Paulhan prevailed: no protest appeared in the January 1932 issue.
However, at this time Gide and Martin du Gard were both thinking that the
*NRF* could and should do more in providing a platform for airing
intellectuals' preoccupations. Again in the New Year Paulhan had to use all
his powers to dissuade Gide from signing a petition in favour of Aragon, who
had been charged with incitement to murder over his poem 'Front Rouge'.[76]
Gide still felt frustrated: 'Je suis comme vous', he wrote to Martin du Gard,
'*j'ai envie de signer quelque chose*'.[77] Afterwards Gide had an important
conversation with Paul Valéry, who was convinced that French politicians
were leading their citizens to the abyss, and all of Europe with them. Both of
them felt that they could not stand on the sidelines and be cowed by what
were the 'disastrous demands of the nationalists'. Martin du Gard thought
that the *NRF* was becoming 'un peu *vieille dame*', as he put it, and said he
was tempted to write elsewhere (especially in *Europe*); there was even talk of
instituting a new section or group where ideas could be debated.[78] In the face
of such determined pressure to give the *NRF* a more distinct political
orientation, Paulhan was not able to resist for long.

### The *NRF*: 'revue engagée'?

One further debate, lasting from April to August 1932, finally tilted the
balance in favour of those wishing to politicize the review. Paulhan found
himself drawn into the centre of the arena in order to argue against what he
saw as the betrayal of the goals of the *NRF* itself, and, in addition, against

---

[75]   JP to Jean Grenier, letter dated 10 December 1931, in *Correspondance 1925-1968*,
       Quimper: Calligrammes, 1984, p. 39.
[76]   For a detailed examination of this 'affair' see C. G. Geoghegan, 'Surrealism and
       Communism: the hesitations of Aragon from Kharkov to the "Affaire Front Rouge"',
       *Journal of European Studies*, VIII, 1978, pp. 12-33. Paulhan wrote to Gide: 'C'est une
       habitude des écrivains assez émouvante que de signer au petit bonheur toutes les
       pétitions qu'on leur présente.' Paulhan objected that the petition for Aragon followed a
       surrealist 'manifeste contradictoire et lâche' which was hypocritical and opportunist;
       letter reproduced in Gide-Martin du Gard, *Correspondance*, vol. 1, p. 716.
[77]   Letter dated 12 February 1932 reproduced in ibid., p. 508 (my emphasis).
[78]   See the crucial conversation of 6 March 1932 reported in *CAG* 5, p. 229.

what he considered to be intellectual bad faith in their rivals' camp at *Europe*. The argument began when Paulhan reproduced extracts from a long letter written by Jean Guéhenno and published in *Europe*.[79] In a commentary on the text in the *Revue des revues*, Paulhan accused his opposite number of bad faith for judging 'par avance un événement qu'il ne connaît pas'.[80] For Paulhan the hypocrisy derived from the fact that Guéhenno had refused to condemn *all* wars; for those intellectuals grouped around the review *Europe* armed violence was acceptable and inevitable in revolution: 'vous en voulez moins aux canons et aux mitrailleuses qu'aux patries et aux nations. [...] Je vois que vous posez mal la question'. In a reply which was placed in the next month's issue, Guéhenno retorted that even if he had put it badly, the important thing was to have dared to raise again the question of war. His premiss was that writers of their generation had survived the experience of the First World War and that it was now essential to explore intellectuals' attitudes 'devant de nouvelles violences *nationales*'.[81]. In a final, rather bitter, exchange (which had sinister resonances for the future), Guéhenno argued that nothing was more likely to cause revolutionary violence than the cowardice and debasement of intellectuals. The issue of war had to be addressed: 'ce monde est si plein de misères que beaucoup d'entre nous se réfugient dans les magnifiques domaines du songe'. Paulhan, on the other hand, pointed to what he considered to be the major flaw in Guéhenno's argument:

> Cet engagement que vous nous demandez de prendre, êtes-vous sûr de la tenir vous-même? Ne lirions-nous pas en tête de l'*Europe*, le jour où Paris serait menacé par quelque armée hitlérienne ou fasciste, un appel aux armes signé Jean Guéhenno? Et croyez-vous donc qu'il soit toujours aisé de décider si une guerre est nationale ou civile? [82]

On reading this exchange Martin du Gard wrote immediately to tell Paulhan that he admired Guéhenno's emotion and honesty and, in short, that he preferred *Europe*'s commitment to the burning issues of the day;

---

79      The letter, entitled 'Les intellectuels et le désarmement', was addressed to 'Messieurs les membres du comité permanent des lettres et des arts de la Société des Nations' in *Europe*, March 1932, pp. 313-327. Guéhenno accused the committee of dilatoriness in confronting war which, he thought, was the foremost preoccupation of the time.

80      *NRF*, April 1932, pp 777-778.

81      *NRF*, May 1932, pp. 942-944.

82      Ibid.

Je préfère sa 'Lettre à Paulhan' à votre réponse. Il s'y engage une fois de plus, il se découvre généreusement; le fond du débat lui importe plus que ce qu'on pourra penser de son attitude, ou ce qu'on pourra critiquer dans le détail. [...] Vous avez pour vous les rieurs de «l'élite»(!), mais l'accent de Guéhenno touche au coeur. *Et il se peut que les temps ne soient plus à éborgner les mouches, et qu'il y ait plus d'urgent à faire.*[83]

Paulhan could only defend himself vigorously, arguing that the greatest danger was intellectual inconsistency; in what was a remarkably strong rebuke to a man who was Gide's long time friend and *confidant*, he warned Martin du Gard against the risk of falling into the same trap:

Je crains un peu que vous n'apparteniez à la race dangereuse des gens qui pour se faire pardonner leur détachement [...] se précipitent de tous les côtés, préfèrent s'engager à savoir précisément sur quoi ils s'engagent et montrent une bonne volonté capable de tout embrouiller.[84]

As Benda had argued in 1928, Paulhan firmly believed that by occupying the higher moral ground of pacifism, by adopting its defence as *their* sole prerogative, Guéhenno, Rolland and their followers on the Left were guilty of their own betrayal.[85]

The final stage of the *NRF*'s inexorable move towards commitment came when Gide insisted that the review should print the text of Romain Rolland's well known call for a world peace congress, 'La guerre vient'. This text was one of the preliminaries to the organization of the Amsterdam-Pleyel peace movement.[86] In this text, Rolland declaimed:

---

[83]    Martin du Gard to JP, letter dated 29 May 1932 (AP).

[84]    JP to Martin du Gard, letter dated 6 June 1932, in *JPC* 1, p. 252.

[85]    In the same forthright exposition of his views, the editor of the *NRF* went on: 'Et quand vous dites que les temps ne sont plus à éborgner les mouches, et qu'il y a plus urgent à faire, vous me jetez dans l'horreur. Les temps ne sont à rien du tout, et il n'y a rien de plus urgent aujourd'hui comme hier et comme il y a mille ans que de ne pas se laisser bourrer le crâne, d'observer que les pacifistes nous content aujourd'hui les mêmes sornettes que le général Cherfils en 1914, et de tâcher d'y voir clair.' *JPC* 1, pp. 252-253.

[86]    On the Amsterdam Congress against Imperialist War, and the Congress against Fascism held at the salle Pleyel held in 1933, see D. Caute, *Communism and the French Intellectuals*, London: Deutsch, 1964, pp. 103ff., and J. Droz, *Histoire de l'antifascisme en Europe, 1923-1939*, La Découverte, 1985, pp. 177-212. For recent examinations of intellectuals' different standpoints regarding pacifism, see N. Ingram, *The Politics of Dissent. Pacifism in France 1919-1939*, Oxford: Clarendon Press, 1991, and C. Prochasson, *Les Intellectuels, le socialisme et la guerre, 1900-1938*, Seuil, 1993.

> *Ce que nous voulons, c'est soulever une immense vague*
> *d'opinion contre la guerre, — quelle qu'elle soit, d'où qu'elle*
> *vienne, et quels que soient ceux qu'elle menace.* [87]

Paulhan objected strongly to the inclusion of this text which, he felt, was not of appropriate quality for the pages of the *NRF*.[88] What is more, the hypocrisy of the declaration was grotesque in Paulhan's eyes: he pointed out to both Gide and Martin du Gard that the pacifist congress was to be co-organized by Henri Barbusse, 'qui n'est pas du tout pacifiste, qui même, étant communiste, est "contre tous les pacifismes", et prêt à substituer aux guerres impérialistes la guerre civile'.[89] Martin du Gard told Paulhan that it was the breakdown of the Lausanne Conference on 19 July which had finally persuaded him to sign, and that the wording of the declaration left him with no further doubts. It is worth quoting at length from Martin du Gard's justification, because he spoke for Gide and other signatories:

> Je n'avais pas attendu ça pour m'apercevoir que les
> gouvernements capitalistes sont aveuglés par la complication,
> très réelle d'ailleurs, des problèmes immédiats et nationaux, et
> incapables de s'entendre sur le plan général [...]. Et je me disais
> que seul un immense mouvement d'opinion pourrait les
> obliger à donner le coup de barre nécessaire. Là-dessus me
> parvient le manifeste de R[omain] R[olland] qui, justement, fait
> appel *à tous*, sans distinction de parti ni de confession, pour
> essayer de provoquer [...] ce sursaut d'effroi et de bon sens qui
> pourraient encore, je crois, sauver la paix. Vous n'êtes pas
> encore parvenu à me faire regretter mon geste. Mais je connais
> vos diableries...[90]

The *NRF* finally printed Rolland's declaration in the issue for August 1932.[91] Thus, by having to yield at last to accumulated pressure from Gide and Martin du Gard to 'politicize' the review, and by publishing Rolland's communist-inspired declaration without critical commentary, the *NRF* followed *Europe* into the fellow-travelling, antifascist camp.

---

87  *Europe*, July 1932, pp. 476-477.
88  See the angry exchange of views between Gide and Paulhan reproduced in Grover, 'Les années 30...', pp. 830-849.
89  Ibid., p. 835.  Cf. JP to Martin du Gard, letter in Fonds RMG, vol. 118 [July 1932].
90  Martin du Gard to JP, letter dated 31 July 1932 (AP).  Both Gide and Martin du Gard were in the process of submitting their own declarations against war to Félicien Challaye; see Gide-Martin du Gard, *Correspondance*, vol. 1 , pp. 528-9, 720.
91  *NRF*, August 1932, pp. 318-319.

In 1928 the serialization of Benda's *La Trahison des clercs* had appeared to fulfil the primary goal of the *NRF*, which was to remain aloof from partisan politics. Instead it worked as a catalyst, sparking off debates on a number of issues which were uppermost in intellectuals' minds at the time. By the summer 1932 Jean Paulhan was forced to accept material which did not fulfil his exacting, literary, criteria and which, moreover, bore a marked political colouring that was sharper than the gentler radicalist tones which had charaterized the review until then. This was directly attributable to events unfolding both at home and abroad, events which awakened intellectuals' fears and stirred them to action. For Paulhan the lessons of the First World War had not been learned; he wrote to Guéhenno:

> Quant à Gide, je crois qu'il accepte nettement aujourd'hui, et souhaite peut-être, la guerre civile. D'ailleurs, avouez qu'il y a maintenant un élan vers cette guerre civile, exactement pareil à l'élan de 1910-1913 vers la guerre nationale. Rolland a remplacé Barrès. A-t-on beaucoup gagné ou changé?[92]

Paulhan's bitterness, or cynicism, as expressed here derives from the fact that he had had to yield to repeated pressures to push the *NRF* into moving with the times: it had to reflect contemporary preoccupations. Afterwards, Paulhan realized that he could not reverse this process and, indeed, the *NRF* went on considering political questions. For example, later that year a special *dossier* presented some of the new ideas and regenerative plans put forward by various small groups of young intellectuals, characterized by their historian as 'non-conformist'.[93] Many of the writers in the *NRF* circle were already beginning to look favourably on the prospect of a 'Front Commun', a movement which would inspire the Popular Front of 1936. And later in the 1930s, as war came nearer, Paulhan himself committed the *NRF* to the anti-Munich cause. Ironically it was his serialization of *La Trahison des clercs* which had cleared the way.

---

[92] JP to Guéhenno [August 1932] (AP).
[93] See the 'Cahier de revendications: onze témoignages', in *NRF*, December 1932, discussed below in chapter 3. Cf. J.-L. Loubet del Bayle, *Les Non-conformistes des années 30*, Seuil, 1969.

# Chapter 3

## Idealism or militancy?
## Radicalism, antifascism and the *NRF*

*L'antifascisme n'est pas seulement le vaste champ où les libéraux se mêlent aux communistes, comme le montrera la guerre d'Espagne [...], c'est un sentiment; c'est aussi une attitude; c'est aussi une politique.*[1]

*Il n'y a plus d'innocents, de nos jours. Et je crains que le manichéisme du fascisme et de l'antifascisme ne trahisse qu'une assez grande paresse d'esprit: mais c'est une paresse quise traîne dans le sang.*[2]

*La politique a discrédité le mot «centre» en lui faisant évoquer des idées d'indécision, de neutralité, de lieu vague où se massent tous ceux du troupeau qu'effraient les aventures.*[3]

The literary primacy of the *NRF* has tended to obscure the important rôle it played in responding to political developments. This rôle has been neglected by historians of French political and cultural life. Jean Touchard, for example, discussing the relationship between the Radical Party and the periodical press in the 1930s, writes:

> Vous ne trouvez pas de revues de gauche de quelque importance dans les années 1930. Il y a *Europe*, qui est fort loin de l'univers radical, la *NRF*, mais la *NRF* est essentiellement une revue littéraire.[4]

This chapter will argue that the intellectuals writing regularly in the *NRF* made a substantial contribution to debates about politics and ideology at a time when they themselves were considering their own responses to the political situation. These debates were conditioned by several factors. To begin with, the stalwarts

---

1    A. Malraux, preface to R. Rolland & J. Guéhenno, *L'Indépendance de l'esprit, Correspondance 1919-1944, Cahiers Romain Rolland* 23, Albin Michel, 1975, p. 7.
2    JP to Suarès, letter dated 15 August 1936, in *CJP* 4, pp. 146-147.
3    J. Schlumberger, *NRF*, August 1936, p. 382.
4    J. Touchard, *La Gauche en France depuis 1900*, Points-Seuil, 1981, p. 111.

of each monthly issue of the *NRF* belonged to an older generation educated during the heroic phase of the early Third Republic. Faithful to the values of radical-republican France, by the early 1930s they had, none the less, become frustrated by the lacklustre performance of the Radical Party in government. There were good reasons for encouraging political renewal, in particular regarding the fortunes and appeal of the Radical Party. There was also a younger generation of writers who had their work published in the pages of the *NRF*. These young authors, profoundly influenced by the First World War – whether they had fought in it or not – had different reasons for wanting to discover new political ideas. Naturally such pressures from his own contributors complicated Paulhan's task during these years. He was forced each month to perform a careful balancing act. On the one hand, he strove to maintain the literary quality of the review, whilst on the other he was forced to take account of the demands of influential figures close to Gaston Gallimard or the *NRF* like André Gide, André Malraux or Pierre Drieu La Rochelle, whose attitudes to politics and publicly expressed commitment risked forcing the *NRF* into the adoption of a biased political position. The difficulties faced by Paulhan are aptly summarized by Claude Roy:

> Quand on les [i.e., les intellectuels] considère aujourd'hui, leurs allées et venues, leurs marches et contremarches, la première image est celle du film 'comique', ou de la fourmilière écrasée. Ils entrent et sortent, vont et viennent, s'agitent entre le communisme, le fascisme socialiste, le maurrassisme, le radicalisme d'Alain, comme si la tarentule les piquait.[5]

Political events at home and abroad came increasingly to determine the stances adopted by French intellectuals. There are four focal points of interest: the renewal of radicalist politics around 1930; the rise of 'non-conformist' political ideas; reactions to the riots of 6 February 1934; and the creation and demise of the Popular Front.

### The renewal of radicalist politics

The *NRF* was perceived as a radicalist organ. It was radicalist both in tone and content, as well as in respect of its personnel and its audience, which comprised members of the teaching and other middle-ranking professions, sectors of the French population which traditionally supported the Radical Party. The primary characteristic of its appeal to teachers was what Jean Touchard has called 'une sorte de très grande nébuleuse radicalisante, [...] ce que Jacques Kayser appelle

---

[5]     *Moi Je*, Gallimard, 1969, p. 214.

«le radicalisme sans frontières». C'est le radicalisme de l'université humaniste, rationaliste, tolérante et gidienne [sic]'.[6]   Even the conservative Sorbonne professor Fortunat Strowski characterized the *NRF* network (*sociabilité*) in similar terms, and it was certainly viewed as radicalist by its more vociferous opponents: Henri Béraud, in his anti-*NRF* polemic of 1923, labelled the review as 'caillautiste'[7], a reference to the stalwart Radical Party politician Joseph Caillaux. Its founders André Gide (born 1869) and Jean Schlumberger (born 1877), as well as its three regular *chroniqueurs* Alain, Julien Benda (born 1867) and Albert Thibaudet (born 1874), all lived their formative years in what Thibaudet came to characterize as the *République des Professeurs*. The Radical Party leader Edouard Herriot presided at the banquets when Paulhan and Benda were honoured by the republic with the *Légion d'honneur*.  In particular the older generation had been profoundly marked by the Dreyfus Affair and the subsequent radicalist 'défense de la République'.[8]  By the early 1930s, however, these intellectuals shared the anxieties of many in politics who feared the stagnation of the French Radical Party.  Serge Berstein sums up the situation confronting the radicals at the end of the 1920s:

> Pendant que les dirigeants hésitent sur la tactique politique à suivre dans l'immédiat, oscillant entre la participation à l'Union nationale et la cure d'opposition, s'opère une très large réflexion sur la doctrine du parti et la place du phénomène radical dans la France de l'entre-deux-guerres.[9]

The poor economic performance of radical-dominated *Cartel des gauches* governments in 1924-1926 undermined the credibility of the radicals and, from 1927-1928 onwards, vigorous attempts were made to rejuvenate the Party's image.[10]  The mainstream Radical Party however, underwent a noticeable shift

---

6    J. Touchard, *La Gauche en France depuis 1900*, pp. 114, 134-135.

7    Strowski wrote: 'Ce serait donc la *NRF* qui exercerait la plus grosse influence sur les jeunes gens. Il n'y a pas à s'en plaindre: l'esprit de la *NRF* est purement universitaire, j'entends dans le sens noble du mot. Son humanisme lui fait concevoir tout sous l'angle du lettré. C'est un véritable mouvement de Renaissance'; *L'Opinion*, 21 August 1920, quoted by L. Morino, *La NRF dans l'histoire des lettres*, Gallimard, 1939, p. 212. For Béraud, see *La Croisade des longues figures*, Editions du siècle, 1924, p. 90.

8    See, for instance, J. Benda, *Jeunesse d'un clerc*, Gallimard, 1968, pp. 114ff, J. Schlumberger, *Eveils*, in*Oeuvres* VI, Gallimard, 1960, p. 335, and C. Jamet, 'Le dreyfusisme radical d'Alain', in *Les Ecrivains et l'Affaire Dreyfus*, textes réunis par G. Leroy, PUF, 1983, pp. 177-184.

9    S. Berstein, *Histoire du Parti Radical*, vol. 2, *Crise du radicalisme, (1926-1939)*, Presses de la FNSP, 1982, pp. 11-12.

10   For example, see Berstein again on the *jeunes turcs*: '[...] un groupe de jeunes intellectuels radicaux ou radicalisants s'efforce de tirer les leçons de l'échec du Cartel et de repenser la doctrine du parti en se fondant sur le réalisme'; *Crise du radicalisme*, p. 12.

from the moderate Left towards the centre and, indeed, the centre-right, as the 1930s progressed.

None the less the Party's political, or electoral, stasis was compensated by the influence and enthusiasm of its intellectual supporters, who looked back nostalgically to the 1900s on what was considered at the time to be the 'golden age' of radicalism. Undoubtedly Alain was the exemplary survivor of this age, and at the time he was regarded as such both by himself and his disciples; for instance, in his *Citoyen contre les pouvoirs* (1926) he characterized himself as the only remaining 'combiste', a reference to Emile Combes, one of the heroes of the 'golden age' of the 1900s.[11] As Jean-Thomas Nordmann has written, the teacher-readership of the *NRF* would have found in Alain 'le miroir idéal qui réfléchit l'image embellie de la république provinciale, familiale et pacifique, la République d'avant 1914'.[12]. By the time Paulhan took over as editor of the *NRF* in 1925, close ties had been established between Gaston Gallimard and Alain, who joined the *NRF*'s regular team of *chroniqueurs* in 1927. Moreover, in 1925, Gallimard collected together a number of texts by Alain dating from before 1914, and republished them as *Eléments d'une doctrine radicale.*[13] Complimentary copies of this publication were distributed at a ministerial meeting of Herriot's cabinet in 1925. Thibaudet relates the episode:

> Deux Lafuma pour les deux Présidents, des ordinaires pour les ministres, et des services de presse pour les sous-secrétaires d'Etat. Ces messieurs retournèrent soupçonneusement le 'document bleu', eurent des sourires, et l'un d'eux rédigea l'impression générale en ce mot: 'S'il y avait vraiment une doctrine radicale, est-ce que nous ne serions pas les premiers à le savoir?'[14]

Despite the humour, Thibaudet's assessment of Alain's Radical 'doctrine' is, on the whole, accurate.[15] Alain's radicalism, reduced to its basic tenet, extolled the virtues of the 'citizen' (*citoyen*) who, whilst in complete obedience to the republic and to its ideals, was encouraged to exercise the rights of the individual 'contre les pouvoirs'; these ideas were intended as a bastion for the 'little man' against

---

[11] See Touchard, *La Gauche en France depuis 1900*, p. 125, and Jamet, 'Le dreyfusisme radical d'Alain', p. 184, both quoting Alain.

[12] J.-T. Nordmann, *Histoire des radicaux (1820-1973)*, La Table Ronde, 1974, p. 144.

[13] Gallimard, 'Documents Bleus' no. 24, 1925.

[14] Thibaudet, *La République des Professeurs*, Grasset, 1927, p. 78; this publicity stunt is also recounted by Robert Aron, Gaston Gallimard's secretary at the time, in *Fragments d'une vie*, Plon, 1981, pp. 49-50.

[15] Cf. Touchard, *La Gauche en France depuis 1900*, pp. 123ff. Jacques Kayser, too, denies that Alain had any real doctrinal influence; see his essay 'Le radicalisme des Radicaux', in *Tendances politiques dans la vie française depuis 1789*, Hachette, 1960, pp. 65-87.

the monolithic State[16]. Raymond Aron remembered admiring Alain's anti-war views during the 1930s more than his 'doctrine': he recalls that 'si la politique d'Alain me tentait, c'est qu'elle m'épargnait la peine de connaître la réalité', and most importantly that 'le citoyen contre les pouvoirs s'arroge immédiatement l'irresponsabilité.[17] The greatest appeal of Alain's thinking lay precisely in the glorification of the individual's rights within the republican State: again, Raymond Aron confessed to being

> pour le peuple contre les privilégiés, pour le progrès contre la tradition, pour la reconstruction rationnelle de la société contre les traditions traditionnelles. Les symbôles républicains ou révolutionnaires me touchaient plus que les symboles conservateurs.[18]

Very rarely were any of the *Propos* overtly political: out of over one hundred to appear between 1927 and 1936, only those of April and September 1934 referred to current events, and even then Alain's conclusion, in April, was typically oblique and non-committal: 'La politique est un jeu de finesse et de précaution, auquel tout citoyen doit être initié.'[19] Coming only a few weeks after the February riots it was clear that Alain's radicalism had little to do with forceful or strident political action. However, Alain was greatly revered and attracted eulogies from former pupils in essays and reviews. Denis Saurat, for example, put Alain alongside Montaigne in a paean of praise published in November 1932.[20]

Outside the *NRF*, however, Alain's thought was often reviled with equal venom at both extremes of the political spectrum. For instance there was a ferocious attack on Alain's presence in the *NRF* in December 1928. An anonymous critic in *L'Action Française* wrote that if the *NRF* had once been a 'haven of repose', it was now 'envahie par les pires passions partisanes'.[21] Having taken to task Léautaud, Henry de Montherlant and Jean Prévost, the author attacked Alain for being 'le professeur de philosophie dont se réclament les jeunes révoltés de Normale, qui [...] poursuit son dangereux enseignement

---

16   Touchard, *La Gauche en France depuis 1900*, p. 125.
17   Raymond Aron, *Mémoires*, Julliard, 1983, pp. 41-43.
18   Raymond Aron, 'Alain et la politique', in *Hommage à Alain*, 1952, p. 157.
19   *Propos*, in *NRF*, April 1934, p. 691.
20   'Alain', *NRF*, November 1932, pp. 760-766. S. de Sacy in June the same year (pp. 1110-1113) also eulogised Alain.
21   *L'Action Française*, 13 December 1928.

par de pesantes ironies.'[22]  At the other end of the political spectrum, Alain's response to a survey entitled 'Pour qui écrivez-vous?', published in the fellow-travelling monthly *Commune*, was savaged by Aragon, who had invited the responses. Aragon wrote:

> [Alain] est l'idéologue du radicalisme. [...]  Il est le grand pourrisseur de gauche des écoles normales.  Alain fait appel à ses élèves pour prouver qu'il n'a jamais cherché qu'à enseigner soi-même.  Nous voudrions espérer [...] qu'ils oublieront les leçons d'un des plus dangereux maîtres que la bourgeoisie donne à la jeunesse...[23]

Alain's real influence lay in his rôle as teacher at the Lycée Henri-IV and the Ecole Normale Supérieure; here his philosophy or, more accurately, his moralism, had a lasting effect on successive generations of pupils and students. Yet if the values they espoused — or even personified — still lingered, electorally-speaking the radicals suffered in the confused political atmosphere of 1930-1932.  Increasingly, 'traditional' radicalism was viewed with disdain, even by those who were sympathetic: it had become a 'passéisme'.[24]

In the *NRF*, as early as 1928 Albert Thibaudet remarked that political renewal had become a priority.  In a perspicacious essay entitled 'Réflexions sur la politique', published as a leading article on the eve of the legislative elections in late April, he detected that 'en France, les elections de 1928 se font ou vont se faire dans la crise, le marasme ou la démission des partis'.[25] The political parties risked being the victims of the lack of ideas, warned Thibaudet.  There was a pressing need for 'un redressement général', as well as a reflexion on the new conditions prevalent in politics:  'Je crois que le problème des partis, partis qui, dans une république parlementaire, sont unis par une certaine règle du jeu, s'efface devant le problème des classes.'[26]  Thibaudet was deeply troubled: he

---

22   Ibid. This example is only one of many assaults by *L'Action Française* on the *NRF* and its personnel; they were to be expected from Charles Maurras, whose very political *raison d'être* was relentlessly to attack the radical republic.  He wrote: 'pour les partis de gauche, il n'est en réalité jamais question de doctrine ni même de programme. Un seul mot d'ordre, un intérêt: la lutte contre la réaction. Jamais un radical bien né ne se laissera enregimenter sous une bannière suspecte de réaction' (*L'Action Française*, 30 December 1927); and, 'le communisme dilué s'appelle socialisme; le socialisme dilué s'appelle radicalisme...' (ibid.).

23   *Commune*, January-February 1934, p. 577. *Commune* was the organ of the Association des Ecrivains et des Artistes Révulutionnaires (AEAR).

24   See J. Goueffon's detailed analysis of Jean Zay's election in 'Le radicalisme entre la crise et le Front Populaire: la première élection de Jean Zay (1932)', in *Revue d'histoire moderne et contemporaine*, 22, 1975, pp. 619-654.

25   'Réflexions sur la politique', *NRF*, April 1928, pp. 433-445.

26   Ibid., p. 442.

considered that since the Russian Revolution, the most urgent task for French political parties was to assimilate the notion of class consciousness, for by doing so they might begin to resolve their own problems:

> On est engagé dans un parti par des opinions et des intérêts. On est engagé dans une classe par une manière d'être. Le radicalisme prête son suffixe à un parti, le socialisme à une classe.[27]

Here he offered an insight into one of the reasons for political stagnation in France, and, in October 1932, Paulhan published another article by Thibaudet. This time it was the conclusion from his book *Les Idées politiques de la France*.[28] Here his tone was even more anxious. Contrasting liberalism and traditionalism in France with the thrusting, new (and apparently very popular) ideologies he identified, he highlighted once more the major shortcoming of French politics:

> Le libéralisme est un système de coexistences dans l'espace. Le traditionnalisme est un système de continuité dans le temps. L'un et l'autre, s'ils étaient dépourvus de fermeté et de l'esprit de dialogue, donneraient ses dimensions à une critique politique passive, miroir, reflet. *L'un et l'autre impliquent en somme la même nature de passivité.*[29]

'Passivity' is the key word in Thibaudet's analysis. He had warned of the need for renewal in his April 1928 article; now, even with the victory of Herriot in June 1932, the long-awaited opportunity to close ranks with the Socialists had been lost. He went on:

> Le nom même de radical-socialisme indique que l'idéologie radicale a besoin d'une rallonge sur sa gauche. [...] C'est pourtant le socialisme qui crée aujourd'hui dans la vie politique l'appel d'air des idées, des problèmes. [...] C'est par rapport au socialisme que s'établissent les positions. C'est sur le Parti que se règlent les partis.[30]

Thibaudet's conclusion was that as part of the heritage of the French revolutionary (i.e. republican) tradition, liberalism was still viable and should be maintained, though it deserved criticism and called for modernization; further revolution, however, should be discouraged. In February 1933, Jean Prévost, one of the *NRF*'s own *jeunes turcs*, reviewed Thibaudet's book; his major criticism

---

[27]   Ibid., pp. 443-445.
[28]   *NRF*, October 1932, pp. 520-538.
[29]   Ibid., p. 527. My emphasis.
[30]   Ibid., pp. 535-536.

was that it lacked understanding concerning the nature of the extreme-Left.[31]
Further analysis was provided by Emmanuel Berl's book *La Politique et les partis*,
published in 1931 and reviewed in June 1933. This book, dedicated to André
Chamson (yet another *jeune turc*), claimed that 'le parti radical à beaucoup
d'égards, c'est la France même'.[32]  In his review Ramon Fernandez pointed to
the fact that 'les partis français poursuivent en gros une même politique'; and the
most arresting part of this appreciation came in the concluding paragraph where,
concurring with Berl that the communists could 'préserver un radicalisme réel',
Fernandez suggested that common ground should be sought upon which to
unite all of the Left in France:

> Qu'il y ait un minimum de choses à changer, sur quoi un radical
> sincère, un socialiste et un communiste pourraient s'entendre, je ne
> songe pas un instant à le nier.[33]

In short, for Fernandez the book highlighted a vacuum in French political ideas.
Thus, with French radicalism coming under sustained critical scrutiny at home,
and with the rise of fascism and communism abroad, anxious intellectuals began
to evaluate alternative ideologies.

### Political 'non-conformism'

The radicals' changing fortunes led to much feverish interest in new political
thinking in France, and the *NRF* took the opportunity to give a sample of the
ideas of numerous so-called 'non-conformist' intellectuals who had begun to
gather around a cluster of small reviews.[34]  Among the first texts to reject both
capitalism and communism in favour of a 'révolution de la personne' was
*Décadence de la nation française* by Robert Aron and Arnaud Dandieu; their book,
published by Rieder, received favourable treatment from the *NRF* in June 1931.
Aron and Dandieu launched a double-pronged attack upon traditional French
political life: their work was at once a critique of radicalist reformism and of
traditional nationalism.  Patriotism could be recuperated, argued Aron and
Dandieu, in a new framework of revolutionary, or *personalist*, individualism.[35]

---

[31]  J. Prévost, 'La critique politique', in *NRF*, February 1933, pp. 338-340.

[32]  Berl, quoted by Touchard, *La Gauche en France depuis 1900*, p. 103.

[33]  *NRF*, June 1933, pp. 997-999.

[34]  On these see in particular J.-L. Loubet del Bayle, *Les Non-conformistes des années 30*, Seuil,
1969; Z. Sternhell, *Ni droite ni gauche: l'idéologie fasciste en France*, Seuil, 1983; M. Winock,
*Histoire politique de la revue Esprit, 1930-1950*, Seuil, 1975; and P. Andreu, *Révoltes de
l'esprit. Les revues des années 30*, Editions Kimé, 1991.

[35]  R. Fernandez, *NRF*, June 1931, pp. 942-945.  Cf. Loubet del Bayle, *Les Non-conformistes des
années 30*, pp. 87ff.

Since Robert Aron was Gaston Gallimard's secretary at this time and thereby able to wield influence, Paulhan found himself under increasing pressure during 1932 to include more 'auteurs de jeunes équipes [sic]', as he wrote to Jean Schlumberger in August. Gallimard had reproached Paulhan for not accepting more material from 'les jeunes équipes politiques: (et particulièrement: aux jeunes équipes révolutionnaires)'.[36] Anxious as ever about the danger of allowing the NRF to be used as a platform for 'revolutionary' ideas, Paulhan explained his misgivings to Schlumberger:

> [...] la verité est en effet que la mode (je ne prends pas du tout le mot au sens péjoratif) révolutionnaire d'aujourd'hui ne me paraît ni moins insensée ni moins dangereuse que la mode nationaliste de 1910-1914, à laquelle elle répond si exactement; et que, s'il s'en suit une guerre civile (qui ne pourrait être qu'internationale) elle passera, je pense, en horreur, la guerre de 14. [...] Ne faut-il pas mesurer la place—étant d'ailleurs revue littéraire—aux révolutionnaires?[37]

Despite these misgivings, preparations began for the important 'Cahier de revendications', which appeared in the NRF for December 1932. Clearly it did not seem unreasonable to Schlumberger to assemble a collection of such texts, especially since he himself was lending support to at least two groups of 'non-conformists'.[38]

Denis de Rougemont was responsible for editing the 'Cahier'. The texts fall into two categories: Henri Lefebvre, Philippe Lamour and Paul Nizan were largely inspired by Marxist materialism, while the others derived their thinking from Emmanuel Mounier's 'personalism'. De Rougemont's principal aim was to attempt to define 'une cause commune de la jeunesse française'.[39] Although on the surface this seemed to be a genuine effort to present a balanced, unified set of new doctrine, the 'Cahier' caused Nizan angrily to dissociate himself from this collection of essays.[40] If the political divergences between the 'personalists' were

---

36  JP to Schlumberger, letter dated 23 August 1932 (BD). In this same letter, Paulhan took the issue planned for September and listed in detail the background of the contributors, and concluded that 'je crois que le difficile serait de découvrir une jeune équipe littéraire ou philosophique d'aujourd'hui qui ne soit pas représentée à la NRF''.

37  JP to Schlumberger [August-September 1932] (BD).

38  See Les Chantiers co-opératifs, Prospectus, numéro hors série, May 1932, and numbers 1 and 2, June and July 1932, where Schlumberger signed a manifesto for the 'Co-opération franco-allemande des nouvelles équipes'; see also Georges Roditi's L'Homme nouveau, no. 1, January 1934, p. 1.

39  'Cahier de Revendications', NRF, December 1932, pp. 801-845 (p. 801).

40  P. Nizan, 'Sur un certain front unique', Europe, January 1933, pp. 137-146, and his correspondence with Denis de Rougemont in ibid., February 1933, pp. 303-304.

only slight, there was an unbridgeable gulf between them and the Marxists. Instead of uniting the *jeunes équipes*, the *NRF* 'Cahier' succeeded in highlighting their fundamental ideological differences over a year before the riots of 6 February 1934. Nizan's counter-attack, on behalf of the communist-backed Association des écrivains et des artistes révolutionnaires (AEAR), berated these 'amateurs distingués', as he called them, insisting that 'nous ne conclurons pas d'accords [...] avec nos plus authentiques ennemis'. The only authentic revolution for Nizan was Marxist and proletarian; though the *personnalistes* might be able to diagnose the shortcomings of bourgeois political ideology, their primary motivation was to 'engage the fight against communism'.[41] Nizan was struck most by their unprecedented search for new political space; drawing on de Rougemont, he quoted this extract:

> Ni à gauche ni à droite, il n'y a rien pour nous. Nous nous plaçons à l'origine de quelque chose d'autre, dont la réalité échappe encore à ceux qui récitent Marx.[42]

Nizan discerned this new space as being fascist: drawing the analogy with Germany where the fascists developed *'en dehors* de l'opposition formelle, [en France] nos nazis naissent [...] dans les revues littéraires'.[43] De Rougemont went on the defensive saying that Nizan had known of 'la composition et l'esprit du 'Cahier' [...] le jour même où nous convînmes de votre collaboration'.[44] Nizan persisted, however, and pointed to what he saw as

> le déséquilibre manifeste qu'il y avait dans l'enquête de la *NRF* entre deux révolutionnaires communistes et tous les autres. Plus d'un s'est étonné de cette disproportion et de la confusion qu'elle n'a pas manqué d'entraîner. [...] Il s'agissait moins de présenter un tableau véritable des revendications présentes que de noyer les revendications communistes parmi les autres témoignages.[45]

Consideration of the problem of political and ideological renewal continued in the pages of the *NRF*: As Thibaudet had noted already, the crux of the problem was to be found in the apparent impossibility of reconciling the institutions of the bourgeois republic, their defenders, the intellectual élites and the masses. Ramon Fernandez reflected on this *impasse* in an important survey

---

41    *Europe*, January 1933, pp. 137-138, 145.
42    *NRF*, December 1932, p. 840.
43    *Europe*, January 1933, p. 146.
44    *Europe*, February 1933, p. 303.
45    Ibid., p. 304.

entitled *Rajeunissement de la politique*. He argued that the true place of the intellectual was within society, and that the myth of the ivory tower had led to the misconception that the *clerc* was somehow a superior being.[46] Although the intellectual had to subordinate himself to the nature of his work, Fernandez repeated that 'rien, dans le développement essentiel de la pensée, de la sensibilité contemporaines ne justifie une opposition radicale entre l'intellectuel et la masse'.[47] At the basis of Fernandez' argument lay the premise that 'l'homme moyen' benefited from the society created and defended by intellectuals; their professional and political roles were inseparable. Fernandez continued in this line of thinking in an article in the *NRF* in March 1933.[48] He believed that any conception of a politico-intellectual élite could not avoid considering the masses, since the new ideologies operating in Italy, Russia and Germany had manipulated the masses 'en utilisant [leur] façon de voir et de sentir'. In France, economic development had altered the political rôle of the masses, he thought, for 'la masse n'est plus ce qu'elle était. [...] Elle exerce une pression nouvelle et surprenante sur les pensées et sur les décisions des élites'.[49] Parliamentarianism was therefore at risk: 'Je frémis', admitted Fernandez, 'en songeant à tant de jeunes héros qui se ruent vers les révolutions de droite et de gauche pour y engloutir le peu qui leur reste de liberté'.[50] Thus *NRF* intellectuals such as Robert Aron and Ramon Fernandez both talked of decadence and of the changing character of political élites; and as Touchard has remarked, these central themes of the early 1930s became linked: 'les jeunes intellectuels des années 1930 pensent que les élites ont une mission et que les clercs ne peuvent pas trahir'.[51] Eager as such young intellectuals were to denounce the rationalism of such as Benda, Jean Paulhan made efforts to prevent the *NRF* from further providing what would have been an extremely influential platform for those he characterized as 'jeunes équipes'. A further challenge to his skills as editor came in the wake of the Stavisky Affair, which exploded in January 1934.

---

46    *Rajeunissement de la politique*, préface de Henry de Jouvenel, Corrêa, 1932, pp. 73-86.

47    Ibid., pp. 80-82.

48    'Sur la formation d'une élite', *NRF*, March 1933, pp. 523-529.

49    Ibid., pp. 526-527.

50    Ibid. Fernandez repeated these fears and anxiety over the masses in his reply to another important survey conducted by Gilbert Comte for *La Grande Revue* in November 1933. The survey asked 'Quels principes et quelles applications assureraient précisément le rajeunissement de la France dans votre vie privée, publique?'. The replies, and there were many, appeared in *La Grande Revue* from January to June 1934. Fernandez' appeared in May 1934, pp. 378-382. By May, however, Fernandez had committed himself to the 'masses'.

51    J. Touchard, 'L'Esprit des années 1930: tentative de renouvellement de la pensée politique française', in *Tendances politiques*, p. 99.

### Reactions to the riots of 6 February 1934

The riots of 6 February 1934 shook the republican political system. Pressure from intellectuals to take account of events grew even stronger and, partly in order to infuse a sense of immediacy into the *NRF*, Paulhan introduced a new rubric in December 1933 called the *Airs du Mois*: he told Jean Grenier that this timely innovation was to be 'une rubrique d'actualité'.[52] After the riots Paulhan had just enough time (between 6 and 15 February, the review's copy deadline for the March issue) to assemble a number of reactions to the events. The critic Benjamin Crémieux wrote eight pages for the *chroniques* section, and over ten pages of the *Airs du Mois* were devoted to the crisis. Crémieux estimated that three-quarters of the crowd had been innocent demonstrators and that they had been manipulated by extremists.[53] He argued that any alliance between the Radicals and the Socialists (SFIO) 'coalise contre elle toutes les forces bourgeoises et petit-bourgeoises, ainsi qu'une fraction importante des electeurs radicaux, surtout les paysans'[54]. The major cause of the troubles were the recent developments of capitalism in France and abroad, and Crémieux found that the French were bewildered by the choices apparently confronting them. He highlighted another factor crucial in this situation: the danger of a fascist takeover was defused by the disunity of the extreme-Right, while in the centre and on the Left the radicals, and even some socialists, refused to unite against fascism because of their anti-communism, or anti-Marxism.[55] Not forgetting the looting of the 7th, the demonstrations of the 9th and the strikes of 12 February, Crémieux insisted that any measures taken by Doumergue would only be interim ones: 'ce ministère d'hommes trop vieux, [...] d'une pureté discutée, sans une idée commune ne peut durer. [...] Ordre-liberté-je m'en-fichisme reste l'idéal du Français moyen', wrote the sceptical critic.[56] Considering authoritarianism on both political extremes, Crémieux felt that either had the potential to damage France irreparably; and significantly enough at this stage he did not hold out much hope for a common or united front: 'aucun signe précurseur d'une large union de ce genre ne se montre encore'.[57] In his concluding paragraph Crémieux revealed that his idealism was tempered with resignation, and even a feeling of impotence:

---

[52]  For further details see above, chapter 1.
[53]  'Hypothèses autour du 6 février', *NRF*, March 1934, pp. 537-545.
[54]  Ibid., p. 538.
[55]  Ibid., pp. 540-541.
[56]  Ibid., p. 542, 543.
[57]  Ibid., pp. 543-545.

> Nous savons aujourd'hui que l'aménagement rationnel du monde
> ne s'est ébauché partout qu'à travers une éclipse de la liberté et de
> l'individu. [...] Nous voudrions que le révolution nécessaire se fît
> sans un sacrifice total des conquêtes de l'individu. [...] 6 février
> 1934: charnière de l'histoire française ou mauvais cauchemar?'[58]

It is crucial to remember that for a great many intellectuals the events of 6-12
February were decisive: many felt obliged to adopt a distinct political position,
and the *NRF* duly reflected these moves. In the *Airs du Mois*, Drieu rejoiced at
the Concorde riots and wished 'que ce moment durât toujours'[59]. Georges
Altman, a communist, provided an emotional eye-witness account; his evocation
of the silence in which the demonstrations of 12 February took place hinted at the
sudden growth of unity among the Left. Julien Benda contributed a series of
meditations by his alter-ego, 'Eleuthère'; in typical fashion he went to the defence
of the republic:

> Méditation d'un chef au matin du 6 février:— Donc je lance mes
> jeunes gens à l'assaut du régime. S'ils gagnent, qu'importe qu'on
> tue quelque mille hommes. L'écrasement de la gueuse vaut bien
> cela. S'ils perdent et qu'on m'en tue seulement un, j'ameute toute la
> France contre le régime de sang. Dans les deux cas, excellente
> affaire.

In short, Benda saw the February riots as a new 'Affaire Dreyfus'.[60] Finally,
Ramon Fernandez made the first of several statements signalling the beginning
of his itinerary of commitment leading him from fellow-travelling on the Left to
support for Jacques Doriot's extreme right-wing Parti populaire français. As he
saw it, 'à Paris en tout cas, les gens qui ont de l'argent forment un front commun
contre ceux qui n'en ont pas'. The Left should unite against the moneyed classes:

> Dans la poursuite de leur unité jusqu'ici chimérique, que les
> gauches songent à cet énorme avantage des droites sur eux: l'unité
> que créent naturellement la possession et l'intérêt.[61]

These were extraordinary words for what what was, supposedly, an aloof
literary review.

58 Ibid., p. 545.
59 'Air de Février 34', *NRF*, March 1934, p. 568.
60 'Sur les conflits de la foule et de la troupe', *NRF*, March 1934, pp. 576-578. Paulhan
reported to Grenier that 'Benda cache assez mal le plaisir que lui ont fait les massacres de
la semaine dernière'; letter to J. Grenier, 12 February 1934 (AP).
61 'Pour l'unité d'action', *NRF*, March 1934, pp. 577-578.

Calls for the unity of the political Left in the March issue of the *NRF* coincided with the publication on 5 March of the manifesto of the Comité de vigilance des intellectuels antifascistes (CVIA) under the triple patronage of Alain, Paul Langevin and Paul Rivet.[62] And in April, Crémieux, clearly aware that things had developed rapidly, returned to the matter of left-wing unity. He wrote:

> La journée du 12 février, l'irritation de la province contre Paris laissent apercevoir la possibilité d'un vaste mouvement de gauche. Et le radicalisme devrait théoriquement prendre la tête, s'il était tel que le définit Alain. Pratiquement, hélas! il n'en va pas de même. Et on peut estimer vain d'espérer une rénovation assez rapide du parti radical pour qu'il redevienne digne de son destin.[63]

The Radical Party risked becoming an 'anachronism'; if it could undertake urgent renewal, a *Front populaire* could be realized.[64] These critical voices culminated in Ramon Fernandez' controversial 'Lettre ouverte à André Gide'. The February riots had forced Fernandez to abandon his 'hope', as he put it, in the right, and henceforth he would work for a unified Left:

> Après le 6 février cet espoir n'est définitivement plus permis. Il n'y a rien, rien, là-bas, derrière leurs grands mots, que des porte-monnaie qui se dégonflent. Marx avait trop raison, je choisis le camp des porte-monnaie vides.[65]

Thus in April 1934 all of the *chroniques* section was preoccupied with the serious side of February events: the reactions were not, however, unified. This was noticed by a reviewer in *Commune*, who wondered why Crémieux had turned a blind eye to a host of germinating proto- or neo-fascist groups, and why he had not joined 'notre camarade Ramon Fernandez, [...] qui fut un des premiers à prendre parti.'[66] Paulhan would have been gratified to read that as yet, *Commune* did not detect a completely partisan stance at the *NRF*; and his inclusion of

---

62    See G. Lefranc, *Histoire du Front Populaire*, Payot, 1965, pp. 46-47, and Annex, p. 433, and N. Racine-Ferlaud, 'Le Comité de vigilance des intellectuels antifascistes (1934-1939)', in *Mouvement social*, 101, 1977, pp. 87-113. Fernandez was elected to the CVIA on 8 May when Paul Rivet stated 'nous devons être présents à toutes les manifestations antifascistes et y affirmer notre position'; Lefranc, *Histoire du Front Populaire*, p. 47.

63    'Partis à prendre', *NRF*, April 1934, p. 700.

64    In the same issue, Thibaudet criticized Alain's radicalism: 'l'esprit radical se définirait volontiers pour Alain comme une opposition et un refus devant les *activismes*, et que le radicalisme [...] ou l'esprit républicain, se définirait presque comme un *passivisme*'; 'Activisme et passivisme', ibid., pp. 692-697.

65    *NRF*, April 1934, p. 708.

66    See Vladimir Pozner in *Commune*, May 1934, pp. 1002-1008.

Schlumberger's *air du mois* the same month showed that he wished to retain a semblance of political balance.[67] Schlumberger departed from Crémieux's view by stating that as soon as one passed Versailles, people in the provinces 'n'ont pas cru devoir conclure que c'en fût fait de la République et qu'on eût passé, le 6 février, d'un ordre du monde dans un autre'.[68]

By the beginning of May 1934 the momentum of intellectuals' *engagement* was gathering. The Union pour la Vérité assembled on 28 April to discuss the problems of 'Libéralisme et communisme'; here, Fernandez defended the 'communist interpretation' of events with special reference to the unity of 9 February, and declared himself in an even more forthright manner than in his 'Lettre ouverte': 'comme je suis marxiste, je dis simplement que c'est une lutte de classes.'[69] And in the *NRF* for May, Fernandez communicated 'Un appel aux travailleurs' in which antifascist intellectuals declared themselves allied with 'tous les travailleurs nos camarades [...], contre une dictature fasciste. [...] Nous sommes prêts à tout sacrifier pour empêcher que la France ne soit soumise à un régime d'oppression'.[70]

By the summer of 1934 the flood of reactions to the February riots had receded. A change of mood was signalled by the publication by Gallimard of the *Plan du 9 juillet*, accompanied by a preface by Jules Romains: here Crémieux's call for a 'programme minimum' seemed to have been answered.[71] The *Plan*, countersigned by nineteen young *fonctionnaires* with an extremely diverse range of political views, 'obtint [...] un gros succès auprès du public [...] et de la presse. Gallimard tira éditions sur éditions de cette petite brochure de 60 pages.[72] Romains' name helped to assure the commercial success of the *Plan*, but in the *NRF*, Thibaudet gave it uncharacteristically severe treatment in September. His objections were that it offered little that was not already present or evolving in other contemporary institutions. Moreover, he believed it was a good example of how Parisian 'cadres' imposed their will upon the provinces. He asked: 'La France ne serait-elle pas encore assez scholocratique?',[73] a sarcastic reference to the *normalien* background of Romains and his associates, as well as to characters

---

67    'Province', *NRF*, April 1934, p. 733. Schlumberger claimed later that this text was intended to introduce a humorous note into the discussion; *Oeuvres*, V, p. 172.

68    *NRF*, April 1934, p. 733.

69    See *Bulletin de l'Union pour la Vérité*, June-July 1934, p. 388.

70    *NRF*, May 1934, pp. 885-886.

71    Crémieux sympathised with Romains' views; see his review of *Problèmes européens*, Flammarion, 1934, in *NRF*, May 1934, pp. 861-863.

72    P. Andreu, 'Les idées politiques de la jeunesse intellectuelle de 1927 à la guerre', *Revue des travaux de l'Académie des sciences morales et politiques*, 2e semestre, 1957, p. 26.

73    'Sur un Plan universitaire', *NRF*, September 1934, pp. 425-430 (p. 427).

in Romains' *roman-fleuve*, *Les Hommes de bonne volonté*. In sum Thibaudet was very dismissive. Later, Paulhan reproduced part of an article by Romains in the *Dépêche de Toulouse* in defence of the *Plan*, as well as a letter from the group's secretary Jean Thomas.[74] Clearly stung by Thibaudet's tone, both of these texts pointed to inaccuracies in his assessment, but, if Thibaudet was willing to admit errors of detail, his opinion of the *Plan* did not change.[75] Whatever opinions were of the *Plan*, its fate was similar to that of other proposals which attempted to distil 'l'esprit des années trente': as J.-M. Mayeur says, their implementation 'se fit surtout ensuite, dans les années de Vichy [...] et jusqu'à la cinquième République'.[76]

It became clear very quickly in the aftermath of February 1934 that the *NRF* was taking risks: criticism of radicalism and calls for completely new political affiliations caused some of the review's readers to cancel their subscriptions.[77] Paulhan felt compelled to try to redress the balance: he inserted an *air du mois* in May's issue in which Drieu La Rochelle declared that 'il y a quelque chose dans le fascisme qui répond à mes tendances naturelles [...]. Ce qui me plaît dans le fascisme, c'est une certaine disposition virile'. He preferred the prospect of a 'révolution anti-parlementaire' to the 'république staviskienne [...] ou soviétique'.[78] At last Drieu had found a political ideology which suited his conception of 'l'homme nouveau' which had once brought him so close to Malraux. This similarity did not go unnoticed by Paulhan, for, from this time, he used work by both Malraux and Drieu to attempt to balance his leading pages. In February 1935 Drieu again revealed his fascist sympathies in the form of the short story *L'Homme mûr et le jeune homme*, just before Malraux's *Le Temps du mépris* began serialization in March that year.[79] At the time Drieu's presence would only have been seen as a token one; the scales were plainly weighted in favour of the Left, although this is not to deny that he wielded influence. For instance, at the Union pour la Vérité debate, Drieu refused to believe that Fernandez was serious when he declared himself a communist:

---

74    *NRF*, December 1934, pp. 936-939.

75    Ibid., note, p. 939. Thibaudet returned to the subject in 'Les Lettres et les classes', *NRF*, February 1935, pp. 274-282.

76    J.-M. Mayeur, *La Vie politique sous la Troisième République*, Seuil-Points, 1984, p. 346.

77    Paulhan told Etiemble that he had received 'quinze désabonnements (dont cinq comtesses)'; see J. Kohn-Etiemble, *226 Lettres inédites de Jean Paulhan*, Klincksieck, 1975, p. 68; he also told the Belgian critic Franz Hellens that 'je reçois des lettres d'abonnés – «quand Fernandez sera dans un camp de concentration», etc. C'est un ton nouveau, qui ne demande qu'à se développer'; letter dated 16 April 1934 (BD).

78    *NRF*, May 1934, pp. 887-888.

79    *NRF*, February 1935, pp. 190-210, and March 1935 to May 1935, respectively.

Je crois que tu es très hésitant, que le dernier mot n'est pas dit, que tu n'est pas une recrue sure, et que ce que tu as dit de tes réserves est très grave. Tu te méfies profondément de la tactique communiste'.[80]

Drieu was proved right, for on 12 June 1934 Fernandez resigned from the AEAR. By May 1935, he was expressing sympathy with the Comte de Paris, a stage on his itinerary towards his commitment to French fascism.[81]

Over the next weeks and months, the public political commitment of intellectuals proceeded apace. Paulhan told the distant Grenier that 'ici l'on se convertit de plus en plus à quelque chose. On fait aussi des manifestes'.[82] The *NRF* was yielding to political pressure and to follow *Commune* and *Europe* into the antifascist, pro-Popular Front camp: the list of *NRF*-associated luminaries who signed declarations like the CVIA manifesto was impressive.[83] The *NRF* had, on the face of things, changed direction.

## The *NRF* and the Popular Front

The *NRF* had shown that it favoured the increasingly likely prospect of an antifascist Popular Front. One of the review's staunchest figureheads, Julien Benda, was certainly willing to make a public show of his commitment by signing declarations and manifestos, despite the stance he had adopted in *La Trahison des clercs*. However, he was only being true to his word: as he had reiterated several times already, Benda's *clerc* did not commit treason when he defended universal values, or, echoing Péguy, when he defended a 'mystique de gauche'. This was Benda's way of signalling his willingness for fellow-travelling. In January 1935 he once again justifed his position:

Ayant récemment signé un manifeste dit «de gauche», j'ai été accusé de manquer à cette éternité que j'exige du clerc. Je réponds

---

80    *Bulletin de l'Union pour la Vérité*, October-November 1934, p. 55.

81    See *CAG* 5, p. 387, entry dated 3 June 1934. Cf. *NRF*, May 1935, pp. 794-795, where Paulhan reproduced an extract from Fernandez' interview with the Pretender taken from *Vu*, 27 March 1935. Cf. also *Commune*, April 1935, pp. 884-890, and J. Plumyène and R. Lasierra, *Les Fascismes français*, Seuil, 1963, p. 133, quoting Fernandez (3 June 1937): 'Après la révocation de Doriot qui est une vilénie et une gaffe formidable, j'adhère au PPF'.

82    JP to Grenier, letter dated 30 April 1934 (AP).

83    Among them were Alain, Benda, Fernandez, Gide, Martin du Gard, Dabit, Daumal, Desjardins and Lalou. A very long list was reproduced in the *Europe* version in April 1934, pp. 601-6; Pierre Gérôme also provided a 'Commentaire' (pp. 584-588) where he noted that party affiliated newspapers *Le Peuple*, *L'Humanité*, *Le Populaire* had followed the initiative of such as Benda, Gide and others (p. 584). See also *Commune*, March-April 1934, 'En marge d'un manifeste'.

> que j'ai signé ce manifeste parce qu'il me semblait défendre des
> principes éternels. [...] Je tiens que je suis dans mon rôle de clerc en
> défendant une mystique, non en faisant de la politique. Zola était
> dans son rôle de clerc en rappelant le monde au respect de la
> justice... On me dit: vous ne deviez pas signer, même pour une
> mystique de gauche. Vous ne devez être ni de droite ni de gauche.
> Je réponds que la mystique de gauche est recevable pour le clerc.[84]

And in March 1935, reflecting on the large demonstration to mark the first anniversary of the February riots, Benda mused on the signs of unity:

> Donc, le 10 février, les communistes ont admis dans leurs rangs ce
> drapeau tricolore. Ils ont compris que leur intérêt est de défendre
> la democratie contre le fascisme.[85]

As the weeks of 1935 passed there were important indications that the Left was gaining in political strength: the municipal elections of 5 and 12 May, the large demonstration of unity on 14 July 1935, and that summer's international Congrès pour la Défense de la Culture organised by the AEAR, all pointed to an eventual Popular Front which would benefit from strong support from intellectuals. That many *NRF* writers were sympathetic to these developments did not go unnoticed. Paul Léautaud, as ever an acerbic observer of the interwar intellectual scene, recorded what many others were witnessing:

> La *NRF* est en réalité un milieu de communistes. [...] On y est
> scandalisé, paraît-il, sur le compte de R. Fernandez, qui, après avoir
> été anarchiste, puis communiste, paraît tourner maintenant au
> monarchiste.[86]

Jean Paulhan was elected as a pro-Popular Front councillor in the Paris suburb of Châtenay-Malabry. To celebrate the victory of Paul Rivet in the fifth *arrondissment*, Benda's leading *air du mois* in June 1935 took the form of an open letter in which he recommended the founding of a new political party which should stand for 'l'antifascisme patriotique'. Benda wanted democratic liberties at home to be defended, but he also urged *active* opposition to Hitlerism abroad. Benda's appeal was strongly worded indeed, and his terms of reference demonstrated how just how deeply entrenched his republicanism was, for he

---

84    *NRF*, January 1935, pp. 170-171, quoted by J.-F. Sirinelli, *Intellectuels et passions françaises*, Fayard, 1990, p. 87.

85    *NRF*, March 1935, 'Donc, le dix février', p. 478.

86    Léautaud, *Journal littéraire*, vol. XI, p. 29, entry dated 7 April 1935.

distanced himself from the contemporary Radical party, whilst at the same time he stood by the old values of Radical-republicanism:

> Vous me dites: ce parti, à la fois antifasciste et patriote, il n'est pas à créer: c'est le parti radical. Je réponds que les radicaux ont voté ces mesures de sûreté en marchandant, en rechignant, comme sous la cravache de la droite. Je veux que vous les votiez fièrement, pleinement [...] par ardeur à défendre les libertés démocratiques contre la menace de l'étranger, comme les eussent voté un Danton, un Gambetta, un Clemenceau, les vrais parrains du parti que je propose.

The conclusion sounded a clarion call: 'Dressez-vous contre le fascisme hitlérien aussi résolument que contre les hommes du 6 février. Tout la France vous suivra'[87].

By 1936 the political atmosphere was as volatile as ever. There was an explosion in the offices of the *NRF* in the rue Sébastien-Bottin, one explanation of which was that a bomb had been laid by the Croix-de-Feu, the right-wing veterans' association.[88] Influenced by such events during these turbulent months, a period marked by the hard-fought campaign leading to the elections early that summer, Paulhan felt very anxious about the direction the *NRF* was taking; he resolved to act. Already he had made it clear that he realized Gallimard and Malraux wanted to politicize the review still further. He confided to Jouhandeau that 'je me sens assez seul, dans cette maison'[89]. To counter these pressures, the editor of the *NRF* was already finalizing arrangements with Jean Grenier, Albert Camus' teacher and mentor in Algiers at this time, to publish his controversial essay 'L'Age des orthodoxies'.[90] Their correspondence shows clearly how concerned both Grenier and Paulhan were to have the text appear as soon as possible: 'il vaut mieux le faire paraître le 1er mars ou 1er avril au plus tard. Tu sais mieux que moi combien l'actualité peut varier'.[91] Paulhan acknowledged receipt of Grenier's proofs on 15 February 1936 confirming, very importantly, that 'je compte donner 'L'Age des O[rthodoxies]' en tête de la *NRF*

---

87     'D'un nouveau parti', *NRF*, June 1935, pp. 949-951.

88     The caretaker's wife was killed as a result of this incident. Gabrielle Gros, an administrator at Gallimard's, recounted that 'les Croix-de-Feu nous avaient menacées, si l'on publiait le livre de Chopine (contre la Rocque), de "faire sauter la maison". [...] La Police et les experts semblaient hier pencher pour l'attentat ...'. 'Du trottoir, jeudi, un monsieur qui passe dit: "Ah, ils ont foutu le feu à la *NRF*"'; *JPC* 1, pp. 361-362, 486.

89     JP to Jouhandeau [February-March 1936] (BD).

90     *NRF*, April 1936, pp. 481-493. Grenier had already passed comment on an ideological trend he characterized significantly as a 'sens unique'; see *Air du mois*, *NRF*, May 1935, pp. 800-801.

91     JP to Grenier, letter dated 5 February 1936 in Paulhan-Grenier, *Correspondance*, pp. 71-72.

du 1er avril. Il ne sera pas trop tard, et Blum, aux dernières nouvelles, n'est pas tout à fait mort'.[92]   In the light of these comments and the proximity of the first round of the forthcoming general election, the timing of Grenier's article was plainly important.  Moreover, at the same time Paulhan was scandalized at the ousting of Jean Guéhenno from the *NRF*'s rival *Europe*, which was about to be taken over by a committee of fellow-travellers and 'orthodox' Marxists.[93] Grenier's article opened with cutting comments on recent trends among Left inclined intellectuals:

> C'est un trait frappant des dix dernières années que le brusque passage d'un doute absolu à une foi totale et parallèlement du désespoir sans limites à un espoir sans limites également'.[94]

Grenier noted that in the contemporary French intellectual scene 'ce qui est urgent n'est plus de se faire une *foi*, c'est adhérer à un *parti*'.[95]  By rallying to antifascism and communism, intellectuals had of necessity adopted Marxist doctrine which, in Grenier's view, was not only an economic theory, it was also a 'theology'.  Grenier's basic critique was that to subordinate the intelligence to materialism, dialectical or otherwise, was to betray intelligence; moreover, the application of Marxist doctrine to the world was a form of intellectual debasement in the search for a new culture.  Marxism as a system was illogical:

> C'est que le marxisme, à la suite de l'hégelianisme, s'appuie sur un système du Devenir qui justifie aussi bien la thèse que l'antithèse en les conciliant dans une «synthèse» supérieure. [...] Mais cet illogisme qui est érigé en méthode suprême pour juger de tout est compensé par une optimisme outrancier.[96]

Grenier was still more outraged by the fact that this 'messianisme' would justify and excuse the death of millions on the way to an earthly paradise.  Similarly, the Congrès pour la Défense de la Culture had provided an illustration of how 'deviation' from the Marxist line was frowned upon; only those writers who toed the line would be tolerated.  Finally, others had perceived this tendency to

---

92    JP to Grenier, letter dated 15 February 1936 (AP).  Blum had just been attacked by right-wing *ligues*.

93    Paulhan told Grenier that 'Ça a été ignoble, le débarquement de Guéhenno d'*Europe*. [...] Il semble que ce soit J. R. Bloch qui reprenne la revue'; JP to Grenier, letter dated 5 March 1936 (AP).  In fact, from May 1936 the *comité de direction* of *Europe* included Rolland, Aragon, J.-R. Bloch, André Chamson, Georges Friedmann, René Lalou and Jean Cassou, who was editor. See *Europe*, September-October 1973, p. 4.

94    *NRF*, April 1936, p. 481.

95    Ibid., p. 482. Cf. Schlumberger's 'Note sur la Politique' *NRF*, December 1934, pp. 866-871.

96    *NRF*, April 1936, p. 487.

subscribe to orthodoxies; he admitted that nothing could be more understandable 'dans le monde de ruines et de mort que nous habitons'.[97] The central point of this withering article was that there was a real danger in espousing communism when its 'faith', Marxism, could justify anything in the name of 'progress'. Appearing at the time of the election of the Popular Front, when not only intellectuals but also political leaders and parties were rallying together with the communists, this article was bound to be controversial. Paulhan told Grenier that even Le Journal des débats had quoted from it and, significantly, Malraux especially was scandalized by what he considered to be a frivolous demolition of Marxism. A number of readers went further and cancelled their subscriptions.[98] By far the most weighty rejoinder to Grenier came some weeks later in Europe, which had moved substantially leftwards. Significantly enough the Marxist Georges Friedmann noted the leading position of 'L'Age des Orthodoxies' in the NRF: he called it a 'manifesto'. He tried to demolish Grenier's argument by pointing to its superficiality:

> Il n'est presque pas une ligne des quatre pages par lesquelles M. Grenier pense condamner l'effort des savants et philosophes marxistes, qui ne porte à faux et ne révèle une connaissance très superficielle des recherches qu'il prétend dominer.[99]

The exchanges rumbled on; encouraged by Paulhan, later that year Grenier based part of a further article on this text by Friedmann. Clearly the NRF had managed to offend many 'orthodox' sensibilities.[100]

This debate unfolded against the electoral victory of the Popular Front: after the second round of voting gave the Left their victory on 3 May 1936, Léon Blum formed his first cabinet on 4 June. In the political upheaval, many intellectuals realigned their own position: André Gide, for instance, an old friend of Blum, lent the new prime minister much support.[101] Even the NRF itself had begun to lose its radicalist aspect: Thibaudet died in early 1936, Alain submitted his last Propos in November and, if Julien Benda still admired republican values, increasingly he came to feel that the communists were the only party to uphold them.

---

[97]   Ibid., p. 492.

[98]   JP to Grenier, letters dated 18 April and 13 May 1936 (AP).

[99]   G. Friedmann, 'Autour d'un manifeste', Europe, June 1936, pp. 228-240.

[100]  See NRF, August 1936, 'L'Orthodoxie contre l'intelligence', pp. 298-314, and 'Question et réponse', NRF, April 1937, pp. 642-644. Grenier gathered these and other texts together and published them under the title Essai sur l'esprit d'orthodoxie, Gallimard, 1938.

[101]  See CAG 5, p. 542, and especially p. 544, for Gide's visit to hear Blum's inaugural speech on 6 June 1936.

In other intellectual *milieux*, however, the *NRF* was clearly seen to have realigned as a pro-Popular Front periodical. The following episode, in which Alfred Fabre-Luce attempted to lure away Jean Grenier as a recognized *NRF* intellectual, is well documented in the correspondence. Fabre-Luce, who in the early 1920s had been associated with the *NRF*, wrote to Grenier asking him to collaborate with his new weekly *L'Assaut*, offering him an attractive monthly fee for a literary column. At this point Grenier asked Paulhan for his advice:

> Le numéro-spécimen qu'il m'envoie contient un article de Brasillach, bon en soi, mais *mauvais* pour l'équipe de *Vendredi*.
> [...] Extrait de la lettre de F.L.: «Peut-être êtes-vous plus à gauche que nous le paraissons actuellement puisque des événements nous situent en opposition avec le Front Populaire, alors que la *NRF* est actuellement sympathisante...» Mais il dit aussi opposition avec conservatisme et que j'écrirai en toute liberté, qu'il y a une distinction entre pages politiques et pages intellectuelles, etc.[102]

This polemical weekly was mobilized against the Popular Front and its intellectual supporters: 'Journal suspect conseille refus—Jean', Paulhan telegraphed on 20 October.[103] A letter followed in which Grenier learned that *L'Assaut* was likely to become a Doriotist newspaper.[104] Grenier confirmed that he had refused on the grounds that although he had liked Fabre-Luce's earlier venture *Pamphlet*, he could not write for a 'journal de combat' because it had a clear political orientation.[105] In the event Grenier *did* contribute, and Paulhan shrewdly assessed the motives behind Fabre-Luce's offer:

> Ce qui me gêne un peu, c'est le parti qu'il veut évidemment tirer de ta présence; et c'est *surtout ce parti* qu'il te paie. (Mais peut-être en effet n'as-tu pas à t'en soucier).[106]

---

102     Grenier to JP, *Correspondance*, p. 89. *L'Assaut* appeared for the first time on 13 October 1936; on p. 7, Jean Prévost interviewed François Mauriac who, referring to Péguy, called for 'un homme qui soit toute la France à la fois'. The article by Brasillach referred to '*Vendredi* et sa famille', qualifying Benda, Gide, Malraux, Chamson and Cassou (among others) as 'un concile de ratés' (p. 6).

103     JP to Grenier, telegram dated 20 October 1936 (AP).

104     JP to Grenier, letter dated 20 October 1936 (AP). Paulhan's intelligence informed him well, because in the issue for 8 June 1937, Fabre-Luce announced that *L'Assaut* 'va fusionner avec *La Liberté*' [Jacques Doriot's newspaper]. For a while *La Liberté du mercredi* provided a platform for the literary staff of *L'Assaut*. Readers were offered a low-cost resubscription to both *La Liberté* and *L'Emancipation nationale*, the main PPF newspaper.

105     Grenier to JP, *Correspondance*, pp. 91-92. All the same Grenier was evidently irritated at having to refuse 1000 francs per month 'sous prétexte qu'il contrarie une politique qui *serait* la mienne si j'en faisais' (ibid., p. 91).

106     JP to Grenier, letter dated 27 October 1936 (AP).

Paulhan was distressed by Grenier's presence in *L'Assaut* precisely because it lent a veneer of *NRF*-inspired respectability to Fabre-Luce's paper; Grenier submitted three articles before withdrawing in January 1937.

## Disillusion with the Popular Front

From October 1936, after its initial successes of the summer, the euphoria surrounding the creation and election of the Popular Front died away. As we shall see, in *NRF* circles Gide was on the point of publishing *Retour de l'URSS*, an apostatical text which infuriated the communists. However, for the time being he continued to support Blum's efforts to hold together the Popular Front. By mid-November he was worried by the attacks on the government coming from all sides, and he even lunched with Blum on at least two occasions in order to underline his support.[107] Paulhan too exhibited signs of continued support; he joined others in sending a modest sum to the pro-Popular Front weekly *Vendredi* when it appealed for financial support in April 1937. It is likely, though, that Paulhan's primary motivation for doing so was that he believed it was worth supporting *Vendredi* so long as it deflected controversial material from the *NRF*.[108]

It was at this time, when the Popular Front began to be perceived as being no more effective than previous governments, that Paulhan sought to recognize the achievements of Charles Maurras. The Action Française leader had returned to the centre of the public stage in 1937. On 6 July he completed his prison sentence for incitement to murder; coming only two weeks after the fall of Blum in June, his release served to remind many of Maurras' status as a right-wing national leader.[109] Believing that he might re-establish political balance by doing so, Paulhan pressed Jean Grenier to write an appreciation of the leader of Action Française. Indeed, Grenier told his editor he had been very impressed with the republication of Maurras' *Mes Idées politiques*.[110] The Action Française movement was undergoing a crisis: there was a risk that because the Comte de Paris and the Duc de Guise severed their links with his movement, Maurras would be discredited as leader of the monarchist cause. The Duc de Guise wrote:

> Si [la] doctrine politique [de Maurras] postule le régime monarchique, les enseignements de son école, par contre, se sont

---

[107]   See *CAG* 5, pp. 567, 570 and 595.
[108]   André Chamson to JP, letter dated 11 May 1937 (AP), thanking him for his contribution. Paulhan's name was listed in *Vendredi*, 7 May 1937.
[109]   See Weber, *L'Action Française*, pp. 392ff.
[110]   Grenier to JP, letter dated 14 November 1937 (AP).

révélés incompatibles avec les traditions de la Monarchie française.[111]

However, Maurras' persistence and instinct for survival ensured that the 'excommunication of 1937 hurt the Pretender more than the Action Française, which received much rallying support from the rest of the Royalist press'.[112] Against this background Grenier's article finally appeared in the *NRF* for February 1938 amid much protest; the text, surprisingly sympathetic, was intended to acknowledge Maurras' influence over the previous 40 years. Grenier deliberately concentrated upon Maurras' achievement, and played down his anti-republican, anti-Semitic, polemical output:

> Sa doctrine pour lui et les siens demeure intacte: elle tend seulement, à force de perdre ses *points d'application*, à devenir une oeuvre d'art.[113]

Some readers praised Paulhan for printing Grenier's article in spite of all the 'jeunes [...] tous "Front Populaire" en diable', and despite the opposition of Benda, one of Maurras' most unforgiving critics.[114]

Time was running out for the Popular Front. Two days before Chautemps' resignation on 10 March 1938, Paulhan sent out a circular letter to a number of *NRF* contributors (including Roger Caillois, Jean Grenier, Etiemble, Georges Friedmann and Denis de Rougemont), asking them for their evaluation of the failure of the Popular Front. Their replies were intended for the April number, but due to the government's fall, Paulhan put the project into abeyance. Judging by the wording of his circular, Paulhan was embittered by the failure of the Popular Front 'experiment'. If there had been changes, they were for the worse: the cost of living had increased; productivity had fallen and workers were demoralized; and abroad, dictatorships were consolidating their position. Moreover, continued Paulhan,

---

111    *L'Action Française*, 23 November 1937, quoted by Grenier in *NRF*, February 1938, p. 292. On 'The Break with Royalty', see Weber, p. 403ff.

112    Weber, *L'Action Française*, p. 408.

113    J. Grenier, 'Réflexions sur Charles Maurras', *NRF*, February 1938, pp. 292-298 (p. 298).

114    Léautaud noted Lucien Combelle's visit to the *NRF*: 'Combelle nous raconte alors le jour qu'il se trouvait dans le bureau de Paulhan. [...] Benda était là et s'est alors élevé dans les termes les plus véhéments. [...] "Vous ne pouvez publier cela. Maurras est un rhéteur, un sophiste, un homme de la plus grande mauvaise foi. Il n'est pas possible qu'on fasse son éloge dans la *NRF*". Paulhan a répliqué qu'il n'y avait aucune raison de ne pas permettre à Jean Grenier de dire ce qu'il pense sur Maurras'; see Léautaud, *Journal littéraire*, vol. XII, pp. 100-101, entry dated 15 February 1938.

> Quand Léon Blum veut former un ministère, il parle à présent d'*Union nationale*. Et du ministère Chautemps, l'on peut tout dire, sauf qu'il est de Front populaire. Il faut avouer que [...] le Front populaire vient d'aboutir à un fiasco complet.[115]

The only response to be printed in the review was from Denis de Rougemont. He used psychoanalytical language to describe the experiment; for him, the 'revolution' of 1936 had suffered a '*refoulement* d'où procèdent les actes manqués'.[116]

It was obvious that the Popular Front was now in decline and that it was only a matter of time before it disintegrated for good. Blum's second cabinet fell on 10 April 1938, after only 26 agonized days in office. Evidently, at least for Paulhan and the *NRF*, the Popular Front could no longer be relied upon to unify France, so severely scarred since 1934. Daladier formed a new cabinet which was no longer a Popular Front, but a government of 'national unity'. And anticipating this new mood, in April's issue Paulhan placed an essay by Armand Petitjean that called unequivocally for a more authoritative approach to government, and as well as for military preparedness: he concluded in a manner which prefigured the anti-Munich stance adopted by the review later that year:

> Nous voulons l'Union, et l'Union totale; et nous demandons aux communistes de déclarer que leur première patrie est la France, dont je ne doute pas un instant qu'ils seront les premiers et meilleurs soldats. [...] Nous voulons des canons pour la France, des avions pour la France, et un gouvernement national. Nous voulons la dictature de la France sur les Français.[117]

Paulhan, in his *Bulletin* for the May issue, achieved ironical effect when commenting on the cluster of manifestos calling for national unity. Desperation and panic seemed to have taken over:

> *Paris*:  Ont signé le manifeste Aragon (pour l'Union nationale): Marcel Arland, Julien Benda. [...]
> *Paris*:  Ont signé le manifeste Alain (contre l'Union sacrée): André Breton, Paul Éluard, Jean Giono [...]
> *Paris*:  Ont signé le manifeste Henri Bordeaux (pour la 'veritable Union nationale'): Abel Bonnard, Drieu la Rochelle, Ramon Fernandez, Thierry Maulnier [...]

---

115  The letter is reproduced in Kohn-Etiemble, *226 lettres*, pp. 152-153.
116  D. de Rougemont, 'Une révolution refoulée', *NRF*, July 1938, pp. 158-159.
117  A. Petitjean, 'Dictature de la France', *NRF*, April 1938, pp. 663-665. The communists heeded this appeal: Aragon referred to it in his opening speech at a conference entitled 'Droits de l'Intelligence' on 1 June 1938. See Jacques Duclos, *Mémoires*, II, Fayard, 1969, p. 299, and annex III, p. 457, where Paulhan's name appears as a participant.

> *Paris*: Bergson, Claudel, Gide and Valéry n'ont jusqu'à présent signé aucun manifeste ...[118]

It is also ironic that in the last half of 1938, from June to December, Paulhan should accept and serialize André Chamson's novel *La Galère*. Apart from Marcel Proust's *Le Temps retrouvé*, this was the longest work that Paulhan ever serialized. *La Galère* evokes the meeting of two former history students, Jean Rabaud and Louis Boulan, on the eve of the February riots in 1934. The two main parts of the novel relate the events of the 6 February and its aftermath, and how they separated the two families so recently brought together. An important 'épilogue', set in November 1934, shows Rabaud, newly *engagé*, haranguing Claire Boulan:

> Au 6 février [...] chacun a été pris par son camp. J'ai été pris par le mien, vous avez été pris par le vôtre. Voyez-vous, Claire, l'homme ne fait quelque chose qu'en luttant contre l'homme.[119]

One friendly critic wondered how such emphasis on the confrontations and divisions in France would be received by readers in the grim atmosphere of early 1939.[120] What the country needed was a genuine effort to unite nationally in the face of fascist aggression abroad. *La Galère* had outlived the Popular Front, and the reader of December 1938 could reflect on the irony that Chamson's fictional alter-ego, Rabaud, in November 1934, had declaimed:

> Je ne sais pas ce que l'avenir nous réserve. La bataille n'est pas achevée. Nous aurons peut-être à traverser des événements plus durs que ceux que nous avons déjà vécus. Je ne déserterai pas mon combat. Je donnerai de moi-même tout ce qu'il faudra donner. Mais je suis sûr de rester ce que je suis.[121]

In 1938 the political emphasis of the *NRF* was different from what it had been in 1934, or in 1930. In 1930 it had been reflective of the idealistic radical-republican tradition that had influenced its main contributors so profoundly. Then it steered a middle course, trying to avoid controversy and upholding the republican values so revered by its *chroniqueurs*. Under pressure, however, it

---

118    *NRF*, May 1938, *Bulletin* [compiled by 'Jean Guérin'], p. 877.
119    *NRF*, December 1938, p. 1031.
120    'Que Rabaud se trompe en pensant que le 6 février a divisé les Français en deux camps, je le crois fermement, quand je songe aux grands périls qu'il nous faut désormais affronter d'un coeur unanime'; review by René Lalou in *Les Nouvelles littéraires*, 1 April 1939.
121    *NRF*, December 1938, p. 1036.

was ready to give a voice to 'non-conformist' ideas; but the controversy that this stirred up only served to underline both its importance as a forum for debate and the dangers it risked in becoming more politically engaged. It reacted to the riots of February 1934 with enthusiasm and an open mind, and continued to urge political renewal. In the ideological magnetic fields of the mid-1930s, some *NRF* intellectuals were drawn towards militancy on the Left, while for others the Right was the pole of attraction. Once the momentum towards the Popular Front had been established, and while many *NRF* intellectuals, including Paulhan himself for a time, favoured it, the review not only recoiled from, but actively criticized Marxist 'orthodoxy' at the very time the Popular Front was celebrating its victory. And once this political 'experiment' was seen to be in decline, and once the political mood had changed in favour of a government of 'national unity', the *NRF* gave sympathetic treatment to Charles Maurras, the republic's most determined enemy at home. By late 1938, the *NRF* had adapted to a new, grimmer, mood of political realism, and signalled again its opposition to fascism. Paulhan's greatest fear of all for the *NRF* was a lapse into *partiality*. In March 1936 he summarized the problem:

> La *NRF* [...] depuis qu'elle existe, a régulièrement paru réactionnaire aux hommes de gauche, mais révolutionnaire aux hommes de droite. Elle a constamment été suspecte aux royalistes, mais aussi aux communistes. [...] L'on n'est jamais tout à fait sûr d'être impartial.[122]

In the stressed political atmosphere of 1930s France, genuine impartiality had become a rare commodity indeed.

---

[122]    'Une lettre de Jean Paulhan à l'universitaire de province', *Combat*, no. 3, March 1936.

# Chapter 4

## A fatal attraction: the *NRF* and Franco-German *rapprochement*

*L'on va recommencer à nous appeler:* La Nouvelle Revue Pro-Allemande. [1]

*En ce moment [...] un article sur les relations franco-allemandes et sur la révision des traités [...] va avoir en Allemagne un retentissement considérable, venant de la NRF.*[2]

Franco-German relations are crucial in the history of the interwar period.[3] Of all the issues — historical, political or cultural — to preoccupy French intellectuals at this time, the question of *rapprochment* with Germany is central to the extent that it underpinned other related issues such as the peace question, the historiography of the First World War, relations with other states (including Britain and the Soviet Union) and, above all during the mid to late 1930s, antifascism. Hitler was very conscious of pacifist tendencies in France, and through diplomatic agencies and intermediaries such as Otto Abetz (who would become Hitler's ambassador in Paris during the Occupation) the Führer exploited intellectual-led pacifism to further his own foreign policy aims.[4] Henri Michel neatly sums up how the issue of pacifism blurred French attitudes and intentions towards Germany, and how French morale could be (and was) undermined from within:

---

[1]    JP to Schlumberger [November 1927] (BD).
[2]    Martin du Gard to JP, letter dated 7 November 1930 (AP).
[3]    For an overview see R. Poidevin and J. Bariéty, *Les Relations franco-allemandes 1815-1975*, Armand Colin, 1977. On the question of intellectuals' efforts toward *rapprochment*, see F. L'Huillier, *Dialogues franco-allemands 1925-1933*, Publications de l'Université de Strasbourg, 1971.
[4]    See A. Kupferman, 'Le Bureau Ribbentrop et les campagnes pour le rapprochement franco-allemand, 1934-1937', in *Les Relations franco-allemandea*, Editions du CNRS, 1976, pp. 87-97, and K. Hildebrand, 'La politique française de Hitler jusqu'en 1936', in *La France et l'Allemagne, 1932-1936*, colloque international, Editions du CNRS, 1980, pp. 339-371.

Ce qui existait en France entre 1932 et 1936, c'était un profond *pacifisme*, qui animait tout le peuple français, sur ce point unanime, et qui, par horreur de la guerre, pour en éviter le retour, poussait les milieux les plus divers à souhaiter une entente avec l'Allemagne; même devenue hitlérienne, elle était, après tout, l'Allemagne, l'ennemie de hier *qui ne devait pas redevenir l'ennemie de demain*. Le paradoxe de cette période est que, au-dehors, et parfois au-dedans, la France est présentée comme une puissance militariste et impérialiste, alors que toute la nation est inspirée par un pacifisme profond, proche parfois du défaitisme.[5]

The problem was a complex one because for the most part the French, including a good number of intellectuals, remained profoundly ignorant of how Germany was evolving during the interwar period, despite the fact that their powerful and mysterious neighbour continued to loom large in the French collective conscious. The true peril of Hitler tended to be masked by such ignorance, and by the persistence of stereotypical images. Jean-Baptiste Duroselle writes:

L'Allemagne vient en tête des préoccupations françaises. On la connaît très mal, parce qu'on y voyage peu, parce que peu d'Allemands viennent en France; outre les sentiments, le contrôle des échanges, établi en 1932, leur interdit pratiquement tout voyage extérieur. Au surplus, l'Allemagne est l'objet de passions mal éteintes et de stéréotypes fondés sur la haine.[6]

### The *NRF* and Franco-German relations

It has long been recognized that from its inception in 1908-9 the *NRF* was responsible for the projection in French intellectual circles of a more realistic image of Germany.[7] In contrast to the deeply held germanophobia of some intellectual *milieux*, for instance the nationalists of the Parti de l'Intelligence, the *NRF*, in the years after 1918, rapidly came to represent a force for *rapprochement* with Germany. Jean Schlumberger recognized this later when justifying their deliberate sorties into the world of politics: he wrote that 'les rares fois où nous avions, Jacques Rivière ou moi, cru devoir introduire dans *la NRF* des réflexions

5    H. Michel, 'Conclusion', in *La France et l'Allemagne, 1932-1936*, pp. 400-401.
6    J.-B. Duroselle, *Politique étrangère de la France: la décadence, 1932-1939*, Points-Seuil, 1979, p. 197.
7    Georges Pistorius writes: 'Il n'est pas douteux que la *NRF* tienne une place de première importance parmi les publications qui ont présenté l'Allemagne au public français [...] Nous voyons se dessiner une nouvelle image de l'Allemagne'; 'L'image de l'Allemagne dans la *NRF* de 1909-1943', in *Connaissance de l'étranger. Mélanges offerts à la mémoire de J.-M. Carré*, Librairie Marcel Didier, 1964, p. 397.

sur la politique, c'était toujours à propos des relations franco-allemandes'[8]. From the very beginning Gide and his comrades had striven to combat what they considered to be the 'nationalization' of literature and culture, a problem relating to French perceptions of Germany in particular: the group did much to promote German culture in France.[9] Germans sensitive to *rapprochement* noted this trend in the *NRF*, and the review succeeded in drawing a figure as important as the author and critic Ernst Robert Curtius toward Gide's circle: Curtius would be a key actor in efforts toward reconciliation after 1919.[10]

When the *NRF* began to reappear in 1919 under Jacques Rivière questions relating to German literature, philosophy and culture continued to be addressed, and a number of writers and critics were assembled to treat them. Jean Schlumberger, one of the founder-members, had direct family ties with Alsace, and nurtured many German friends and associates. Alfred Grosser has stressed that Schlumberger's background and understanding of the problem singled him out as a highly qualified spokesman on Franco-German affairs.[11] The eminent Germanist Félix Bertaux (1881-1947) throughout the interwar period dominated the literary *chroniques allemandes*. Bertaux's penetrating notes and review articles were of central importance to the *NRF* from 1919, when he was brought in regularly. Apart from his long and close association with Schlumberger and Rivière, Bertaux had dealings with many German writers and intellectuals, including especially the Mann brothers, Thomas and Heinrich.

The philosopher Bernard Groethuysen (1887-1946) studied and taught philosophy in German universities, and was particularly conversant with trends in German philosophy. Invited to contribute to the *NRF* from 1920, Groethuysen grew especially close to Jean Paulhan, with whom he became acquainted through having rooms in the same block of apartments in Paris.[12] As an *éminence grise* at the *NRF*, Groethuysen was a convinced Marxist who exerted an influence over Gide and Malraux.[13] His politics made it difficult for him to live in safety in

---

8     J. Schlumberger, *Oeuvres*,V, Gallimard, 1960, p. 171.

9     See Gide's articles on 'Nationalisme et littérature', in the *NRF*'s June, October and November issues, 1909. Cf. also L. Richard, 'L'image de l'Allemagne dans la *NRF* de 1909 à 1914', *Mosaic*, VII, 4, 1974, pp. 71-98.

10    Richard, 'L'image de l'Allemagne dans la *NRF* de 1909 à 1914', quoting Curtius' memoirs of 1952. See also C. Foucart, 'Ernst Robert Curtius et André Gide: les débuts d'une amitié (1920-1923)', *Revue de littérature comparée*, juillet-septembre 1984, pp. 317-339.

11    A. Grosser, 'Jean Schlumberger, l'Allemagne et la morale politique', *NRF*, March 1969, pp. 334-349.

12    On Groethuysen, see J. Paulhan, 'Mort de Groethuysen à Luxembourg', in *NRF*, May 1969, pp. 946-976. Charles Du Bos paid him the compliment of having 'the greatest metaphysical mind I know'; C. Du Bos, *Journal 1920-1923*, Corrêa, 1948, p. 29.

13    Gide was struck by Groethuysen after his meeting with Walter Rathenau in 1921; see his 'Feuillets', in *Journal*, I, pp. 712-713. For Malraux, Groethuysen was 'peut-être l'homme qui j'ai le plus admiré'; J. Lacouture, *Malraux: une vie dans le siècle*, Seuil, 1976, p. 145.

Germany as the Nazis came to the fore, and he left in 1932 to live in Paris. Groethuysen did much to introduce Kafka into France, and he often advised Paulhan on the quality of German writers. In addition to these regular contributors to the review, the *NRF* had close ties with the Mayrisch family of Colpach in Luxemburg. Mme Mayrisch (under the pseudonym of Alain Desportes) provided some articles crucial to preliminary moves towards Franco-German reconciliation in June 1919, and with her husband Emile Mayrisch, she opened her home as a 'neutral' meeting-place for French and German intellectuals, politicians and industrialists. It was here that Gide was able to meet Curtius and the German economist and foreign minister Walther Rathenau, both of whom were enthusiastic to exploit early French moves towards *rapprochement*.[14]

Against this background Rivière introduced his own personal analysis of Franco-German problems into the *NRF*: Daniel Durosay has studied this in the context of Rivière's political evolution, and finds that the three articles in question 'font en un raccourci frappant la mutation d'un discours politique qui se déplace cette fois très nettement de l'idéalisme au réalisme, de la psychologie à l'économie'.[15] These texts no longer sprang from Rivière's personal war experience, an experience that had traumatized him deeply and whose effects may be felt in his book, *L'Allemand* (1924).[16] Significantly enough they were all written in response to contemporary political developments during negotiations over reparations. Rivière abandoned his previous, more affective, approach and, in the third article, without explicitly criticizing French policy, pointed to all the 'excesses, annexionist ambitions and perils of stalemate' inherent in the French occupation of the Ruhr. By this time, Rivière was converted to co-operation and even to active economic collusion with Germany, instead of being content merely to accept the empty charade of 'les principes moraux qui avait cours depuis Versailles'[17]. The time had come to grasp the political nettle.

---

14     Gide met Rathenau at Colpach in September 1920; see *CAG4*, pp. 45ff, and Gide, *Journal*, I, pp. 711f. On Rathenau's rôle, see D. Felix, *Walter Rathenau and the Weimar Republic*, Baltimore and London: The John Hopkins Press,1971, J. Joll, *Three Intellectuals and Politics*, New York: Pantheon Books, 1960, and E. Schulin, 'Rathenau et la France', in 'Cent ans de relations franco-allemandes', *Revue d'Allemagne*, IV, 3, 1972, pp. 547-557.
      Gide met Curtius for the first time in June 1920; see *CAG4*, pp. 87ff. For his achievement, see A.J. Evans, *On Four Modern Humanists*, Princeton, Princeton University Press, 1970, pp. 85-145.

15     D. Durosay, 'Les idées politiques de Jacques Rivière', *Bulletin des amis de Jacques Rivière et d'Alain-Fournier*, nos. 20-21, 1980, pp. 21-70 (p. 56.).

16     The articles are: 'Note sur un événement politique', *NRF*, May 1921, pp. 558-571; 'Les dangers d'une politique conséquente', ibid., July 1922, pp. 5-11, and 'Pour une entente économique avec l'Allemagne', ibid., May 1923, pp. 725-735.

17     Durosay, 'Les idées politiques de Jacques Rivière', p. 57. These proposals produced a long response from Heinrich Mann ('Antwort Nach Frankreich', in *Sieben Jahre*, Berlin:

André Gide, too, contributed an important article on the absolute necessity of re-establishing contact with Germany.[18] This was a direct result of the talks Gide had had with Curtius in 1921: aware of his own personal influence, Gide backed a number of ideas on how to restore communications between French and German writers. Their essential thrust was that international relations should be approached as humanistically and as non-contentiously as possible. Gide agreed with Thibaudet:

> Il y a une vie internationale, dans laquelle les individus et les nations sont baignés [...]. Sachons la considérer non d'un point de vue internationaliste, mais d'un point de vue international, c'est-à-dire d'un point de vue humain.

Thibaudet stressed that *intellectuals* could initiate reconciliation. Gide added his own conclusion: 'Puisse la *NRF* y aider: *il n'est peut-être pas aujourd'hui de tâche plus importante*'.[19] This article had predictable repercussions: under its *Revues* rubric the *NRF* reproduced extracts from various sections of the press. The press debate echoed familiar divisions: the liberal conservative Paul Souday, supporting Gide, criticised 'la xénophobie intellectuelle', while the right-wing nationalist Fortunat Strowski condemned *any* collaboration with Germany.[20] In June the same year the *NRF* gave extracts from an important article on the subject by a young Jean Guéhenno who, writing in *La Grande Revue*, argued the internationalist case.[21] Although it endorsed his attacks on French nationalist propagandists, the *NRF* did not, however, reproduce Guéhenno's lines on Gide's dilatoriness:

> A quoi bon tant de gloses et tant de reprises? M. André Gide toujours semble écrire dans les marges. [...] Il craint les pensées brèves et les mots trop rapides. [...] *Ce sont des gens de cénacle.* Leur pensée, comme leurs livres, est à tirage restreint. Ils redoutent, par dessus tout, les collusions politiques, et seraient navrés si on les soupçonnait d'avoir, un jour, voulu parler du monde.[22]

Guéhenno referred to the *NRF* to illustrate how, in his opinion, intellectuals risked merely pontificating in a void when they ignored or denied the

---

Zsolnay, 1929, pp. 129-41). Rivière gave a shorter version in the *NRF* for August 1923 as 'Co-opération économique seulement?', pp. 248-253. Here Mann pointed to the risks of failing to broaden *entente* beyond economics.

[18] 'Réflexions sur l'Allemagne', *NRF*, November 1921, pp. 513-521.
[19] A. Thibaudet, in *L'Opinion*, 13 August 1921, quoted in *NRF*, November 1921, p. 521 (my emphasis).
[20] 'Les relations intellectuelles franco-allemandes', *NRF*, February 1922, pp. 252-255.
[21] *NRF*, June 1922, pp. 762-763.
[22] *La Grande Revue*, April 1922, pp. 335-343 (p. 337).

importance of *political* commitment. Thus the debates which would be inspired by the publication of *La Trahison des clercs* are already prefigured here in attitudes to the German question.

If Guéhenno and other 'internationalists' saw the *NRF* as ineffectual, nationalist intellectuals such as Camille Mauclair and Henri Béraud saw it as pro-German. In his bombastic anti-*NRF* 'crusade', Béraud had already accused the review of abusing its diplomatic connections at the Quai d'Orsay to obtain preferential treatment in the distribution of French books abroad.[23] Yet Béraud would have struck a chord with many when he asserted that the *NRF* was unfairly biased towards Germany. In his *Croisade des longues figures*, Béraud reproduced extracts from a constellation of provincial newspapers that delighted in attacking what they considered to be part of the Parisian *avant-garde*. Camille Mauclair set the tone thus: 'C'est, pour parler net, la tendance obstinée de la *NRF* à prôner le rapprochement intellectuel et économique avec les Boches'[24]. Adapting his text for the *Eclaireur de Nice*, Mauclair objected that the *NRF* dominated not only the literary scene, but that it also had a clear pro-German political bias. He referred directly to what was Rivière's latest article (May 1923) and suggested that the *NRF* should change its name to '*La Nouvelle Revue Franco-Allemande*'. This was a jibe that Paulhan would not forget, as the epigraph to this chapter shows.

### Jean Paulhan and the Franco-German question

Thanks to the efforts of Gide, Schlumberger and Rivière, and to the attacks of their opponents, by the time Paulhan took over as editor in 1925 the *NRF* exerted considerable influence in the area of Franco-German relations. The extent of the late Rivière's interest in Germany was reflected by the *NRF* in its tribute published in April 1925; no less than eight *témoignages* and articles were devoted to the question, and an extract of his war diary was inserted. As in other areas, Paulhan attempted as far as possible to perpetuate Rivière's editorial policy — notwithstanding its ambiguities — particularly in the political arena. Yet there is evidence in his correspondence relating to editorial decisions to demonstrate that, from the beginning of his editorship, Paulhan felt different about the inclusion of material on international issues as sensitive as the German question. He believed it to be unsuitable and campaigned to restore consistency to the review's policy, basically because he had observed some of the dissonances of

---

23    See H. Béraud, *Croisade des longues figures*, Editions du siècle, 1924. Among other things Béraud accused Jean Giraudoux of being an *NRF* 'infiltrator'. Giraudoux refuted these allegations in his interview with F. Lefèvre, *Une heure avec...*, Gallimard, 1924, pp. 141-153.

24    In *Le Phare de la Loire*, 14 May 1923, in Béraud, *Croisade des longues figures*, p. 82.

Rivière's direction at close quarters. For example, in the case of the refusal of a 'political' essay by the Belgian critic Franz Hellens, Paulhan felt that it had been highly inconsistent to invoke editorial policy in this refusal when it was being broken each time Rivière wrote or accepted an article on Germany.[25] With this experience in mind, he determined to prevent the review from following the same path as Rivière.

At the time Paulhan took over, Edouard Herriot had been in power since May 1924 and had placed relations with Germany on to a more congenial footing. In what was to prove to be a historic speech, and one with profound significance for Paulhan's review, on 28 January 1925 Herriot called for a national union in foreign policy: the speech signalled to Germany a spirit of *détente* which would ease negotiations preceding the Locarno Conference of October that year. Herriot's biographer takes up the story:

> Dans une péroraison pathétique, il lance un appel prophétique aux Etats Unis d'Europe et à la réconciliation avec l'Allemagne: "La France n'a pas de haine, la France garde au milieu de tous les périls [...] son sang-froid. [...] Mon plus grand désir est de voir un jour apparaître les Etats-Unis d'Europe. [...] Dans la grande institution de la Société des Nations, je voyais la première esquisse de ces Etats-Unis." [26]

This speech encouraged those intellectuals who were campaigning in favour of a policy of reconciliation, and therefore marked the beginning of Paulhan's problems. Sometime between the beginning of April and July 1925, an article by Pierre Viénot was submitted to the *NRF* for consideration.

Viénot, a diplomat, had just returned from Germany, and published an important article in a review which propagated the *'esprit de Genève'* of the League of Nations: 'République allemande et Allemagne nationale'.[27] Here Viénot emphasized both the necessity of changing French perceptions of Germany, and how efforts needed to be made to understand their neighbour without prejudice. At the same time, Viénot, linked by marriage to the Mayrisch

---

25    This letter is important as an illustration of the way Paulhan himself wished to apply policy: 'Vos considérations, si intéressants soient-elles, entrent trop dans le vif de la politique. Nous ne pouvons guère sans inconvenance à la *NRF*, nous mêler de porter un jugement sur la nation belge. [...] Je suis d'accord avec vous—bien que connaissant peu la question—sur son caractère factice [...] mais ce n'est pas vraiment à nous qu'il appartient de le faire ressortir. *C'est sur des tendances purement littéraires que nous avons besoin d'être renseignés; ne laissez pas croire qu'elles se confondent à ce point avec les tendances politiques'*. (My emphasis.) JP to F. Hellens, 4 April 1922 (BD).

26    M. Soulié, *La Vie politique d'Edouard Herriot*, Armand Colin, 1962, pp. 207-209.

27    *Revue de Genève*, April 1925, pp. 405-425. See J.-P. Meylan, *La Revue de Genève, miroir des lettres européennes*, Geneva: Droz, 1969.

family, approached Schlumberger, and discussions began to set up the Comité
d'Information Franco-Allemand.[28]. If the *NRF* had wanted to take the lead in
these initiatives, then an article by Viénot would have presented the ideal
opportunity. Four letters to Schlumberger, however, written between the spring
and August 1925, reveal much about how Paulhan was determined to re-
establish what he saw as the *literary* primacy of the review, and how he applied
literary criteria to justify the refusal of 'non-literary' texts. With apparent
approval, Gaston Gallimard passed on Viénot's text; at this point Paulhan sought
Schlumberger's advice:

> Si vous dirigiez la revue, publieriez-vous l'article de Viénot?
> Gaston me l'a remis ce matin... Je le trouve comme vous
> extrêmement intéressant, juste presque toujours, aussi mal écrit que
> possible. [...]
> Autant enfin il me semble propre à amorcer heureusement,
> dans quelque revue politique, une longue discussion, au cours de
> laquelle ses véritables traits se dégageraient peu à peu—autant je
> lui prête difficilement ce caractère «définitif» que prend un article
> politique publié par une revue littéraire.

Worried about the potential impact of Viénot's article, Paulhan wrote again to
develop his reasons for refusing it:

> [...] Vraiment, un tel article est-il à sa place dans une revue
> littéraire? —si encore il était l'application dans le domaine
> politique d'une méthode, d'une philosophie qui par ailleurs nous
> pourrait toucher (comme c'était le cas pour les autres articles
> politiques qu'a donnés la *NRF*), j'admettrais bien que l'on pût à la
> rigueur oublier une telle incorrection de forme—mais un article
> qui n'est et ne peut être que politique, qui n'a point d'autre intérêt,
> ni d'autres ambitions, que lui reste-t-il comme excuse? Je serais
> bien désolé qu'il vous parût mériter d'être retenu.[29]

Paulhan prevailed: Viénot's article changed destination and appeared in *La Revue
européenne*.[30] Clearly anxious to avoid a repetition of recent nationalist attacks,
Paulhan was relieved that the article could be deflected to a periodical which was
not only committed to but also financed by interests working for the Comité

---

28   On this committee see F. L'Huillier, *Dialogues franco-allemands* , pp. 29-37.
29   JP to Schlumberger [1925] (BD).
30   See 'Enquête sur l'Allemagne — a sécurité par la compréhension d'autrui', *La Revue
     européenne*, 1 July 1925. Viénot criticized French revanchist attitudes as embodied in the
     'diktat' of the Versailles Treaty and concluded—'[il faut] nous libérer de l'obscur instinct
     qui nous fait condamner ce qui est différent de nous et d'exiger d'autrui notre
     rationalisme'; ibid, p. 14.

d'Information Franco-Allemand.[31]  However worthy Viénot's stance was, and however attractive it was both to German intellectuals and as a promotional exercise to Gallimard and Schlumberger, Paulhan felt he was right and explained himself once more:

> Mais ignorez-vous donc quelles menaces nous ont valus, et même de la part de nos abonnés les plus fidèles, l'article de Jacques [Rivière] sur les relations franco-allemandes, la campagne de Mauclair nous accusant, dans dix journaux de province, de toucher l'argent allemand?  Combien de désabonnements nous sont parvenus, combien d'«amis» de province, qui s'occupaient à ce moment d'organiser des conférences de la *NRF*, nous ont écrit qu'ils ne pouvaient plus s'intéresser à nous?  Bien entendu, il nous était facile de répondre: l'article était de Jacques...

This letter reveals that some within the *NRF* had been willing to make allowances for the refractory Rivière on such matters; Paulhan, however, did not feel able to tolerate the inconsistency that this state of affairs engendered.  He was keen to follow through the disagreement with Schlumberger because he only had the best interests of the *NRF* at heart:

> Vous me direz qu'il faut d'abord faire la revue selon notre coeur, et ne songer aux abonnés qu'ensuite.  Oui et je ne voulais que répondre à votre remarque sur les abonnés allemands que nous aurait valus l'article Viénot.  Et je n'insisterais pas non plus, si je n'étais bien sûr de défendre contre vous ce qui a toujours été l'esprit de la *NRF*.
>
> Je ne parle même pas de la première revue, la vôtre, qui n'a jamais dit un mot de politique en un temps malgré tout infiniment plus dangereux, plus «exposé» que le nôtre.  Mais la seconde, celle de Jacques, quels obstacles ne devait pas franchir, avant d'y pénétrer, une étude relevant d'une autre discipline que la discipline littéraire.  Vous le savez comme moi, mieux que moi.

And in a passage couched in thinly veiled sarcasm, Paulhan indicated that the review might be accused of further inconsistency if it did not open itself up to other areas:

> Me direz-vous que les problèmes politiques se présentent avec un caractère d'urgence tel, qu'il faut les traiter, quitte à les traiter mal.  Mais il n'y a pas que les problèmes de politique étrangère, qui

---

31     On Charles de Rohan and the *Revue européenne*, see F. L'Huillier, *Dialogues franco-allemands* , p. 36.

> soient urgents. Devrons-nous parler aussi, sans choix, de la
> dépopulation, de la syphilis, de l'alcoolisme?[32]

The heart of the matter for Paulhan was that Viénot's article risked turning the
*NRF* into a 'revue de combat', because his ideas were so clearly opposed to the
nationalists that former animosities surrounding the Parti de l'Intelligence debate
might be revived:

> Si nous publions sur la politique étrangère un article médiocre, un
> article «plein de bonnes citations», ce seront les disciples de Jean
> Schlumberger [...] que nous jetterons dans les bras de Maurras ou
> des communistes. [...] Est-ce Viénot que nous opposerons à
> Bainville?[33]

The last letter of this sequence refers once more to the doctrinal content of
Viénot's study: Paulhan felt that simplistic or spurious psychologizing could
only damage genuine diplomatic efforts to improve relations with Germany. At
last he wrote to suggest a policy stipulation:

> A propos des relations franco-allemandes, ne pensez-vous pas que
> nous devrions refuser énergétiquement tout article, ou note, fondé
> sur le détestable «mieux on se connaît, plus on s'aime» ou tout lieu
> commun analogue?[34]

Paulhan's insistence kept the *NRF* free from similarly controversial material for
some months to come, despite the pressure being applied from interested parties
within the review.

Although Paulhan had succeeded in playing down the issue, it is
inaccurate to claim that Franco-German interests received no further attention in
the *NRF* until 1933.[35] In January 1926, Thomas Mann came to Paris on a semi-
official visit. Among other functions he was to speak at the Union pour la Vérité
and at the Union Intellectuelle Française.[36] Following the ratification of the
Locarno Pact just over a month earlier, this visit announced a further warming of
relations. Consequently Paulhan appeared to make concessions to his earlier
hard-line, and on 21 January 1926, the day of Mann's two speeches, Paulhan
wrote: 'il me semble qu'il serait bon de donner dans la *NRF* le discours qu'a

---

[32]  JP to Schlumberger [July 1925] in *JPC* 1, p. 97.
[33]  Ibid., p. 98.
[34]  JP to Schlumberger, letter dated 16 August 1925 (BD).
[35]  Cf. L. Richard's article 'L'Image de l'Allemagne dans la *NRF* de 1919 à 1939', *Revue de psychologie des peuples*, 25, 1970, pp. 197-210.
[36]  Cf. C. Du Bos, *Journal 1926-1927*, Corrêa, 1949, pp. 21ff, and T. Mann, 'Pariser Rechenschaft', in *Gesammelte Werke*, Band XI, Hamburg, 1974.

prononcé Mann à l'Union Intellectuelle'.[37]. Later, however, he explained that this idea would be dropped because the text had been given elsewhere: its inclusion would be superfluous. The speech would have represented a *coup* for the *NRF*, because both Mann brothers were seen in world intellectual circles as the 'ambassadors of Weimar'.[38] At the same time, there was a possibility that Heinrich Mann might contribute material for the review as well. Groethuysen, however, was hostile to any such contribution, pointing out rather sweepingly that Mann 'a justement coulé auprès de tous les intellectuels allemands un peu sérieux'. Paulhan agreed:

> Cette dernière raison n'avait pas été sans me toucher: les réconciliations entre peuples tendent assez naturellement à devenir des réconciliations avec la mauvaise littérature—et tout ce que j'ai lu de Mann m'a donné le sentiment d'un Georges Lecomte, un peu plus «à la page».[39]

Franco-German relations were steadily improving at this time. The efforts of Aristide Briand, one of the architects of *rapprochement*, found wide support, and the Pope's condemnation of Action Française drove Maurras' catholic support behind Poincaré. What is more, the negotiations to establish the Comité d'Information Franco-Allemand were coming to fruition: in July the French executive committee met for the first time, and offices were opened in Paris and Berlin in November 1926.[40] Once Gide had returned from his journey to the Congo, he too gave his attention to the problem. The momentum had become such that Jacques Bariéty has written: 'au cours de ces années naît [...] une sorte de mystique du rapprochment franco-allemand'.[41] By September 1926 Germany had been admitted to the League of Nations, with Briand and Stresemann continuing their interminable negotiations over reparations.

## Julien Benda and the German question

If most leading *NRF* intellectuals were expressing support for Franco-German reconciliation during these months, in his serialization of *La Trahison des clercs* Paulhan manifested a desire for balance. This catalytic work[42] was important for the question of relations with Germany because Benda paraded an anti-

---

37    JP to Schlumberger, letter dated 21 January 1926 (BD).
38    The phrase is Nigel Hamilton's; see *The Brothers Mann*, London: Secker & Warburg, 1978.
39    JP to Schlumberger [1926] (BD).
40    F. L'Huillier, *Dialogues franco-allemands*, pp. 34-37. Curtius came to the Paris opening; see *CAG* 4, pp. 293-295.
41    R. Poidevin and J. Bariéty, *Les relations franco-allemandes* , p. 272.
42    See above, chapter 2.

Germanism which, paradoxically enough, aligned him with the nationalists. Benda blamed unequivocally 'les clercs allemands' for the 'nationalization' of culture; what is more, 'le clerc nationaliste', continued Benda, 'est essentiellement une invention allemande'. This view was central to his thesis, and it would not be an exaggeration to say that Benda accused Germany of hatching a Europe-wide conspiracy:

> C'est d'ailleurs un thème qui reviendra souvent dans cet ouvrage [i.e., *La Trahison des clercs*]; que la plupart des attitudes morales et politiques adoptées depuis cinquante ans par les clercs en Europe sont d'origine allemande et que, sous le mode du spirituel, la victoire de l'Allemagne dans le monde est présentement complète.[43]

Like the Action Française historian Jacques Bainville, Benda saw Germany as a perpetual threat to France, the difference being that Benda considered German irrationalism and its moralism of violence as the real menaces to French rationalism and republicanism. As a universalist however, Benda would want to be interpreted as attacking *nationalism* first, and Germany second: in this perspective, *La Trahison des clercs* was, equally, an attack upon French nationalist intellectuals. Consequently the right-wing press was already in uproar because of the serialization of Benda's essay. Against this background, Paulhan found himself in a quandary once more. He had to make a decision on Curtius' anti-nationalist essay 'Restauration der Vernunft'. Given Curtius' proximity to Schlumberger, Viénot and Gide, and his active rôle in the Comité d'Information Franco-Allemand, Paulhan was caught in a delicate position: he firmly believed, however, that to accept Curtius' essay would attract still more fire towards the review. As he put it: 'si la 'Restauration der Vernunft' entame une campagne, je crains que ce ne soit une campagne riche et d'idées vagues [sic]. Mais opportune, peut-être. En tous cas, terriblement inopportune à la *NRF*'. Paulhan concluded by advising against inclusion of the essay, because Benda's *La Trahison des clercs* was nearing completion in serial form. Moreover, knowing how quickly such material could be rendered obsolete by publication elsewhere, Paulhan distanced himself from Schlumberger, to whom he wrote:

> Mais pensez-vois qu'il soit possible, dans un moment où nous malmenons assez durement les intellectuels français [...] de leur faire encore faire la leçon impérieuse et sèche! Peu d'articles ont soulevé plus d'emotion que *La Trahison des clercs*.

---

[43]    *NRF*, September 1927, p. 319.

Paulhan was anxious to avoid what would have appeared as a two-pronged attack led by both Benda and Curtius upon the nationalists; remembering Mauclair's 1923 invectives, he concluded by warning that 'l'on va recommencer à nous appeler: *La Nouvelle Revue Pro-Allemande*. Vraiment ce moment serait mal choisi d'accueillir Curtius'.[44] Once again Paulhan prevailed: his committee refused the Curtius article, and it appeared elsewhere, although it received a brief mention in the *NRF*'s 'Revue des Revues'.[45]

The debate over Benda's stance on Germany echoed within the *NRF*. Albert Thibaudet devoted a significant part of one of his *Réflexions* to reprimanding Benda for his anti-Germanism. Thibaudet saw the book as 'un livre de guerre, ou plutôt un livre de *la* guerre, [...] et il l'a pensé d'abord comme une défense contre l'Allemand'.[46] It was a polemic in the literal sense of the word. Thibaudet had other criticisms, but most importantly he turned his attention to Benda's underlying assertion that nationalism was a German invention: Thibaudet did not like Benda's distortion of history— 'le fait général, c'est la création des nationalités, non par l'imitation des clercs allemands, mais par la Révolution française'.[47]

The next year, 1928, marked the beginning of difficulties in relations between France and Germany. The effect of the Briand-Kellogg Pact, signed on 27 August, was to weaken France. Briand had wanted a unilateral pact with the United States, but Kellogg, by making it multilateral, allowed Germany to undermine France's military strength.[48] Against this background, Paulhan began publishing Benda's *La Fin de l'éternel*, with the September number in particular placing responsibility for the First World War squarely upon Germany.[49] This coincided with Thibaudet's article on the Demartial affair and the correspondence it provoked. Demartial, an ex-colonial minister, distinguished himself by blaming Russia and France entirely for the First World War.[50] The result of the ensuing scandal was that Demartial was suspended for five years from the Légion d'Honneur. Thibaudet insisted that even liberal Germans

---

44     JP to Schlumberger, November 1927 (BD).
45     See 'The Restoration of Reason', in *The Criterion*, November 1927, pp. 389-397, and *Revista de Occidente*, vol. 17, September 1927, pp. 257-267. Curtius concluded by exhorting intellectuals to revive the spirit of Reason: 'only then will we overcome the various types of radicalism [...] and attain the objective which is the most important of all today: the reconstruction of the European man. All those who do not want to surrender to Americanism or to Bolshevism must take their share in this task'; *The Criterion*, p. 396.
46     *NRF*, December 1927, pp. 810-819.
47     Ibid., p. 817.
48     R. Poidevin and J. Bariéty, *Les relations franco-allemandes* , p. 273-274.
49     *NRF*, September 1928, pp. 353-360. Cf. also above, chapter 2.
50     'L'Affaire Demartial', *NRF*, August 1928, pp. 261-270.

would find it difficult to agree with Demartial that it was France's entry into war which provoked German aggression. Secondly, it was patently not true that Germany was innocent of having started the war. Thirdly, and most importantly, Demartial was guilty of oversimplification. Thibaudet borrowed an image from Bergson's *Matière et mémoire* and applied it to the complex question of war responsibilities:

> Pour ma part, j'en verrais les plans réels comme autant de coupes sur un cône. [...] Plus les coupes sout éloignées de la pointe du cône, plus le problème se dilue, se confond avec la profondeur, les ondulations, les rythmes de l'histoire européenne.[51]

Turning to the vexed question of the Versailles Treaty, Thibaudet displayed his optimism; whereas Demartial devoted all his efforts to applauding those who 'stigmatized' the Treaty, Thibaudet resigned himself to its existence. As far as he was concerned, France should continue to seek a fairer negotiated settlement with Germany; this was something which should have remained possible in the still optimistic climate of mid-1928. Thibaudet concluded by affirming his faith in the League of Nations. Thibaudet believed that the French obsession with retribution was holding back moves towards disarmament. Yet he appears to have ignored the growing belligerence of the national-socialists in Germany. In November the *NRF* reproduced a letter from Demartial, who questioned Thibaudet's optimism, particularly his opinion that the article of the Versailles Treaty concerning responsibility for the war was now a 'dead letter'.[52] The 'ex-enemies' of Germany should abandon their impossible position and consign the question of responsibility to history: they should desist from making it central to international politics. Predictably enough, this 'affair' had considerable repercussions in the French press. In December 1928, Thibaudet briefly examined one sample reaction. Replying to Pierre Bernus, who had referred to Renouvin's book *Les Origines de la guerre*, Thibaudet stressed that he had found nothing in this objective study totally to condemn Demartial. Without being explicitly critical of the nationalists, Thibaudet, drawing a parallel with the Dreyfus Affair, insisted that 'il s'agit en effet d'une affaire qui nous occupe ordinairement ici [i.e. 'la *NRF*']: *celle de la différence et de l'incompréhension entre générations*'.[53] He ended by calling for continuing reconciliation.

---

51    Ibid., p. 264.
52    *NRF*, November 1928, pp. 751-752.
53    *NRF*, December 1928, pp. 845-849 (my emphasis). Bernus' article had appeared in the *Journal des débats*, 14 August 1928.

The years 1928 and 1929, ten years after the Armistice and the Versailles Treaty, witnessed attempts to achieve a new honesty regarding the First World War. Yet although the experience was gradually passing into history, historians, novelists and essayists, including those associated with the *NRF*, continued to grapple with the myths surrounding the causes and the conduct of the war.[54] On the international scene, however, the prospects for any lasting settlement of differences were becoming less bright. The Young Plan, drawn up between February and May 1929, rescheduled the Germans' reparation payments over the next sixty years, with, in return, a stipulation that France and the Allies should withdraw from the Ruhr by mid-1930.[55] The Plan further weakened the Weimar Republic, already under threat from Hitler, who scored a propaganda victory by claiming that reparations would enslave Germany for generations to come. These important changes were observed by Pierre Viénot, then in Germany attempting to strengthen Franco-German understanding. But he encountered so many obstacles and hesitations, and such reluctance on the part of the French press to take any lasting initiatives, that Viénot resigned from his post on 31 December 1929.[56] The Second Conference on reparations in The Hague put the finishing touches to the Young Plan, and when the French withdrew from the Rhineland, there were violent nationalist demonstrations in Germany. Finally, the Wall Street Crash meant that American credits backing the Young Plan would no longer be forthcoming, and the Nazis, as a direct result, scored a highly significant electoral victory. Significantly, the election of an additional 107 Nazis to the Reichstag on 14 September 1930 at last spurred several German and French intellectuals into action, action which not only signalled the beginnings of an awareness of German national-socialism, but which also had direct consequences for the *NRF*.

In the October issue for 1930 Thibaudet responded to some of these changes, and examined them in the light of the recent history of the Franco-German relationship. The September elections results in Germany somewhat

---

54      See the exchange between Crémieux and Drieu La Rochelle on E.M. Remarque's novel *A l'ouest rien de nouveau* in *NRF*, October 1929, pp. 568-569, November 1929, pp. 725-730, and the 'Revue des revues', *NRF*, January 1930, pp. 146-148, where Paulhan encapsulates the mood: 'L'on nous a assommés, tant que durait la guerre, de romans belliqueux, où les soldats tenaient joyeusement de petits discours à leur baïonnette, qu'ils appellaient Rosalie. Les poncifs ont changé: l'on nous écrase aujourd'hui de soldats désespérés, qui ne parlent que suicide, catastrophe et révolution. Cette nouvelle mode n'est pas plus déplaisante que l'autre: il arrive qu'elle soit pleine de bonnes intentions. Mais l'on en abuse un peu'.

55      R. Poidevin and J. Bariéty, *Les relations franco-allemandes* , p. 273-276.

56      F. L'Huillier, *Dialogues franco-allemands* , pp. 71-97.

diluted the optimism of this article, but it is a notable analysis.[57] Thibaudet highlighted the fact that as early as 1873, the philosopher Charles Renouvier had had the foresight to consider the Alsace-Lorraine question as a European problem. He had also anticipated a 'future assemblée européenne', leading Thibaudet to criticise the persistent gallocentrism of successive governments. France, in 1930, needed to be far more generous of spirit because opportunities to modify the Versailles Treaty had not been taken. He remained optimistic regarding the future rôle of the League of Nations, but advised against complacency:

> Ce programme ne manque pas de difficulté, mais moins encore de necessité. Il est resté, jusqu'à présent, à peu près étranger à ce qu'on appelle l'esprit de Genève. Le moment ne viendra-t-il pas de parer à cette carence de la cléricature?[58]

There was, clearly, a distinction to be drawn between the theory and practice of the *esprit de Genève* and the League of Nations. If confirmation were needed of such ineffectiveness, it was already to hand: the electoral successes of the Nazis had shaken many in Germany, and the French press at last began to take notice. One literary paper ran a series of statements by German intellectuals who all pointed to the urgency of revising the Versailles Treaty, and they all spelled out the dangers to democracy in Hitler's Germany.[59] Heinrich Mann castigated Hitler and national-socialism, and called for renewed efforts of opposition:

> La masse du parti national-socialiste, qui n'a rien de socialiste ni de national, est formée par les désespérés, qu'en ce moment on compte par millions, et par une jeunesse anarchique [...]. Nous nous battons pour notre peuple contre ces ennemis intérieurs; et ce faisant nous défendons des intérêts communs à la France et à l'Allemagne.[60]

Thomas Mann also called for 'une alliance franco-allemande pour la paix', as well as for the revision of the iniquitous Treaty which the Nazis had so long exploited.

---

57  'Appel au concile', *NRF*, October 1930, pp. 542-554. Paulhan considered that this was the best article to have been submitted by Thibaudet for some time; JP to J. Schlumberger, letter dated 23 September 1930 (BD).

58  *NRF*, October 1930, p. 554.

59  *Les Nouvelles littéraires*, 11 and 25 October, and 1 November 1930 gave interviews with Gérald Bauer, Alfred Kerr and Heinrich Mann respectively.

60  *Les Nouvelles littéraires*, 1 November 1930.

## The *NRF* speaks out

Already the *NRF* was preparing to comment on this alarming state of affairs. Roger Martin du Gard put pressure on Paulhan by stressing that he fully approved of the idea that Schlumberger should make a statement, especially in view of the distress signals he had read in the French press:

> Je ne cesse de penser à l'article de Jean. [...] J'aurais aimé être bien certain qu'il se rend compte de toute l'importance de son geste. En ce moment [...] un article sur les relations franco-allemandes [...] va avoir en Allemagne un retentissement *considérable*, venant de la *NRF*.[61]

In a statement of supreme importance, Martin du Gard felt he could not overstate the scale of the impact that the *NRF's* view would have in Germany:

> [Le] retentissement dépassera sans doute les milieux intellectuels. Jean sera considéré comme le porte-parole du groupe de la *NRF* et davantage encore - *comme représentant les intellectuels français*. Il va jouer là-bas le rôle que jouent pour nous, Français, les frères Mann. Cette chronique, qui risque de faire là-bas figure de manifeste intellectuel français, doit être *impeccable*, pesée [...], purgée de toute possibilité de malentendu. [...] Encore une fois, elle nous engage tous. C'est un geste très heureux, amis assez gros de conséquences, me semble-t-il. Je voudrais être sûr que notre modeste Jean s'en rende compte, et qu'il porte, en notre nom à tous, un coup magistral.[62]

From the tone of Martin du Gard's exhortation, Paulhan realized that the *NRF* would be making a momentous gesture by publishing this statement on Franco-German *rapprochement*, and that it would appear to many as a desperate attempt on the part of French intellectuals to improve relations. Thus, on 1 December 1930, the *NRF* carried Schlumberger's text as the leading article.[63]

Schlumberger strove to show restraint in his criticism of French policy towards Germany. He interspersed his commentary with an imagined dialogue between the author and an interlocutor in order to add depth to his statement by anticipating potential objections. The implications of hasty political action and panic reaction on the part of the public had to be carefully contemplated, because war remained a threat. The central premiss was that France had failed to adapt to 'un monde où tout s'est déplacé'.[64] If peace was illusory, it was the fault of the

---

61    Martin du Gard to JP, letter dated 7 November 1930 (AP). The article in question is 'D'un certain manque d'imagination', which would appear in December 1930; see below.
62    Ibid. Emphasis in the original.
63    'D'un certain manque d'imagination', *NRF*, December 1930, pp. 757-771.
64    Ibid., p. 759.

Versailles Treaty. He underscored the difference between *peace* and *peace-treaties*, and was certain that a choice had to be made between them; such a choice was crucial in understanding how Europe had become a dangerous place, because nations were attached to each other like 'mountaineers'. Should one of them fall, the result would be catastrophic. This was not necessarily the central problem; France, in common with other countries, was suffering a lack of self-confidence. He shared Thomas Mann's belief that each nation was also suffering from what Freud had called an 'inferiority complex'. Europe was in extreme peril because it was afraid of the unknown; France, which should have been a pathfinder, preferred to remain introverted. France had been reluctant to adapt to the postwar world, and technological advance made it ever more dangerous to procrastinate over strategic decisions. A new sense of realism was long overdue because in spite of the somewhat illusory concessions France had made over the previous decade, Europe was poised on the brink of disaster:

> Entre une Amérique trop puissante et une formidable Asie, il sera laborieux de nous tirer d'affaire, et toutes nos chamailleries sont bien risibles entre ces deux gueules ouvertes. C'est quelque chose que dix années dans la vie d'une civilisation dont l'existence même est en jeu.
> —C'était les payer cher.
> —La paix vaut cher.[65]

The article met with much praise, and helped to impel a debate that would evolve into the 1930s. Martin du Gard told Paulhan that the text, 'imprimé en tête du numéro, et relu attentivement, m'a fait *la meilleure impression*, et je suis très sûr qu'il a porté'.[66] Paulhan himself remained unconvinced, believing still that a literary review was the wrong place for such pronouncements: 'le défaut des articles politiques que publient *Europe* ou la *NRF* est, il me semble, qu'ils peuvent parler de tout, sauf de leur sujet'.[67] Some *NRF*-associated writers launched into debates at the Union pour la Vérité,[68] and these discussions provided the context for a further article in the *NRF* on the subject in January 1931 by Ramon Fernandez.[69]

---

[65]    Ibid., pp. 766-767.
[66]    Martin du Gard to JP, letter dated 20 December 1930 (AP).
[67]    JP to Martin du Gard, Fonds RMG, vol. 118, letter dated 24 December 1930.
[68]    These important debates were published in a separate volume: see *Problèmes franco-allemands d'après-guerre*, Valois, 1932. Among the participants at these debates were Raymond Aron, Benjamin Crémieux, Georges Demartial, Ramon Fernandez, Jean Guéhenno, Jules Isaac, Jacques Kayser and Pierre Viénot, as well as several German writers and academics.
[69]    'L'autre impasse', *NRF*, January 1931, pp. 113-122.

### The blurring of Franco-German relations and antifascism

The issues of peace and reconciliation, and continuing calls for European unity became central preoccupations in the minds of many intellectuals, as signalled by the publication of the *Notre Temps* manifesto.[70] Gide, for instance, was becoming obsessed by such problems.[71] However, the Franco-German problem was also beginning to be viewed against the achievements of the Soviet Union: in this way the questions of peace and relations with Germany and attitudes towards communism and antifascism all became interlinked around this time.[72] In November 1931 Gide confided to his diary that he was attracted to communism, even if he disliked its means; already he was preparing for his support of the Amsterdam-Pleyel Peace movement.[73] As though to endorse Franco-German understanding, the *NRF* published in translation selected letters written by German students who had been killed during the war.[74] To this correspondence was added a French post-scriptum in which Paul Desjardins hoped that their publication would demonstrate how the Germans had suffered equally in the carnage of the First World War: they stood as a universal andshameless plea to the emotions and implied unequivocal support for pacifism: 'La paix est une chose non point rêvée, mais secrète, comme un germe sous des enveloppes. [...] Voilà à quoi le recueil de ces épaves aura servi quant à la pacification. Autrement, à rien'.[75] These tragic letters contained a bitter irony: the students had had to die before they could, as Germans, ever be understood.

The year 1932 saw the failure of attempts to re-establish equitable relations between France and Germany. Preliminary talks at the Geneva disarmament negotiations began in February, and Herriot, returned to power in May, presided over the Lausanne Conference, where German reparation payments were

---

70  See the 'Manifeste de *Notre Temps* contre les excès du nationalisme, pour l'Europe et pour l'entente franco-allemande, signé par 186 écrivains'. The signatories believed that Franco-German reconciliation was the 'keystone' in the construction of a new, peaceful, Europe; cf. above, chapter 2. (*Notre Temps* was a 'Briandist' weekly co-funded by the Quai d'Orsay and Wilhelmstrasse.)

71  'A cette époque [1931] Gide s'occupait surtout du rapprochement franco-allemand. Il échangeait une correspondance suivie avec E.R. Curtius et Thomas Mann, et me dictait, pour les journauz allemands, des articles dans lesquels il exaltait les motifs d'une union intellectuelle entre la France et l'Allemagne'; M. Epron-Denegri, *Le Figaro littéraire*, 3 December 1955, p. 5.

72  For another case study of such developments, see N. Racine, 'La revue *Europe* 1923-1939. Du pacifisme rollandienne à l'antifascsime compagnon de route', in *Matériaux pour l'histoire de notre temps*, no. 30, January-March 1993, pp. 21-26.

73  See Gide's *Journal*, I, p. 1091, entry dated 8 November 1931. On Amsterdam-Pleyel, see above chapter 2; for the way Gide and the *NRF* were drawn into support for the Soviet cause, see below, chapter 5.

74  'Lettres d'étudiants allemands tués à la guerre', *NRF*, November 1931, pp. 673-692.

75  'Postscriptum français daté de 1931 à des lettres allemandes', *NRF*, November 1931, pp. 693-710 (p. 709).

abandoned for good; finally, Jacques Bariéty and Charles Bloch have detailed the last efforts of French and German industrialists to settle their countries' differences within the context of the so-called 'Comité Mayrisch'.[76] As for Gide, during one of several visits to Berlin in 1932, he declared himself very pessimistic regarding Franco-German reconciliation, telling Heinrich Kessler that 'le projet de désarmement d'Herriot n'est pas sérieux, il ne l'a déposé que pour la galérie, dans l'espoir qu'il sera rejeté. Et pourtant, un accord était tout à fait possible entre les deux peuples'.[77] The NRF switched its attention to the international Peace Movement and to the debate it provoked, as well as to Gide's declarations of sympathy for the Soviet Union, yet this did not detract form the success of the Goethe centenary tribute in March 1932, which sold out very rapidly.[78]

### The NRF and Hitler's Germany

The NRF remained silent on Germany until August 1933, some months after Hitler's coming to power on 30 January. Some in the NRF circle considered that a new war was inevitable, thanks to French hypocrisy regarding disarmament.[79] Others, including Gide and adherents of the Association des écrivains et des artistes révolutionnaires (AEAR), were driven to protest at the alarming repression of the opposition in Germany.[80] In a shift that was becoming increasingly common among intellectuals on the Left, Gide believed that Soviet communism was infinitely preferable to Hitlerian barbarism, because under the Nazis Germany embodied fascist totalitarianism, whereas the Soviet effort

---

[76]  R. Poidevin and J. Bariéty, Les relations franco-allemandes, p. 280, and J.-B. Duroselle, Politique étrangère de la France: la décadence, 1932-1939, pp. 29-43. The disarmament talks lasted from February 1932 until 14 October 1933, when Germany withdrew from the League of Nations. It is worth recalling that the failure of the Lausanne Conference finally persuaded such as Martin du Gard to adhere to Amsterdam-Pleyel; see above, chapter 2.
On the 'Comité Mayrisch', see J. Bariéty and C. Bloch, 'Une tentative de réconciliation franco-allemande et son échec, 1932-1933', La Revue d'histoire moderne et contemporaine, XV, July-September 1968, pp. 433-465.

[77]  H. Kessler, Les Cahiers du Comte Henri Kessler, Grasset, 1972, p. 273.

[78]  Paulhan invited essays from a number of writers, including Curtius, Thomas Mann and Gide; the overall tone showed how Goethe was admired for his interpretations of the French Enlightenment, but Fernandez, in an essay entitled 'Réserves', questioned the legitimacy of praising Goethe's achievement in 1932; NRF, 'Hommage à Goethe', NRF, March 1932, pp. 321-578.

[79]  After a gathering of NRF luminaries on 12 March, Léautaud reported that all the assembled company expected war, some in two months, others in two years. He berated the 'tartufferie d'Herriot qui, élu pour faire une politique de paix, fait la politique de Poincaré. Tous concluent que nous sommes tous de pauvres zéros, bernés, trompés, entretenus dans le mensonge par la presse, toute la presse'; Journal littéraire, X, pp. 151-152.

[80]  See 'Fascisme', text read to the AEAR, in Gide, Littérature engagée, Gallimard, 1950, pp. 20-25.

crystallized the struggle of a new sort of humanism. Henceforward, the Franco-German question would, inevitably, be realigned with the opposition between fascism and antifascism.

In August 1933, the *NRF* introduced a new rubric entitled 'Textes et Documents'; the first to appear were 'Documents sur le national-socialisme'.[81] Extracts from a variety of sources were selected and commented on by Brice Parain and Georges Blumberg. Their intention was to be objective, for the authors stressed at the beginning that the national-socialist movement in Germany was widely misunderstood. They provided a brief historical outline in which the crucial events after the 1918 defeat were the Ruhr occupation, the rationalization of German industry from 1925, and the Nazis' electoral successes of 1928 and 1930. The early phase of national-socialism had succeeded because of its responses to the agricultural crisis, in which Parain and Blumberg detected most of the Nazis' strength. Underlying Nazi anti-industrialism was a profound anti-rationalism, and this was the subject of the first of four sections of documents. The electoral successes of 1928 and 1930 were, according to Parain and Blumberg, due to peasant support, which explained the success of the 'Blut und Boden' doctrine, introduced by Walter Darré in 1929-30. Finally, the predominance of the agricultural question explained early moves towards what was read as a plan for disindustrialization. The Nazis idealized the peasantry because of their hatred of the Left, as embodied in the proletarianized masses, many of whom were unemployed as a result of the rationalization of industry. Hitler's attitude and policy towards industry was still uncertain at the time Parain and Blumberg prepared their dossier, for in their conclusion they detected vacillation in the most recent Nazi declarations. What was clear was that Nazism was 'une révolution contre la raison, contre l'industrie, et c'est pour avoir mis en question les valeurs du rationalisme industrialisateur qu'il a remporté son succès politique'.[82]

Gide was pleased by the publication of these documents, for they fulfilled the rôle of the *NRF* as he saw it, which was to 'éclairer impartiellement l'endroit ou l'envers des pensées, des systèmes'.[83] Others however, like Alix Guillain, Bernard Groethuysen's partner, violently disapproved of the objective treatment that Nazism had received in the pages of the NRF.[84]

---

[81]    *NRF*, August 1933, pp. 234-262.
[82]    Ibid., p. 262.
[83]    Gide to JP, letter dated 13 August 1933 (AP).
[84]    'Certains sont beaucoup affectés [...] de ces documents hitlériens. [...] Je ne les avais malheureusement pas lus encore lorsque j'ai entendu Alix Guillain s'élever contre eux. Lorsque je la reverrai je ne manquerai pas de lui dire que je ne puis désapprouver cette publication'; ibid.

As far as Franco-German relations were concerned, the worst fears were confirmed when the Germans withdrew from the League of Nations on 14 October 1933. Hitler's brutal repression of the antifascist opposition provoked protests in France, and was the pretext for Gide and Malraux's journey to Berlin the following January to plead for the communist militant Dimitrov's release. At this time there were growing signs of a widening gulf at the heart of the *NRF* regarding Germany: while Gide believed that *rapprochement* with Hitler was untenable, Schlumberger felt that France could still strive for peace without necessarily protesting at the conduct of Germany's internal affairs. Schlumberger put his point of view in an *air du mois* for January 1934. Reviewing the confusion of press opinion on Germany, Schlumberger criticised the Left for resorting to the familiar 'thèmes sur la barbarie germanique' and for ignoring Hitler's appeals to France. As for the Right, the general feeling was that this last chance should not be wasted. Yet he sounded a warning note: there was a marked tendency in public opinion to blame the Jews for preventing *rapprochement* with Hitler— 'l'antisémitisme progresse à pas très rapides. [...] L'opinion oscille, tâtonne, dans un extrême malaise', concluded Schlumberger.[85]

This difference of opinion between Gide and Schlumberger highlights again how the issues of Franco-German relations and the opposition between fascism and antifascism overlapped. Indeed, chronic confusion and misinterpretation on the French side made it ever more necessary to penetrate the smokescreen surrounding Germany. In February 1934, the *NRF* produced what was ostensibly a special number on Gobineau; but there was one very important additional text beside the usual *airs du mois*. This was an essay by Leon Trotsky, whom Malraux, at this time an enthusiastic sympathizer with the exiled revolutionary, had invited to contribute.[86] The article was dated 10 June 1933, at Prinkipo, but a paragraph was appended dated 2 November, 1933, after Trotsky's arrival in France.[87] National-socialism had prospered on the disillusion of the *petite-bourgeoisie*. By exploiting their familiar grievances, the Nazis had managed to weld the disinherited petty bourgeois together in a common hatred of the proletariat. Shunning Marxism, materialism and rationalism, the Nazis had turned to racial theory in an attempt to elevate the nation above History. Trotsky wrote: 'Hitler a dû emprunter de seconde main les

---

85      'Faut-il causer?', *NRF*, January 1934, pp. 145-146.
86      See J. Lacouture, *André Malraux*, p. 205. Malraux met Trotsky at Royan on 26 July 1933; the Russian was expelled from France soon after the February riots of 1934.
87      'Qu'est-ce que le national-socialisme?', *NRF*, February 1934, pp. 311-322. For the provenance of this essay, see B. Knei-Paz, *The Social and Political Thought of Leon Trotsky*, Oxford: OUP, 1978, p. 411, note 120.

idées du racisme à un Français [...], le comte de Gobineau',[88] as though to underscore the relevance of including this essay in a 'tribute' to the nineteenth century racial theorist. Trotsky further believed that once in power, Nazism no longer represented the *petite bourgeoisie*; on the contrary, it was transformed into the ruthless dictatorship of monopoly capital. The inevitable outcome would be imperialism—the 'true historical mission of fascist dictatorship'. In retrospect, this prognosis is remarkably accurate. Trotsky spoke for many on the intellectual Left when he concluded the addendum thus:

> Le délai qui nous sépare d'une nouvelle catastrophe européenne est déterminé par le temps nécessaire au réarmement de l'Allemagne. Il ne s'agit pas de mois, mais il ne s'agit pas non plus de dizaines d'années. Quelques annés suffisent pour que l'Europe se trouve de nouveau précipitée dans la guerre, si Hitler n'est pas arrêté à temps par les forces internes de l'Allemagne elle-même.[89]

In a remarkable contrast, a few pages further on Paulhan inserted an *air du mois* by Drieu La Rochelle celebrating 'l'Allemagne, ce beau monstre industriel qu'avait choyé le capitalisme international'[90]. This text, whose poetic prose reflected Drieu's idealized conception of national-socialism, heralded a longer text which appeared in March, alongside Crémieux's analysis of France's internal problems after the February riots.[91] Drieu's impressions were based on a recent journey to Berlin; he found that the overwhelming atmosphere was one of material poverty and sacrifice which dissembled 'une richesse morale' in which the Germans took great pride. Drieu himself rejoiced in this, and affirmed that 'le fascisme n'est pas de la crotte comme se contentent de diagnostiquer sommairement la plupart des anti-fascistes'. The Nazis had learned much from the Russian Revolution, and socialism was 'en fermentation dans le monde fasciste'.[92] At the same time, capitalism was being subsumed into the Nation-State, and Drieu saw European capitalism and socialism as having entered their final phase of decline: he believed there were two lessons to be learnt from this process. Firstly, all efforts and hopes had to be made under the sign of a new form of 'stoicism', a euphemism for individual sacrifice to the demands of the State. Secondly, Germany was a microcosm of Europe to the extent that both

---

88    Ibid., p. 317. On Gobineau's influence on European anti-Semitism, see L. Poliakov, *Histoire de l'antisémitisme*, Calmann-Lévy, 1981, and the same author's *The Aryan Myth. A History of Racist and Nationalist Ideas in Europe*, London: Chatto-Heinemann, 1974.

89    *NRF*, February 1934, p. 322.

90    Ibid., pp. 393-394.

91    'Mesure de l'Allemagne', *NRF*, March 1934, pp. 450-461.

92    Ibid., pp. 451-542.

capitalism and socialism had failed. By May 1934, Drieu felt confident enough in fascism to write:

> Or moi, je suis séduit par le courage des fascistes [...]. Je veux espérer encore qu'ils emploieront ce courage à faire le socialisme. Car si les fascistes ne font pas le socialisme, qui le fera? [93]

Drieu, however, did not celebrate the *autodafés* in Hitler's Germany. In June 1934, the *NRF* drew attention to the establishment of a 'Bibliothèque allemande des livres brûlés' under the auspices, among others, of Gide, Heinrich Mann, Romain Rolland and H.G. Wells.[94]

Paulhan serialized André Chamson's novel *L'Année des vaincus*, written after his own journey to Germany.[95] Although Chamson's novel was weakened by stock characterizations and stereotypical images, the central point was clear. It was necessary to travel to Germany to appreciate fully the menace of Nazism; it had to be resisted at all costs, for the inevitable result of its gathering strength would be war. In addition the *NRF* gave the first of two extracts from a work by André Suarès, *Vues sur l'Europe*.[96]   Benda's anti-Germanism seems mild by comparison:

> Vous vous étonnez de l'horreur que l'Allemagne nous inspire depuis deux ans. [...] Vous n'êtes donc pas sensible à la Barbarie? La voici qui va du Rhin à la mer du Japon; et celle de Berlin l'emporte sur celle de Moscou, parce qu'elle se vante d'y être contraire. [...] Je ne suis pas suspect si je reconnais dans l'Allemagne présente la perfection de la Barbarie. [...] Les brutes Hitler, Goering, Goebbels, toutes les sortes de Hesse [sic] et de Rosenberg triomphent dans le plus vil orgueil de la violence et de la haine.[97]

Suarès' undiluted venom provoked Schlumberger to protest in the review itself: he believed that such concentrated abuse was out of place in the *NRF*.[98]

During 1935, the *NRF* consolidated its antifascist, pro-Popular Front image, and most references to Germany were subordinated to the opposition between fascism and antifascism. Indeed the Saar plebiscite (13 January 1935) and Hitler's restoration of military service in Germany (16 March 1935)

---

93   'Guerre et révolution', *NRF*, May 1934, p. 888.
94   *NRF*, June 1934, pp. 1038-1039.
95   August to November inclusive, 1934.
96   *NRF*, November 1934, pp. 641-655, and December 1934, pp. 851-865. The volume was finally published by Grasset in 1939.
97   *NRF*, November 1934, pp. 647-648, and p. 650.
98   'Note sur la politique', *NRF*, December 1934, pp. 869-870. On Suarès' germanophobia, see L. Richard, 'Suarès et l'Allemagne', *André Suarès 2*, Minard, 1976, pp. 484-490.

underlined the Nazis' warlike intentions. Julien Benda, by now a convinced antifascist, rejoiced that Edmond Vermeil's new book on Germany avoided the commonplaces which had misled the French public for so long.[99] Quoting from a speech made by a leading Nazi reported in *Le Temps*, Benda was mystified by the continuing and blatant self-deception of certain French 'demagogues' who insisted that Franco-German understanding was still possible. In the May issue, Benda referred specifically to the restoration of German military servic. Anticipating his call for an 'antifascisme patriotique',[100] he found that the pacifism of the Comité de vigilance des intellectuels antifascistes (CVIA) was dangerously weak in its policy of 'peace of all costs' with Germany. Dismissing their claim that the French refusal to disarm had caused the Germans to rearm, Benda predicted that 'l'Allemagne nourrit des revendications territoriales'.[101] Benda repeated his long held conviction that Germany had deserved the 'humiliation' of the Versailles Treaty, because 'Germany had wanted the war and had lost it', and concluded with a fierce attack on the Radicals for allowing such as Henri de Kérillis and Charles Maurras to usurp the defence of Western civilization: 'la vérité est que [les radicaux] ont perdu tout sentiment de la France de la Révolution, toute perméabilité à la moindre idée générale et ne s'émeuvent plus que de misérables intérêts électoraux'.[102] The Radicals' incompetence in foreign policy had thus provoked Benda to savage the Party which supposedly represented the ideals he stood for: his disillusion drove him to favour first the Popular Front and then the communists as the best qualified to defend republican ideals.

The nature of national-socialism was such that it was becoming increasingly difficult for some intellectuals (Drieu La Rochelle within the *NRF* is a case in point) to avoid the 'magnetic pull' of fascism.[103] In view too of how close leading personnel of the *NRF* were to supporting the nascent antifascist Popular Front in 1935, Paulhan feared that the *NRF* could, like *Europe* or *Commune*, become a partisan review. Where Germany was concerned, silence was the only real alternative. Félix Bertaux, writing in January 1937, helps to explain this attitude:

> Il faut avouer que depuis trois ans nous avons perdu contact avec
> l'Allemagne. Sur tous les terrains, et en particulier sur celui des

---

99    *NRF*, March 1935, pp. 462-464. The book was *L'Allemagne du Congrès de Vienne à la révolution hitlérienne.*

100  See above, chapter 3.

101  'La gauche devant l'Allemagne', *NRF*, May 1935, pp. 801-802.

102  Ibid., p. 802.

103  P. Burrin, 'La France dans le champ magnétique des fascismes', *Le Débat*, no. 32, November 1984.

idées. La politique du national-socialisme, tant à l'intérieur qu'à l'extérieur, nous a mis dans un état de choc. [...] On dirait que le monde allemand est devenu l'autre monde, une sorte de fatalité qu'il faut accepter ou rejecter en bloc, sans pénétration possible.[104]

Hitler's Germany had become the evil, 'other world' in a Manichean universe: understanding was impossible because national-socialism was simply unacceptable. France and Germany had again become adversaries, and, after the Munich crisis (which would again impel Paulhan and the *NRF* to oppose fascist aggression), it would be only a matter of time before war broke out.

Despite efforts to reestablish the literary primacy of the *NRF*, Jean Paulhan had been powerless to prevent the intrusion of the Franco-German question into the review; the long standing interest in Germany of such as Rivière, Gide and Schlumberger challenged his authority. His experience made him acutely aware of the risks incurred by the *NRF* in its making statements which, on the outside, were clearly regarded as being representative on a question which belonged, strictly speaking, to the domain of international or diplomatic relations. Its early stance against French intellectual nationalism had marked the *NRF* as a review sympathetic to Germany, but at the same time it had tended to view French culture as pre-eminent. By virtue of the zeal and idealism of its contributors on both sides of the Rhine, the *NRF*, albeit in good faith, sometimes helped perpetuate a rather naive approach to reciprocal understanding between France and Germany. It was only after events had forced the review and its contributors to come to terms with the true menace of Hitler, and only after they had begun to reconsider the problem from an antifascist standpoint, that the *NRF* adopted a more realistic attitude. Yet events in Soviet Russia, and the consequent attractions of fellow-travelling on the Left, also exerted an influence on *NRF* intellectuals, and it is towards an examination of the 'great glow in the east' that we should now turn.

---

[104]    '*L'Allemagne nouvelle*, par Henri Lichtenburger [Flammarion]', *NRF*, January 1937, pp. 128-130.

## Chapter 5

## The 'great glow in the East':
## the *NRF*, Gide and the Soviet Union


*Je voudrais crier très haut ma sympathie pour la Russie.*[1]


*Si l'on prend parti, aussitôt le parti vous prend.*[2]


*Je doute qu'en aucun autre pays d'aujourd'hui, fût-ce l'Allemagne de Hitler, l'esprit soit plus courbé, plus craintif (terrorisé), plus vassalisé.*[3]


Although the relationship between France and Germany dominated the course of interwar history, Franco-Soviet relations and the image of the Soviet Union as it was perceived in France were hardly less important.[4] Faced by the growing national-socialist threat in Germany, as the 1930s went on the support of the USSR for antifascists in western Europe became increasingly important. From mid-1935 onwards changes in Komintern policy contributed directly to the formation of the Popular Front in France.[5] Communist front organizations found willing adherents among French intellectuals, many of whom became fellow-travellers: with André Gide and André Malraux among the most eminent

| | |
|---|---|
| 1 | A. Gide, *NRF*, September 1932, p. 369, entry dated 27 July 1931. |
| 2 | A. Gide, *NRF*, April 1935, p. 500. |
| 3 | A. Gide, *Retour de l'URSS*, Gallimard, 1936, p. 59. |
| 4 | See J.-B. Duroselle, *Politique étrangère de la France: la décadence, 1932-1939*, Points-Seuil, 1979, and M. Mourin, *Les Relations franco-soviétiques*, Payot, 1967. |
| 5 | There is an abundance of literature in this area: see especially I. M. Wall, *French Communism in the era of Stalin*,Westport & London: Greenwood Press, 1983, esp. pp. 9-28; T. Kemp, *Stalinism in France*, Vol. 1, *The first twenty years of the French Communist Party*, London: New Park Publications, 1984; D.R. Brower, *The New Jacobins: the French Communist Party and the Popular Front*, New York: Cornell University Press, 1968; and N. Racine and L. Bodin, *Le Parti communiste français pendant l'entre-deux-guerres*, Armand Colin, 1972. |

supporters of the Soviet effort, the *NRF,* for a time, inevitably followed the same path.[6]

In the case of *rapprochement* with Germany, it had been the intellectuals — with the *NRF* in the vanguard — who had made the first moves. While Poincaré and the Right staunchly resisted reconciliation and occupied the Ruhr, Gide and Curtius represented intellectuals on both sides of the Rhine who favoured *rapprochement.* With regard to the Soviet Union, however, the reverse is the case. It was the Radical Party leader Edouard Herriot who initiated recognition of the Soviet state after first travelling there. Apart from a handful of pro-Soviet French revolutionaries who had remained in Russia after the upheavals, intellectuals only began to overcome their scepticism and satisfy their curiosity by travelling there *after* official recognition in October 1924.[7] There are two important reasons for this. Firstly, geographically speaking, Russia seemed very distant from France, and was generally considered as Asiatic rather than European. Secondly through treaty ties Russia had been an ally before the war, but was considered as having betrayed France in particular and the Allies in general by concluding the treaty of Brest-Litovsk in 1918; the subsequent behaviour of the Bolsheviks only served to compound this perceived betrayal. Consequently France launched into military intervention in eastern Europe: faced with the resolve of the Red Army, however, intervention failed, and the result was completely counter-productive:

> Loin d'avoir nui au bolchevisme, [la France] avait conféré au gouvernement soviétique, qui n'avait reçu aide militaire ni subsides de personne, un caractère national et jacobin que lui-même n'avait pas recherché et qui lui assurait, avec un plus large appui populaire, les chances de la durée.[8]

## French perceptions of Russia

Brice Parain, who would gain employment with Gallimard in 1927, was one among many young intellectuals returning to his studies after the First World War; in his memoirs he describes the nature of French perceptions of Russia at this time, against a background of extreme political and military hostility:

---

6    On fellow-travelling, see D. Caute, *Communism and the French Intellectuals,* London: A. Deutsch, 1964, and *The Fellow-Travellers: a Postscript to the Enlightenment,* London: Weidenfeld & Nicolson, 1973. See also H.R. Lottman, *La Rive gauche,* Seuil, 1981; J.-P. Bernard, *Le PCF et la question littéraire, 1921-1939,* Presses universitaires de Grenoble, 1972; J. Touchard, 'Le PCF et les intellectuels', in *Revue française des sciences politiques,* June 1967, pp. 468-483.

7    See F. Kupferman, *Au pays des Soviets: le voyage français en Union Soviétique, 1917-1939,* Collection archives, 1979.

8    M. Mourin, *Les Relations franco-soviétiques,* p. 123, and M.J. Carley, 'The Origins of the French intervention in the Russian Civil War, January to May 1918: a reappraisal', *Journal of Modern History,* 48, 1976, pp. 413-439.

> Quand j'ai commencé à faire du russe, en 1920, ce qui se disait chez nous, c'est que nous étions les gens les plus raisonnables, les plus intelligents du monde et que la Russie était un pays de fous. On avait eu la victoire, on avait évité la Révolution, on vivait comme il faut, on touchait des dommages pour la moindre chaise démolie out pillée pendant la guerre, on était des rois partout à l'étranger, là-bas c'était le genre famine, massacres, théories, tout cela ne faisant d'ailleurs que continuer les extravagances des boyards, qui, auparavant, n'avaient pas arrêté de se saouler et de se ruiner aux cartes, de perdre toutes leurs batailles, de se signer pour un oui ou pour un non.[9]

After French recognition in 1924, the mythical image of revolutionary Russia as the focus of hope for a great many western intellectuals (and potential fellow-travellers) crystalized and began to evolve. The power of this mythical image is well illustrated by one of Jules Romains' fictional characters, Clanricard, who summarizes the view of many intellectuals spellbound by *Cette Grande Lueur à l'est*:

> Je ne suis pas communiste [...] sur bien des points, je me sens même très éloigné des thèses communistes [...]. Je crois plus à la révolution russe qu'au communisme, plus à l'élan qu'elle incarne qu'à la doctrine qu'elle prétend appliquer. Ce qui m'attire, moi, c'est l'idée qu'il se dépense là-bas une force de renouvellement de création, une enthousiasme, une foi en l'avenir de l'homme, un héroisme, parmi peut-être des excès terribles... J'ai envie malgré moi d'en approcher, d'y participer.[10]

Romain's title — *Cette Grande Lueur à l'est* — is also appropriate when considering fellow-travellers' perceptions of the Soviet experiment: as David Caute points out, it was seen by many as a historical extension of the Enlightenment. This interpretation finds its political counterpart in the leaders of the Parti communiste français (PCF), who were happy to be portrayed as new 'Jacobins', and who came eventually to be perceived as such by none other than Julien Benda, that staunch defender of the ideals and legacy of the *French Revolution*.[11]

Once the *NRF* had resumed after the war, Rivière acknowledged the fact of the Bolshevik Revolution in an important article, 'La Décadence de la liberté'.[12]

---

9   B. Parain, *De Fil en aiguille*, Gallimard, 1960, p. 186.
10  *Les Hommes de bonne volonté*, XIX, *Cette Grande Lueur à l'est*, Flammarion, 1944, pp. 259-260.
11  See D.R. Brower, *The New Jacobins*, passim.
12  *NRF*, September 1919, pp. 498-522.

Rivière pondered the notion that liberalism and liberty might be decaying concepts, particularly when viewed in the context of the barbarity of the recent war. Rivière ended the first part of his meditation on liberty with a comment which, in retrospect, had far reaching implications:

> La liberté n'aura peut-être été qu'une phase dans l'évolution de l'humanité. De même que l'existence humaine semble avoir revêtu d'abord la forme collective, de même il est possible qu'elle tende maintenant à la reprendre. *Peut-être entrons-nous aujourd'hui dans un âge collectiviste.*[13]

Although Rivière believed that French humanistic individualism was diametrically opposed to socialist collectivism, the Russian experience was proving to have invaluable lessons for socialism: 'grâce aux Russes commence pour le socialisme une ère [...] de réalité', he affirmed. In a remarkably bold statement in the circumstances, he concluded:

> Il faut voir les choses en face: même s'il est vrai que le peuple russe subit en ce moment d'affreuses misères, même s'il repent d'être bolcheviste, un fait subsiste: c'est qu'il l'est, et que, par lui, en un point du globe, l'existence socialiste a commencé.[14]

Within the *NRF*, Rivière's tentative view was fiercely opposed by Henri Ghéon, one of the original founder-members of the *NRF*; Ghéon had recently converted to catholicism, and was a supporter of the Action Française. In his counterattack on behalf of the Parti de l'Intelligence, he stated his primary belief: 'le monde entier a intérêt à la restauration de l'esprit français, ferment, moteur, animateur de la seule civilisation que nous regarde, [...] celle des Occidentaux'.[15] Another fear was that Bolshevism was not confined to Russia: it was already being imitated by France's neighbours. In the face of this supposed threat from just across the Rhine, France's duty was to strive to reimpose political and cultural hegemony in Europe: if it failed to do so, catastrophe lurked in the guise of 'confusion, contradiction, asiatisme'.[16] Ghéon spoke for a narrow, gallocentric, form of nationalism: his views were so distanced from the *NRF* that he would soon cease his contributions. Yet Jean Schlumberger was as antipathetic to Bolshevism as Ghéon; it was only his protestantism which had prevented him from signing the Parti de l'Intelligence manifesto. Moreover, approving of

---

[13]  Ibid., p. 506.
[14]  Ibid., p. 522.
[15]  'Réflexions sur le rôle actuel de l'intelligence française', *NRF*, November 1919, pp. 953-964.
[16]  Ibid., p. 962.

Weygand's intervention in Poland, he felt that the *NRF* had committed a gross error of judgement in welcoming Dada at such a difficult time.[17] Thus at this early stage — *before* recognition of the Soviet State — within the *NRF* there was considerable animosity towards Bolshevism.

After the election of Edouard Herriot's *Cartel des Gauches* government in 1924, the French gave official recognition to the Soviet Union. Herriot and Anatole de Monzie set up a commission to investigate the vexed question of Franco-Russian debts, and, in October 1925, de Monzie employed Brice Parain to help set up a Centre de Documentation Russe. By the time his various missions to Russia ended in 1927, Parain had become a communist, and through the Education Ministry in Paris he came to know Jean Paulhan, who then introduced Parain into the Gallimard publishing house.[18] The Gallimard publishing house exploited the new atmosphere of *détente* with Russia and established two important collections of books under the direction of Boris de Schloezer[19]; the Gallimard publishing-house had a considerable interest in presenting a favourable view of the Soviet Union.

At the time Paulhan assumed the editorship of the *NRF* in 1925, in the USSR the policy of 'Socialism in One Country' was being adopted; the risk of world revolution seemed to have diminished. In spite of the hardening anti-Sovietism accompanying the return to power of Poincaré in August 1926, a growing number of French intellectuals were making the journey to Russia. Most of these 'fashionable journeys' occurred between mid-1926 and the end of 1927, and, for the first time, the *NRF* began to devote space to the Russian question. Yet as we shall see, the image of Soviet Russia projected in France was distorted by the fact that as these travellers returned to write accounts of their experiences, Stalin's first Five Year Plan dramatically displaced the New Economic Policy at the end of 1927.

---

17    Referring to Gide's and Rivière's articles of April and August 1920, Schlumberger comments: 'Une si candide déclaration de partialité pour les "iconoclates" [i.e., the Dadaists] avait lieu dans cet angoissant mois d'août 1920, où les Bolsheviks, envahissant la Pologne, marchaient sur Varsovie. [...] Dans un moment pareil, la consécration littéraire accordée aux "entrepreneurs de démolition" me semblaient d'une inopportunité provocante'; Schlumberger, *Oeuvres*, II, p. 202.

18    B. Parain, *Entretiens avec Bernard Pingaud*, Gallimard, 1966, pp. 68, 78-79.

19    These were 'Les Classiques russes', launched in 1925, and 'Les Jeunes Russes' in 1926. In 1934 *NRF* publicists boasted that 'les éditions de la *NRF* [...] ont été les premières à publier les jeunes écrivains soviétiques, [et] sont restées les seules à continuer systématiquement une collection de la littérature sovietique'; *NRF*, January 1934, publicity brochure, p. 18.

### Reflecting images of Russia

The most illustrious pair to make this journey during these months were Luc Durtain and Georges Duhamel. To coincide with the tenth anniversary of the October Revolution, Paulhan inserted the first fifty pages or so from Durtain's forthcoming book, *L'Autre Europe, Moscou et sa foi*.[20] Durtain's text, dedicated to the socialist artist Franz Masereel, is highly impressionistic. The reader is asked to imagine that he is accompanying Durtain in the railway compartment on the journey east. At the end of the text in the *NRF*, Durtain apostrophized his reader:

> Voyageur, réfléchis. [...] Où situer ce Moscou d'aujourd'hui et le pays dont il est le résumé et la capitale? Ni en Europe, tu viens de la constater. Ni hors d'Europe, tu l'avais reconnu. Cet amalgame, unique au monde, de nouveauté hardie et d'habitudes archaïques... *l'autre Europe*.

Russia was another world where the visitor (and by extension the reader) had to suspend their occidental disbelief, a requirement which applied also to the political question. The designation *l'autre Europe* was preferable to

> les mots URSS et Russie [qui] véhiculent en eux tant de passions politiques! Quelles que puissent être celles que tu partages, un nom frais ne peut-il t'aider à les mettre un temps à l'écart: m'aider aussi à oublier les miennes, au cas où j'en posséderais sans le savoir? [21]

Durtain saw the new system in Russia as a new form of humanism: even the way his book is written and constructed demonstrates his liberal, humanist optic. The new Russia was 'un motif de plus d'aimer et de redouter l'homme. Une façon de plus de le connaître'.[22] Through the publication of this extract Gallimard no doubt wished to exploit the literary event of that summer, the publication of Duhamel's version of the journey, *Le Voyage de Moscou*.[23] Duhamel praised communism in Russia, but argued for its avoidance in France. His position provides a good example of what David Caute calls 'remote control radicalism', involving commitment 'at a distance', because Duhamel applied the 'convenient double standard' of the western liberal idealist, something which distinguishes the fellow traveller's commitment from the communist's 'because his disillusion with western society is less radical, less total'.[24] All in all, the implication was

---

20    'Arrivée en Russie', *NRF*, October 1927, pp. 444-462. The volume was published by Gallimard in 1928.
21    Ibid., p. 462.
22    *L'Autre Europe, Moscou et sa foi.*, p. 340.
23    *Voyage de Moscou*, Grasset, 1927. *Les Nouvelles littéraires* also serialized the book between July and October 1927.
24    D. Caute, *The Fellow-Travellers*, pp. 3, 5.

that communism might be admirable in Russia, but it was certainly not appropriate in France.

Intellectuals writing in the NRF had a chance to assess the nature of what seemed to be an alluring new phenomenon in a number of review articles which dealt with the latest books.[25] Commenting on this first, optimistic, phase of liberal reportage on Soviet Russia, Fred Kupferman writes:

> Un aller-retour suffit pour rapporter en France une certaine image de la Russie. Chacun a la sienne, on s'en doutait un peu. Partis le même été [...] Duhamel et Fabre-Luce reviennent avec des certitudes bien différentes. Le processus est bien connu, depuis que les Français ont perdu leurs derniers pays imaginaires. Le voyageur élabore, à partir de matériaux qu'il a inconsciemment triés, l'image qui renforce son sentiment de sécurité.[26]

The NRF, in its assessments of writing and reporting on the USSR, was no exception: Thérive disliked Bolshevism as much as he thought Duhamel's liberalism was outmoded; Drieu La Rochelle found in Fabre-Luce's account the reflection of his own political aspirations, and Fernandez, schooled in the French liberal, philosophical tradition, could admire what he believed to be Durtain's 'objective', if impressionistic, approach. Of course what was absent from all this was a faithful representation of the Soviet Union: the process had begun whereby a skein of fact, misrepresentation and misguided interpretation became ever more entwined and difficult to unravel.

The reality was that during 1928 and 1929, collectivization was proceeding apace. Trotsky, having already been excluded from the Party, was expelled from from his internal exile in Kazakhstan on 20 January 1929. Lacouture recounts the legendary story of how the impressionable Malraux — also now working for Gallimard — wanted to lead an expedition to rescue Trotsky. After the success of his novel Les Conquérants (serialized in the NRF), Malraux was embarking on his 'Trotskyist-adventurer' phase.[27] Yet if Malraux admired Trotsky, he was in the minority among nascent fellow-travellers, for 'Trotsky wanted a permanent world revolution and the fellow-travellers didn't'.[28] Thus another important process had begun within the NRF whereby a younger generation of intellectuals

---

25     See A. Thérive, 'Le Voyage de Moscou, par Georges Duhamel', in NRF, December 1927, pp. 825-827; Drieu La Rochelle, 'Russie 1927, par A. Fabre-Luce', NRF, February 1928, pp. 252-255; and R. Fernandez, 'L'Autre Europe, par L. Durtain', NRF, April 1928, pp. 549-552.
26     F. Kupferman, Au pays des Soviets, pp. 20-21.
27     J. Lacouture, Malraux: une vie dans le siècle, Seuil, 1976, pp. 194-195.
28     D. Caute, The Fellow-Travellers, p.88. See also the exchange between Malraux and Trotsky, whose article 'La Révolution étranglée' appeared in the NRF for April 1931, pp. 488-500, and Malraux's reply, ibid., pp. 501-507.

exerted influence on the older generation: just as the appeal of Trotsky for such as Berl and Malraux was making itself felt during the early months of 1929, so their enthusiasms were, in turn, beginning to make an impression on André Gide. Although at first a little unsettled by their tendency towards iconoclasm, there is no doubt that Gide was impressed by Berl and Malraux.[29]

### The Roussakov Affair

On the international scene during 1929, relations between France and the USSR became strained. At home Tardieu's government took rigorous preventive measures against the PCF, measures which included a wave of arrests. In France few details were known regarding the extent of the repression and liquidation of the Kulaks and Nepmen during these months. That is, until October 1929, however, when the *NRF* published, as the leading article, a long extract from a forthcoming book by the Romanian author, Panaït Istrati. Istrati, a protégé of Romain Rolland, had travelled extensively within the Soviet Union during late 1927.[30] After his return to Paris in February 1929, Istrati remained silent until his article exploded in the pages of the *NRF*.[31] His long excoriation of the Soviet system sprang from what he felt to be the injustice meted out to dissidents Roussakov and Serge, and the subsequent calumnies and mendacity of the authorities. The article opened by making two forceful points about what was to follow. Firstly, the treatment of Roussakov was only a microcosmic example of what was going on in the Soviet macrocosm. Secondly, Istrati believed that the 'proletariat' was the victim of its own 'dictatorship' which was, in reality, being imposed by a dominant 'caste' above the proletariat. The GPU police, keeping the 'subversives' Victor Serge and his father-in-law Roussakov under surveillance, brought charges against Roussakov which were then published in Party organs in order to remove him from his employment. In the *NRF* Istrati summarized the terrible logic of this sequence of events:

> Le *Jakt* ('la Co-opérative du Logement') provoque une agression; la *Pravda* relate l'agression, fulmine, demande la mort du coupable; le *syndicat* lit la *Pravda* et exclut Roussakov; la fabrique *Samoilova*

---

[29]   See Gide, *Journal*, I, p. 912; Lacouture, *Malraux*, pp. 176-185, and D. Boak, 'Malraux et Gide', in *André Malraux 3, Revue des Lettres modernes*, Minard, 1975, pp. 31-49.

[30]   Rolland, recently converted to the Soviet cause, and anxious to lend it the support of *Europe*, had already suggested that Istrati should submit a text which, he assumed, would be a paean of praise for the USSR. For Rolland's fellow-travelling, see Caute, *Communism and the French Intellectuals*, pp. 104ff, and correspondence with Guéhenno, in *Indépendance de l'esprit, Cahiers Romain Rolland*, 23, p. 38.

[31]   'L'Affaire Roussakov, ou l'URSS aujourd'hui', *NRF*, October 1929, pp. 437-476. This text was incorporated in P. Istrati, *Vers l'autre flamme*, Reider, 1929, republished by Editions '10/18', 1980, pp. 149ff.

> [Roussakov's work-place] chasse un homme que le syndicat avait
> exclu; la *Pravda* prend acte des déclarations de la fabrique; le *Jakt*
> tient ensuite des assemblées où il lit la *Pravda* et demande
> l'exécution immédiate du monstre.[32]

Scandalised by this injustice, Istrati launched a counterattack upon the Soviet
authorities: it was only his status as a foreigner which prevented his own arrest:
'Eh bien, tas de salauds! Assassins d'ouvriers! Oui, ce sont des ignominies, ce
que vous faites, et je protesterai ici et à l'étranger!'[33] With persistence, Istrati
managed to remonstrate with Party chiefs. However, after one trial, which
resulted in the acquittal of the Roussakov family, other charges were conjured
up, leaving them without bread rations or the right to work. Exhausted by his
efforts, Istrati left the USSR, 'plus misérable qu'au temps où j'étais moi-même un
de ces ouvriers qu'on écrase sous tous les régimes'.[34] He learned later that in
spite of his protests, the Roussakovs had been sentenced. For Istrati, the gulag
already existed:

> D'un bout à l'autre de l'empire, maté par la trique du fascisme
> communiste, les Sibéries sont pleines de Roussakov. [...] Il n'est
> plus question là-dedans de socialisme, mais d'une terreur [...] dont
> on se sert pour le triomphe d'une nouvelle et monstrueuse caste qui
> raffole de fordisme, d'américanisation.[35]

Such powerful material, articulated in colourful and sometimes extreme
language, with whole sections of text italicized or in block capitals, would have
surprised many readers of the normally restrained *NRF*. Predictably, the PCF
daily *L'Humanité* lost no time in mounting a scorching counter-offensive in which
Istrati was so vilified that he never truly recovered before his suicide in 1935. On
4 October *L'Humanité's* front page indicated that 'la presse bourgeoise fait grand
bruit [...] autour d'un article publié par Panaït Istrati dans la *NRF*, dans lequel cet
haidouk parjure hurle contre la Russie soviétique avec les chiens bourgeois et
social-démocrates.' For days after, insults continued to be heaped on the
perpetrators of this 'social-fascism'.[36]

    In the absence of concrete evidence one can only speculate on the motives
for publishing this polemical attack. It may be difficult to identify distinct
political motives, but the publicity given to this sensational *rentrée* issue in the

---

32    *NRF*, October 1929, p. 465.
33    Ibid., p. 450.
34    Ibid., p. 472.
35    Ibid., pp. 474-475.
36    See *L'Humanité*, 4, 5 and 13 October 1929. Cf. the rehabilitation 'Justice pour Panaït
      Istrati',*Vers l'autre flamme*, 1980, Annexe no. 2.

press would have ensured that it was a commercial success. Jean Grenier approved and felt the article was an excellent counterbalance to Benda, who responded to the 'Affaire Roussakov' in the November issue. He felt far enough removed from the Soviet situation to write: 'je dois avouer que cette nouvelle affaire Dreyfus me laisse assez froid'.[37] For Benda, history was repeating itself; there was nothing new in the fact that 'un groupement [here, the Soviets] ne peut être fort que dans l'injustice et le mensonge'. Maintaining his established position, Benda defined the rôle of the intellectual thus: 'c'est votre affaire et non la mienne', and went on to give a display of his gymnastic logic:

> Les nécessités de l'ordre social, les conditions vitales d'une nation, c'est là des choses que vous savez et qui ne me regardent pas. Je n'empêche pas les États de pratiquer le mensonge, s'ils le croient nécessaire; je les empêche seulement de dire qu'il est la vérité.[38]

Benda's antipathy for the bourgeoisie led him to excuse the brutal exigencies of history of which Istrati's account provided only one example. The proletariat's violent repression of the bourgeoisie had exploded because of centuries of accumulated injustice. Benda appeared to annex this Soviet example to the exposition of antibourgeoisism given in *La Trahison des clercs*, yet he remained indignant that so many in France could (hypocritically) lambast the Soviet State for its betrayal of the revolutionary ideal.[39] Similar 'historical exigencies' would, with time, erode Benda's idealism; later in the 1930s he rallied together with the fellow-travellers.

In the same issue, Paulhan inserted another corrective to Istrati, this time from the pen of Brice Parain, himself a communist and familiar with the situation in the USSR. He picked out the inconsistencies of the polemic, referred to Istrati's 'instinct d'agitateur', and called him a 'trotzkiste' because of his association with Victor Serge.[40] Parain's appeal for impartiality shows how orthodox he was at this time:

> Soyons impartiaux: le gouvernement soviétique n'a pas proclamé la démocratie en URSS estimant prématuré de relâcher des rigueurs de la dictature. On ne peut donc exiger de lui ni la liberté de presse, ni la liberté de répandre [...] des propos contrariant l'effort en cours.[41]

---

[37]   'Sur l'affaire Roussakov', *NRF*, November 1929, pp. 696-702 (p. 696).
[38]   Ibid., p. 697.
[39]   Ibid., p. 702.
[40]   'A propos de l'affaire Roussakov', *NRF* November 1929, pp. 730-732.
[41]   Ibid., p. 731.

Istrati was a 'bourgeois liberal' who, conveniently ignoring the true political significance of the issue, had produced 'un réquisitoire contre l'URSS du point de vue bourgeois'. No one would be fooled by Istrati's accusations: 'Aucun des lecteurs de la *NRF, parmi lesquels on relèverait peu de prolétaires*, j'imagine, ne s'y sera trompé'.[42] In Parain's view Istrati could not at the same time be a revolutionary *and* maintain his liberal concerns.

## Towards *engagement*

At this time it began to be widely reported in the French press that thanks to the first Five Year Plan, the Soviet Union was making fantastic progress in its efforts to industrialize. However, because French commerce was suffering from the 'dumping' of cheap Russian goods, and because French countermeasures soured relations further, by the end of 1929 the two countries had almost reverted to the enmity prevalent before 1924. In short, apart from the PCF, the French political class continued to parade its anti-Bolshevism.[43]

It was against this background of Soviet progress and French suspicion and hostility that Gide, already aware of the effect that revolutionary ideas had had on the likes of Malraux, Parain, Berl and Groethuysen, began to take an obsessive interest in the USSR. Gide seems to have been totally captivated by reports of the 'success' of the first Five Year Plan. For instance, he read in *Europe* Michael Farbman's *Piatiletka, le plan russe*[44], and one of his companions, Maria Van Rhysselberghe, recorded its effect:

> [Gide] entre avec un numéro d'*Europe*. [...] "Ce que je lis est passionnant, c'est peut-être le premier article sur la Russie qui m'emballe vraiment; *ce sont de simples statistiques* sur le plan quinquennal, c'est tout simplement prodigieux et je ne puis m'empêcher de souhaiter de tout mon coeur qu'il réussisse. Ah! vraiment après tout ce que les Russes se sont entendu dire! quel triomphe! toute l'Europe sera à leurs genoux!"[45]

---

42    Ibid., p. 732 (my emphasis).

43    'La presse conservatrice continuait à exprimer son hostilité à la signature d'un pacte de non-agression franco-soviétique, qui selon elle renforcerait le prestige du gouvernement soviétique et faciliterait l'activité subversive des bolchevistes à l'étranger. [...] Les partis de gauche [...] à l'exception du PCF, demeuraient prudents, [...] attentifs à déceler les moindres symptômes d'un affaiblissement des nationalistes allemands qui rendrait moins urgent le rapprochement avec l'Union soviétique'; M. Mourin, *Les Relations franco-soviétiques*, p. 170.

44    *Europe*, April 1931, pp. 526-557, and May 1931, pp. 76-118. Also, Marc Chadourne lent Gide a work on the Soviet Plan by the Amercian economist Knickerbocker, leading Gide to write: '*Je voudrais crier très haut ma sympathie pour la Russie*'; *Journal*, I, p. 1066, entry dated 27 July 1931 (my emphasis).

45    *CAG* 5, p. 142, entry dated 14 May 1931. Cf. Gide, *Journal*, I, p. 1044.

'Statistics were the sacred digits of socialism', writes David Caute[46], and Gide was clearly mesmerized by them. They formed the basis of his commitment to the Soviet cause. In an important conversation on the subject with Jean Schlumberger and Roger Martin du Gard, Gide countered their objections, arguing that it was Russian moral dynamism which attracted him. He even went so far as to admit that 'ce qui se passe en Russie me passionne beaucoup plus du point de vue moral, et je crois que pour individualiste que je sois, je me soumettrais très bien à la contrainte soviétique.'[47] Further conversations, and notations in his *Journal*, show that Gide managed to think of Russia in a surprising variety of contexts, so much so that Martin du Gard was led to confide anxiously: 'Vous savez, il file à gauche, notre ami, tout à fait à gauche.'[48] In November 1931 Gide told the Soviet Embassy that he was thinking of making public his pro-Soviet feelings, a move which would have delighted the communists' front organizations.[49] By the end of February 1932, his mind was made up; after another conversation with Martin du Gard, he declared: 'Je vais publier dans la *NRF* mon journal actuel, puisque cela devient presque ma seule façon de produire'.[50] And two weeks later, the harassed editor of the *NRF* received instructions from Gide: 'Mieux vaut remettre d'un mois le début du *Journal* dans la Revue. Cette publication est (pour moi du moins) fort importante et je serai soulagé si je ne me sens plus talonné.'[51] At last, starting in June 1932, and running each month until October, Gide's 'Pages de Journal' began to appear. It was July's issue which carried the bombshell: in the last page, he wrote:

> Mais surtout j'aimerais vivre assez pour voir le plan de la Russie réussir. [...] Jamais je ne suis penché sur l'avenir avec une curiosité plus passionnée. Tout mon coeur applaudit à cette gigantesque et pourtant toute humaine entreprise. [...] La première condition pour que ce projet réussisse, c'est de croire obstinément qu'il réussira. Loin de défier l'intelligence il l'appelle et c'est la raison qui doit ici triompher.[52]

46  Caute, *The Fellow-Travellers*, p. 64f.
47  *CAG* 5, p. 164, entry dated 5 October 1931. There is evidence in his *Journal* which lends credence to the view that Gide's *engagement* resembles a sort of ' non-conformism'; see for example Gide, *Journal*, I, p. 1087, and J.-P. Bernard, *Le PCF et la question littéraire, 1921-1939*, pp. 153-176.
48  *CAG* 5, p. 168, entry dated 18 October 1931.
49  Ibid., p. 186, entry dated 7 November 1931.
50  Ibid., p. 224, entry dated 28 February 1932.
51  Gide to JP, letter dated 12 March 1932 (AP).
52  *NRF*, July 1932, p. 42.

These pages coincided with moves among intellectals to support the communist-led Peace Movement, and caused Paulhan to worry that the *NRF* might lurch further leftwards. Martin du Gard reported Paulhan's misgivings to Gide who, in turn, told Paulhan that the review had to remain impartial despite his declarations of support for the Soviets.[53] This would prove to be easier said than done.

In the issue for September, only a few sentences signalled Gide's new stance. He repeated his admiration for the Five Year Plan, for Soviet workers' endurance of sub-human mining conditions, and exclaimed: 'comme je comprends leur *bonheur*'. These pages included Gide's most forthright declaration of sympathy, in which he hoped to live long enough to see such efforts succeed.[54] These few sentences in the *NRF* unleashed a raging storm of protest in intellectual circles which did not subside until Gide's 'apostasy' in late 1936. The inclusion of these lines also signalled a new phase for the *NRF*, because in addition to the peace question, henceforward Paulhan had to contend with the inevitable political bias which these declarations imposed on the review.

### Reactions to Gide's *engagement*

Among the first reactions was that of Jean Guéhenno. The editor of *Europe* wrote on 2 September 1932 that 'J'aime [...] les pages de *Journal* de Gide. [Mais] toutes ces réflexions sur les Soviets, sur Barrès, me paraissent venir un peu tard'. In reply, Paulhan felt that there was 'de l'enfantillage — d'ailleurs touchant — dans l'adhésion de Gide aux Soviets'.[55] Yet Paulhan was anticipating far worse reactions, because he had already read the proofs of the 1932 'Pages de Journal': he wrote protesting that Gide's declarations were all too easy, and pondered the wisdom of making such strong affirmations of faith when Gide had not even travelled to Soviet Russia: 'pourquoi n'allez-vous pas en Russie?', he asked.[56] Also in *NRF* circles, Fernandez spread the rumour that Gide was the victim of communist manipulation through his exposure to Groethuysen, and particularly through the latter's companion, Alix Guillain; Martin du Gard believed there was some substance in this.[57]

---

53     Gide to JP, letter dated 21 July 1932, quoted by Grover, 'Les années 30...', p. 834.

54     *NRF*, September 1932, pp. 369-370. Cf. above, epigraph, and note 44.

55     Guéhenno to JP, and reply, letters dated 2 and 5 September 1932 (AP).

56     JP to Gide, letter dated 3 September, in *JPC* 1, p. 267.

57     In a meeting at Pontigny Fernandez had alleged that 'une militante sectaire et bien connue [i.e., Alix Guillain] sans nul doute a reçu du Parti mission d'"avoir" André Gide! On comprend bien [...] quelle importance cette conversion peut avoir pour la cause. Malraux [...] croit qu'il a dû prendre naissance à la *NRF*. "On voit très bien", dit-il, "comment ce bruit a pu naître et le parti qu'en tirent ceux que cette conversion de Gide gêne"'; *CAG* 5, pp. 248-249, entry dated 3 September 1932.

The fifth and final part of the 'Pages de Journal', those dating from 1932, gave a more substantial impression of Gide's commitment to the Soviet cause. Gide admired the communist effort for personal, emotional and humanistic reasons.[58] His greatest reservations about communism concerned individualism. He could not share Valéry's fear that communism risked ending civilization as they knew it, protesting 'je ne parviens pas à me persuader que les Soviets doivent fatalement et nécessairement amener l'étranglement de tout ce pour quoi nous vivons'.[59] One passage gives a clear idea of the intellectual sleight-of-hand which was so common among fellow-travellers: individualism and communism could, in an ideal world, coexist:

> Un communisme bien compris a besoin de favoriser les individus de valeur, de tirer parti de toutes les valeurs de l'individu. Et l'individu n'a pas à s'opposer à ce qui mettrait tout à sa place et en valeur; n'est-ce pas seulement ainsi que l'état peut obtenir le meilleur rendement de chacun?[60]

For Gide communism represented a type of 'alternative theology' to Christianity. The Church had corrupted and perverted Christ's mission on earth, and it was partly in response to his own need for belief in a faith that Gide turned to the USSR. He interpreted the Soviet reality in a manner conditioned by his own protestant background. The suggestion that Gide's rallying to communism was motivated by personal needs and responses — both in terms of the social question and the theological one — was confirmed by repeated insistence on his political ineptitude.[61] And there is a telling remark which suggests that there is a 'literary' dimension to Gide's statements on Russia. Answering Paulhan's objections on his stated willingness to die for the Soviet cause, Gide wrote : 'Toutes ces déclarations de mon journal devraient être endossés par quelque héroïne ou héros d'un roman [...] que je m'etais promis d'écrire et où j'eusse purgé ma pensée'.[62] Such comments challenge the seriousness of Gide's pro-Soviet statements; indeed, this private admission explains Paulhan's feeling that Gide was guilty of 'enfantillage'.

This spectacular entry into the domestic and international political arena provoked a steady stream of comment outside the review. In particular, large

---

[58] *NRF*, October 1932, p. 485.
[59] Ibid., p. 491.
[60] Ibid., pp. 491-492.
[61] See ibid., p. 498, entry dated 22 April 1932.
[62] Gide to JP, quoted in Grover, 'Les années 30...', p. 835. Cf.: 'Je l'ai déjà dit: je n'entends rien à la politique. Si elle m'intéresse, c'est à la manière d'un roman de Balzac, avec ses passions, ses petitesses, ses mensonges, ses compromissions'; *Journal*, I, p. 1175 (June 1933).

sectors of the right-wing press lost no time in savaging Gide's 'conversion' to communism.[63] François Mauriac was among the first to commit himself to print: on 10 September his article 'Les esthètes fascinés' appeared in *L'Echo de Paris*. Significantly Mauriac broadened his attack to include the whole circle of *NRF* intellectuals: it was risible, hypocritical and inconsistent for this group of 'grands bourgeois' to commit themselves to the Soviet cause:

> Ce petit groupe de beaux esprits, ces grands bourgeois de lettres, vêtus comme de luxueux voyageurs, et munis des mirobolantes valises de Barnabooth, chiffrées *NRF*, s'approchent à pas comptés de l'ogre bolcheviste avec forces salamalecs.

André Rousseaux, writing in *Je Suis Partout* (12 September), saw Gide's *Journal* as the 'literary event' of that summer, and Camille Mauclair, in *La Dépêche de Toulouse* (16 September) gave an imaginative interpretation of 'le corrupteur-né qu'est M Gide' in an article entitled 'D'Oscar Wilde à Lénine'. Emile Henriot, meanwhile, in *Le Temps* (10 October; 'André Gide communiste') called the October 'Pages de Journal' a 'manifesto', while Thierry Maulnier (in *Action française*, 10 November) chose to berate Gide's so-called 'conversion'. On the Left, the PCF remained rather bemused, even though *L'Humanité* reprinted some extracts from the *Journal* (10 and 14 October 1932). One tangible way in which the impact of Gide's declarations could be measured was in terms of cancelled subscriptions; and Paulhan's worst fears were soon confirmed.[64] Despite these Paulhan published a text he had commissioned from publisher and novelist Jacques Chardonne who, impressed by reports of technical progress, was equally enthusiastic about the scale of the Soviet achievement:

> Pendant dix ans, un million d'hommes ont édifié une oeuvre originale, dans des conditions très difficiles, construit des usines, restauré un pays, géré d'immenses entreprises, sans l'attrait du gain personnel, sans aucun intérêt propre, simplement pour le bien du prochain, ce qu'on ne croyait pas possible.[65]

Chardonne clung to the belief that in Europe, despite the coming phase of communist dominance, 'des retours d'indiscipline sont probables, des révolutions de bourgeois, inspirées par la France'.[66] Again, such declarations did not pass unnoticed; for some left-wing intellectuals such as Jean Guéhenno they

---

63    A helpful source of material here is 'Gide et le communisme', a dossier of press cuttings from the Fonds Gide held at the Bibliothèque Littéraire Jacques Doucet (A. II.14).

64    Gide reported 'plusieurs désabonnements à *la NRF* depuis mon dernier Journal'; *CAG* 5, p 254, entry dated 11 October 1932.

65    'Petits-bourgeois', *NRF*, November 1932, pp. 703-711 (p. 709).

66    Ibid., p. 711.

meant that 'les vrais écrivains ont besoin d'accompagner au moins la masse humaine', while further over on the Left *L'Humanité* remarked that they were symptomatic of 'le désordre radical de l'économie capitaliste'.[67]

One result of Gide's pro-Soviet pronouncements was that the front organization, the Association des écrivains et des artistes révolutionnaires (AEAR), received increased support from intellectual circles, now that Gide had lent fellow-travelling such respectability. This support came so quickly that the AEAR was able to launch a high quality periodical, *Commune*, in July 1933, with Gide as a member of the 'comité directeur' alongside Paul Vaillant-Couturier and Henri Barbusse.[68] It should not be forgotten either, as Paul Léautaud astutely noted, that Gide's status as a 'maître à penser' rallied many younger intellectuals to the cause; he would sorely disappoint them later.[69]

### The *NRF*: 'revue engagée'? (reprise)

The *NRF* seemed to be following Gide's lead. The January 1933 issue opened with a curious selection of documents on 'La Jeunesse russe'.[70] These texts, 'entretiens, lettres, journaux intimes', were introduced by the Paris correspondent of *Izvestia*, Ilya Ehrenburg. In his opening remarks, using vocabulary which would become more familiar as the decade progressed, Ehrenburg celebrated the joint efforts of Soviet engineers and writers in the search for 'l'homme nouveau'. Coinciding as they did with reports of the results of the first Five Year Plan, the documents seemed to provide confirmation of Gide's faith in the Soviet effort. The picture Ehrenburg drew was an heroic one in which Russian students struggled on very limited resources in order to complete their studies. These texts provided material good enough for a novel, insisted Ehrenburg, but they also foreshadowed and illustrated the nature of the new doctrine of 'socialist-realism'. The changes in the USSR were seismic:

---

[67] Cf. *Europe*, December 1932, p. 614, and *L'Humanité*, 6 January 1933.

[68] N. Racine, 'L'Association des écrivains et des artistes révolutionnaires (AEAR): la revue *Commune* et la lutte idéologique contre le fascisme, 1932-1936', *Mouvement social*, no. 54, 1966, pp. 29-47.

[69] 'Chez Gide, [...] c'est à la fois une manifestation de curiosité intellectuelle et de sensibilité morbide. Dans quelques années, il [...] fera une pirouette, cela n'a aucune importance. C'est autre chose pour les jeunes gens de vingt-cinq ans qui suivent Gide. Il a une extrême influence sur eux. Ils seront séduits par sa curiosité. Ils le suivront. Ce peut être très fâcheux pour eux'; P. Léautaud, *Journal littéraire*, X, p. 78, entry dated 29 December 1932.

[70] *NRF*, January 1933, pp. 5-35. The documents were included by Paulhan to satisfy Gide's request, but sarcasm betrayed his attitude: 'Je ne sais trop si les Russes ont déjà fait leur homme nouveau. Tu verras des choses curieuses dans la prochaine *NRF*'; JP to Grenier, letter dated 20 December 1932 (AP).

> [Ces documents] aident à comprendre ce phénomène qui, maintenant, ramène à lui l'attention de l'univers, ce grand mouvement humain qui peut être comparé [...] au déplacement des couches géologiques.[71]

After Hitler came to power at the end of January 1933, attention was again focused on Germany. The establishment across the Rhine of a national-socialist régime helped to bolster the Soviet cause in France, and political issues tended increasingly to be viewed in a perspective opposing fascism and antifascism. There was certainly no exception in Gide's case: on 21 March 1933, he delivered his speech 'Fascisme' at the Salle Cadet in Paris.[72] A valuable gauge of how far Gide was moving to the Left at this time is provided by his comments on a text inserted in the *NRF*'s 'Revue des revues' for April 1933. Gide stressed that he would have happily signed this text himself, a remarkable statement, considering its orthodox Marxist vocabulary.[73] Martin du Gard noticed the shift, and warned Gide to beware that he might be manipulated by forces beyond his control:

> Vous êtes embarquée. On souffle dans vos voiles, on trique votre gouvernail. Vous avez dû abandonner votre naturelle démarche, qui, quarante ans de suite, a été de zigzaguer entre les extrêmes. Très habilement, ou vous manoeuvre; on vous fait dire plus que vous ne pensez.[74]

Gide was sensitive to such criticism, and consequently rejected a suggestion that the *NRF* might publish an appeal on behalf of Victor Serge, who had been arrested and jailed in Russia. He wrote to Paulhan:

> Mon avis est très net: n'insérez pas. En publiant cet appel, si légitime qu'il puisse être, la *NRF* s'aventure sur un terrain glissant et des plus dangereux. Ce n'est point là son rôle. J'ai du reste refusé ma signature personnelle, bien que sollicité de la manière la plus pressante. N'empêche que je ferai volontiers, si possible, une tentative en faveur de Serge; mais je voudrais éviter qu'on se servît de mon nom (comme le ferait celui de la *NRF*) pour diviser le parti et fortifier l'opposition.[75]

These political differences relative to the Soviet Union were beginning to show that they had the potential to split the *NRF*: Gide and Malraux, encouraged by

---

71    *NRF*, January 1933, p. 7.
72    Reproduced in *Littérature engagée*, pp. 20ff.
73    The extracts were from André Muret's article in the *Revue des belles-lettres* (Lausanne); *NRF*, April 1933, pp. 699-702.
74    Gide-Martin du Gard, *Correspondance*, vol. 1, p. 556f, letter dated 3 April 1933.
75    Gide to JP, letter dated 9 May 1933 (AP).

Guillain and Groethuysen on the one hand, opposed Paulhan and Martin du Gard on the other. This tense state of affairs soon came to a head: in late June, Gide read a review in proof form by the Swiss author Charles-Albert Cingria on two works by Trotsky, *Ma Vie*, and *Histoire de la Révolution russe*.[76] Gide was so incensed that he intervened directly. He admitted to being baffled by the article, and by its inclusion in the review. He was particularly annoyed that Cingria had used sarcasm and irony to deal with such a serious subject, so much so that 'vers la fin, [il] tourne à la bouffonnerie'.[77] Gide insisted that if — against his wishes — Paulhan wanted to turn the *NRF* away from current social and political issues, he should at least do so less flippantly. Cingria had touched a raw nerve. Paulhan wrote back defensively, arguing that Cingria met with the approval of Paul Claudel and Gaston Gallimard among others; personally he found Cingria's *notes* to have an 'ironic delicacy'.[78] This episode illustrates how Paulhan felt compelled to play games with the review in order to try to reestablish equilibrium; for even if one ignores the capriciousness of the article, it had a distinct political flavour because Cingria was an avowed anti-communist and encouraged Paulhan to exploit it.[79]

The 6 February riots of 1934 brought further rallying calls from left-wing intellectuals, as well as from those supporting the Radical Party, to unite against fascism; and the *NRF* followed the trend.[80] Most important of all, the PCF manoeuvred and improved its political appeal, and in Moscow the February riots 'appear to have tipped the balance in favour of Dimitrov on the Komintern Executive', the upshot of which was that Thorez was called to Moscow in April, and by June 1934, formal instructions on the 'United Front' policy were issued and agreed with the French Socialist Party (SFIO).[81] This sequence of events, and the rôle played in them by intellectuals, seemed to provide further vindication for Gide's position, which continued to be regarded with intense fascination by the younger generation of intellectuals. This fascination is reflected in a text by Etiemble (under the pen-name Jean Louverné) inserted in the *NRF* for April

---

76   *NRF*, July 1933, pp. 150-153.
77   Gide to JP, letter dated 25 June 1933, in *NRF*, January 1970, p. 76. Cingria compared the Soviet 'empire' with that of Venice, '[qui] a non seulement vécu longtemps sans statistique agraire, mais sans agriculture du tout'; *NRF*, July 1933, p. 152.
78   JP to Gide, letter [misdated as 1937], in *NRF*, May 1969, p. 1005; cf. also *JPC* 1, p. 298.
79   C.-A. Cingria, *Correspondance générale*, Vol. 3, *Lettres aux amis de la* Voile latine, Lausanne: Editions de l'Age d'Homme, 1977, pp. 154ff.
80   See above, chapter 3, for details.
81   I. M. Wall, *French Communism in the era of Stalin*, p. 15; cf. J. Haslam, 'The Comintern and the origins of the Popular Front, 1934-1935', *The Historical Journal*, 22, 1979, pp. 673-691.

1934.[82] The article shows that Gide's influence over the younger generation remained weighty, and that his *engagement* gave a lead to many such young writers who were wishing to make up their minds politically. Etiemble argued that for Gide there had been no sudden conversion to a political cause, rather a politicization of moral preoccupations which Gide had written about since *Les Nourritures terrestres* and *Le Roi Candaule*. His premiss was based upon Gide's statement in the recently published volume *Pages de Journal* that 'communiste, de coeur aussi bien que d'esprit, je l'ai toujours été, même en étant chrétien'.[83] Etiemble conjoined the 'non-conformist' interpretation of Gide's 'communism' with the literary preoccupations expounded in the preface to *Le Roi Candaule*. Gide's 'communism' was a consequence of his 'humanism', and, as such, it amounted to a moral position rather than a political choice. In conclusion Etiemble felt that far from being hypocritical, Gide's literary moralism was highly consistent.

In the same issue of the *NRF* appeared Fernandez' important 'Lettre ouverte à André Gide'.[84] This article reflects again how intellectuals were responding to the temptations of publicly expressed political commitment; it is virtually a profession of faith: 'il est des moments, dans la vie publique, où l'on se voit forcé de prendre position afin de sauver son honneur d'homme, même si cette position entraîne des acceptations auxquelles l'esprit s'astreint difficilement'. Very suddenly, Fernandez appeared to brush aside his former objections to communism, to proclaim this 'essential point': '*l'intellectuel a besoin de la classe ouvrière pour se connaître lui-même complètement*'. Fernandez precipitately overtook Gide's position, declaring that 'le libéralisme est mort: c'est aujourd'hui un chèque sans valeur'.[85] The remaining obstacle was the prickly problem of accepting the discipline of a Party: yet this was the most indispensable element of the fellow traveller's position, and one with which Gide had already come to terms. Gide had not joined and would not join the PCF: as David Caute has shown, the very essence of the value of fellow-travelling was for the writer in question to remain in liberal circles where he would bring greatest prestige. Moreover, this characteristic of fellow travelling was not inconsistent with Stalinist thinking.[86] Despite these reservations, as soon as the proletariat

---

82      'Conversion?', *NRF*, April 1934, pp. 628-648. Etiemble traces the origin of this article in *Lignes d'une vie*, Arléa, 1988.
83      Ibid., p. 628.
84      'Lettre ouverte à André Gide', *NRF*, April 1934, pp. 703-708.
85      Ibid., pp. 704-705 (Fernandez' emphasis).
86      'Le prolétariat ne peut atteindre la Révolution que par une seule voie qui est celle du Parti; mais chaque intellectuel peut rejoindre la Révolution par sa propre voie'; Stalin, quoted in the epigraph to Maurice Sachs' work *André Gide*, Denoël et Steele, 1936.

was endangered by its enemies, then Fernandez would be ready to act on its behalf. His realignment had been motivated by his reaction to the nationalists' agitation during the 6 February riots; and once again, the moral justification could be traced to the new 'humanism' in the USSR.[87] For a period thereafter Fernandez became active in the AEAR.

Reactions from the Right to these renewed professions of faith in the NRF were vituperative and numerous.[88] Even Paulhan himself intimated to Jean Grenier what he felt to be a more 'realistic' image of the USSR, and informed Etiemble that the two April texts had brought a number of cancelled subscriptions.[89] Even Thibaudet could not avoid discussing the question — 'dans ce numéro de la NRF où nous descendions tous dans la rue' — in his June 'Refléxion'.[90] On the Left, Aragon's indulgence towards Gide (in L'Humanité, 25 June 1934) showed that through the changes in Komintern policy, Moscow had revised its antipathy towards French bourgeois intellectuals. Indeed relations between French fellow-travelling intellectuals and the Soviet Union were now reaching their zenith: Gide allowed Ehrenburg to take a message to Moscow to be read at the Soviet Writers' Congress (the French delegation included Nizan, Malraux, J.-R. Bloch and Vladimir Pozner).[91] At last, in September, the USSR was admitted to the League of Nations.

### The NRF and socialist realism

In Paris the 1934 literary rentrée was dominated by reports of various statements which had been made at the Congress. Jean Grenier, in an air du mois, identified the doctrine of socialist realism as the central issue. Although sceptical, and even scathing of such as Radek, Grenier's view was not entirely negative: quoting Malraux — 'tout homme s'efforce de penser sa vie, qu'il le veuille ou non' — he concluded: 'c'est ainsi que le communisme ne laissera pas perdre inutilement ses grandes forces d'enthousiasme et de création et qu'il rejoindra vraiment

---

87     NRF, April 1934, pp. 703, 708.

88     For instance, see Thierry Maulnier, who characterized Etiemble's article as 'une grossièreté de pensée presque incroyable'; La Revue universelle, 15 April 1934, pp. 244-246. In common with many on the Maurrassian Right, Maulnier saw the NRF as a radical-republican organ with 'revolutionary' tendencies. See also Jean de Fabrègues, La Revue du siècle, May 1934.

89     Cf. JP to Grenier, letter dated 28 May 1934 (AP): 'Songe aussi à l'Air du mois. N'y faudrait -il pas des "nouvelles"? Par exemple: «L'industrialisation de la Russie se poursuit heureusement. On trouve, au matin, dans chaque ville, 50 cadavres de paresseux. La doctrine marxiste et l'argent américain continuent à donner satisfaction, etc».'; see also J. Kohn-Etiemble, 226 lettres, p. 68, letter dated 18 or 25 May 1934.

90     'Conversions et conclusions', NRF, June 1934, pp. 997-1003.

91     See H. Lottman, La Rive gauche, p. 128ff, and Gide, Littérature engagée, p. 52ff.

l'expérience humaine'.[92]  The November issue carried an even longer report, which showed that all the Soviet writers were of one voice, and endorsed Ehrenburg when he affirmed: 'le nouveau roman commence à prendre forme', based as it had to be upon '[le] récit documentaire, toutes ces annotations sténographiques, toutes ces confessions, ces procès-verbaux et journaux intimes'.[93]  Ivanov was enthusiastic for a rigid socialist realism, while Radek, referring to non-Russian authors, showed much more indulgence towards their concern for style and content.  Given the context of the Congress, none of this was particularly surprising; what was much more shocking for many *NRF* readers was Gide's attitude in the 'Message'.  In a bizarre mixing of terms, Gide wrote:

> [La tâche de l'URSS] est aujourd'hui d'instaurer, en littérature et en art un *individualisme communiste*. [...] Chaque artiste est nécessairement individualiste, si fortes que puissent être ses convictions communistes et son attachement au parti.[94]

The stream of vilification from the right-wing press was predictable, and even more violent than before.[95]  Gide's 'Message' even drove Schlumberger to protest in his 'Note sur la politique' of December 1934.  When Rivière had treated political questions, he had a least been free from what Schlumberger called 'la pensée enrôlée'.  The *NRF* was not a suitable organ for what amounted to professions of faith, so in effect Schlumberger was making a tacit apology to the review's subscribers on Gide's behalf.  In his message Gide had ignored the worrying reports of 'déportés, affamés, Guépéou, propagande qui ne recule devant aucun mensonge' which were, at last, coming from the USSR. Schlumberger managed both to criticise Gide and to explain his motives.[96] Ironically enough, this 'Note sur la politique' appeared the same day that Kirov was assassinated, 1 December 1934, a date which marks a sea-change in the course of interwar Soviet history.

---

92    'Le Congrès des écrivains de l'URSS', *NRF*, October 1934, pp. 631-632.
93    'Le Congrès des écrivains soviétiques', *NRF*, November 1934, pp. 721-750. These reports ended with Gide's message, retranslated from the Russian, since the original was unavailable.
94    *NRF*, November 1934, p. 750.
95    E.g. Camille Mauclair: 'Un célèbre propagandiste de l'homosexualité, riche, avide, gavé de succès et de faveurs par la bourgeoisie dont il est issu, proclame, en haine de la famille, de la propriété dont il jouit, de la religion dont il se réclame depuis longtemps, son éclatante adhésion au soviétisme'; *L'Eclaireur de Nice*, 8 November 1934.
96    'Ce que la foi remplace nécessairement, c'est une certaine attitude critique à l'égard de son objet. Elle est un élan vital plus qu'un jugement; elle bondit par-dessus les objections; elle accepte le risque qu'elle court s'il lui arrive de manquer son saut'; *NRF*, December 1934, p. 869.

The most notable intellectual event in January 1935 was the debate which took place at the Union pour la Vérité. This meeting gave Gide the opportunity to face his opponents and to explain himself to them. He reaffirmed his essentially 'non-political' position, and repeatedly stressed the humanistic nature of his gesture towards the USSR. By this stage, Gide was evidently influenced by Malraux's fellow-travelling rationale, for he readily adopted it himself. Schlumberger, reporting the debate for the *NRF*, praised Gide for confronting his opponents, reminded readers of his admirable concern for the 'question sociale' as exemplified by his visit to the Congo, and explained away Gide's fellow-travelling by reference to his uniqueness of spirit.[97] Gide was as keen as ever to refute charges that he had become a 'revolutionary', and although his published *Pages de Journal* continued to show support for the cause, he repeated again and again that he would never join the Party.

### Gide's journey to the USSR

By now it seemed essential that Gide should travel to the Soviet Union to see conditions there for himself; in previous months Paulhan, Schlumberger, Martin du Gard and Gabriel Marcel had all suggested that Gide owed it to his own intellectual credibility to experience the USSR at first hand. Preparations went ahead; but in spite of increasing pressure from Malraux and Ehrenburg, Schlumberger managed to dissuade Gide from allowing himself to be manipulated.[98] These discussions and deepening misgivings even led Gide to temper his pro-Sovietism. Schlumberger was relieved momentarily that Gide had postponed his journey, but the delays were due both to the imminent winter, and to the fact that Gide had not finally decided who was to accompany him.[99]

On 5 May 1936, two days after the victory of the Popular Front, Gide, albeit unenthusiastically, finally decided to travel to Russia.[100] He arrived in Moscow on 17 June, joining his five companions later; there followed a lengthy tour which, despite its favourable aspects, proved to be an experience which led directly to Gide's renunciation of the Soviet cause.[101] Significantly enough the *NRF* observed a period of silence before, during and after Gide's journey. This

---

[97]   The debate took place on 26 January 1935; the audience included several representatives of the intellectual Right, among them Henri Massis, Thierry Maulnier, Jacques Maritain and François Mauriac. The proceedings merited publication in *André Gide et notre temps*, Gallimard, 1935. For Schlumberger's report, see 'Gide, rue Visconti', *NRF*, March 1935, pp. 482-484.

[98]   *CAG 5*, p. 475, and pp. 478ff, entries for 2 and 14 October 1935.

[99]   Ibid., p. 491, entry for 28 October 1935. See also R. Maurer, *André Gide et l'URSS*, Berne: Editions Tillier, 1983.

[100]   *CAG 5*, p. 539, entry dated 5 May 1936.

[101]   See R. Maurer, *André Gide et l'URSS*, especially the section headed 'Gide apostat'.

indicated a change in fellow-travelling attitudes, since it was no longer tenable to print favourable perceptions of the USSR in the review because of rumours of the purges there.

The visit to the USSR was overshadowed by the death during the journey of the novelist Eugène Dabit. On Gide's return, both he and Paulhan were scandalized by the way that the communists claimed that Dabit was one of their own, and that he had been favourably impressed by the Soviet Union, a view which Paulhan forcefully contradicted:

> [Dabit] est mort seul, dans un petit hôpital de Sébastapol, sans un médecin près de lui qui parlât français, sans pouvoir lui-même dire ou écrire le moindre mot. Gide avait regagné Moscou. Dabit avait pour l'hôpital l'horreur qu'ont tous les ouvriers; et peut-être le besoin de parler, qu'ont tous les intellectuels, aux derniers moments. [...] Je ne me défais guère de la pensée que Dabit a *vu* en URSS la ruine des valeurs dans lesquelles il voulait mettre son espoir [...] et que de cela aussi il est mort.[102]

What the literary and intellectual world was waiting for was Gide's account of his journey; after several delays, caused primarily by Ehrenburg, Gide's *Retour de l'URSS* exploded on to the public stage on 13 November 1936 (the volume went through nine printings to September 1937, totalling some 146,300 copies).[103] Paulhan lost no time in sending his congratulations, and he told Grenier that Gide believed the book would provoke a 'scission communiste'; the reason for the delay in publication had been caused by the insistence of such as Ehrenburg that Gide should temper his hostile attitude by at least mentioning the Soviet effort in Spain.[104] Yet whatever the continuing political implications of *Retour de l'URSS* would be, Gide felt a 'terrible disorientation' which many, Léautaud among them, would interpret as a 'moral defeat'.[105]

---

[102]  JP to Suarès, letter dated 4 September [1936], in *JPC* 1, p. 409. In another letter to his anti-communist friend Jouhandeau, Paulhan was less restrained: 'Après trois semaines en URSS, Schiffrin, Guilloux, décident de revenir en France: ils sont éreintés, (On ne dort pas à Moscou, à cause du bruit et des punaises. Si Gide dort, c'est qu'un avion l'emmène chaque soir dans un sana à 40 kil. de Moscou), inquiets, agacés (ils ne peuvent faire un pas sans se sentir surveillés). Mais Gide et Dabit poussent jusqu'à Sébastapol, où Dabit tombe malade. [...] On interdit Gide de le voir. Gide revient à Moscou, et Dabit meurt quatre jours après, seul, déçu...'; [27 August 1936] *JPC* 1, pp. 402-403.

[103]  *CAG* 5, pp. 560-563, entry dated 23 October 1936. See also Kupferman, *Au pays des Soviets*, p. 182.

[104]  JP to Gide, quoted in Grover, 'Les années 30...', p. 840, letter dated 12 November 1936; see also JP to Grenier, letter dated 16 November 1936 (AP).

[105]  Cf. Gide, *Journal*, I, p. 1252, entry dated 3 September 1936, and Léautaud, *Journal littéraire*, XI, p. 278, entry dated 25 November 1936.

Predictably there was a flood of reactions to *Retour de l'URSS* from all sides of the political spectrum.[106]  As far as the *NRF* was concerned, Benjamin Crémieux reviewed it in a long, balanced account. Crémieux seemed prepared to accept the picture drawn by Gide, but remarked that if he had cared to, Gide could have discovered all he needed to know long before 'par une masse de reportages et de documentaires'.  In what was an exemplary exercise in *NRF*-style objectivity, Crémieux identified the central paradox in Gide's 'apostasy':

> En résumé, Gide est profondément froissé par la méconnaissance de certaines valeurs éternelles: vérité, beauté, justice, liberté, et par la renaissance de certaines valeurs bourgeoises qu'il déteste: famille, argent, conformisme, inégalité.
>
> Mais qui aurait imaginé qu'André Gide, avant son voyage, ignorât tout de ces caractéristiques soviétiques?[107]

It was all a question of perspective: Crémieux underscored the crucial and irreconcilable differences between the French and Soviet social and cultural systems:

> Peut-être arrive-t-on au coeur du débat quand on constate que Gide se refuse à sacrifier certaines des valeurs conquises par la révolution bourgeoise de 1789 et que l'expérience stalinienne se refuse à reconnaître ces valeurs.[108]

Gide, a product of that 'golden age' of radical republicanism, had been ripe for fellow-travelling, because the ideology underlying his intellectual make-up could, with effort and zeal, be extended to embrace the new revolutionary 'humanism' in the east.  Once again, Crémieux, reminding his readers of the political experiment being undertaken in contemporary France, restated the liberal view that communism might have been appropriate, admirable even, in the USSR, but that it was inappropriate in France.  The final sentence of the review encapsulates the problem: 'Lénine pensait avec raison que la Révolution russe devait être une exemple, non un modèle pour l'Occident'.[109]

While the political Right delighted in Gide's *volte-face*, the left-wing press erred between outrage and disappointment; many of the articles assisted Gide in preparing his *Retouches à mon retour de l'URSS*.[110]  It was published on 2 July

---

106    R. Maurer, *André Gide et l'URSS*, pp. 129-148.
107    *'Retour de l'URSS*, par André Gide', *NRF*, December 1936, pp. 1071-1077 (p. 1072).
108    Ibid., p. 1076.
109    Ibid., p. 1077.
110    Cf. the following: Lion Feuchtwanger, 'Opinion d'un esthète sur l'Union Soviétique, *Journal de Moscou*, 5 January 1937;   Romain Rolland, 'Lettre aux ouvriers de

1937; once again, amid renewed protest from the Left regarding the book, Crémieux was called upon to review it for the *NRF*.[111] This work added little to the previous volume, believed Crémieux; its primary concern revolved around Gide's objections to the Soviets' inescapable need to excuse the unimaginable terrors and repression inherent in Stalin's revolution and to mask them by lying. The consequence of Gide's experience was to wonder whether Soviet *étatisme* was any less barbaric than the Nazi version. And, echoing Benda in *La Trahison des clercs*, Crémieux predicted that the forces created by the coexistence of these two opposing ideologies could only explode in cataclysm: 'La crise des idéologies d'après-guerre, communisme compris, est plus proche qu'on ne le croit. Fascistes, nazis et soviétistes ne vivront pas éternellement d'enthousiasme collectif et d'espoir'.[112]

Now that the 'truth' was out, the *NRF* observed an uneasy silence regarding the USSR: the debate raged on elsewhere.[113] An indication that the poise of the review had been restored came a year later. The *NRF*, which was becoming increasingly patriotic and committed to 'national unity', included in the same number a vituperative anti-Soviet essay by Paul Claudel, with Benda's *chronique* 'Anticommunisme et patriotisme'.[114] The juxtaposition of these two articles signalled to *NRF* readers that the brutality of the Soviet régime should continue to be condemned, but also that patriotism and unity at home were above party differences, and should be encouraged. Despite the efforts of the antifascist Left, including the PCF, after the Munich accords of 30 September 1938 'appeasement' politics came to the fore; as discussed below in chapter seven, the *NRF* joined the anti-Munich faction. And with the conclusion of the Nazi-Soviet pact just under a year later, the government banned the PCF.

---

Magnitogorsk', in ibid., 12 January 1937; André Wurmser, 'L'URSS jugée par André Gide', in *Commune*, January 1937, pp. 567-583, and Georges Friedmann, 'André Gide et l'URSS', *Europe*, January 1937, pp. 5-29.

111    '*Retouches à mon retour de l'URSS*, par André Gide (Gallimard, 1937)', *NRF*, August 1937, pp. 339-341.

112    Ibid., p. 341.

113    See the following: *La Flèche*, 20 November 1937, and 25 December 1937; *Vendredi*, 16 and 24 December 1937, and throughout January 1938.

       The literary supplements of *Le Figaro* also carried the reactions of several intellectuals to Gide's change of heart (14 August 1937 and successive weeks); Schlumberger summed up the mood of many at the *NRF*: 'Depuis que Moscou affecte d'avoir dépassé la phase où de telles contraintes étaient indispensables, on se meut manifestement dans le mensonge' (14 August 1937). Benda, however, was entering a period in which he believed that the *French* Stalinists, whom he characterized as 'new Jacobins', should be supported (21 August 1937). See also the replies from Paulhan (18 September 1937) and Arland (11 September 1937).

114    Claudel, 'Une saison en enfer', *NRF*, August 1938, pp. 210-224, and Benda, 'Anticommunisme et patriotisme', ibid., pp. 307-309.

Compared to treatment of the Franco-German issue in the *NRF*, Paulhan, despite encouragement to retain a balance, momentarily lost control over the review's equilibrium because of Gide's pro-Soviet pronouncements. The *NRF* reflected the tendency of French liberals and radical republicans to interpret the Soviet Union at a distance as a land of hope, where a new, socialistic humanism was in the process of replacing a feudal serfdom with an egalitarian paradise. It soon became clear, however, as exemplified in the *NRF* by Istrati's *reportage*, that the road to the new utopia (as it was conceived in the west) would only be constructed at enormous cost to human effort and lives. For a time, such sacrifice and 'justifiable' brutality seemed to have been rewarded by the breathtaking achievements obtained. So much so, indeed, that Gide, seen by his contemporaries as one of Europe's leading humanists, felt able, initially without equivocation, to publicize his enthusiasm; he even declared, admittedly from the safety of French soil, that he too was willing to sacrifice himself for the cause. The issue of intellectuals' support for the communist cause then became increasingly absorbed with not only the effort at home to unite the Left, but also with the international antifascist movement.

Gide's journey and subsequent change of heart coincided with the beginning of the purges; thereafter, 'great glow in the east' grew dim and ever more sinister. Gide's fellow-travelling (whether one characterizes it as 'revolting hypocrisy' or as 'a transferred masochistic fantasy'[115]) may have tarnished for a time the non-partisan reputation of the *NRF*, bringing a number of cancelled subscriptions. All the same, like Gide, it survived, thanks to the in-built defence mechanisms of fellow-travelling. After the disillusion of Soviet reality had been experienced at first-hand, recuperation was permissible if the recantation was seen to be agonized and sincere. History had forced the *NRF* to take account of the new ideologies in the USSR and Germany. In the case of Nazi Germany, ideology embraced and promoted a racist philosophy which, inevitably, raises the Jewish question and anti-Semitism.

---

[115]    Caute, *The Fellow Travellers*, p. 72.

# Chapter 6

## The *NRF*, the Jewish question
## and anti-Semitism

*Le Juif est un mythe, comme la femme. La question juive ne soulèvera chez nous que des polémiques.*[1]

*J'ai été élevé dans le goût de la République et des principes démocratiques [...] L'attachement de mon père à la Révolution était fait en partie de la reconnaissance qu'il lui portait parce qu'elle avait émancipé sa race, donné aux Juifs les libertés civiles et politiques.*[2]

Anti-Semitism, by its very nature, is complex and protean. As noted by Saul Friedländer, it operates on a number of levels — the cultural, the social, the psychological. Cultural factors, drawn themselves from theological differences, formed the historical foundations of the myths associated with anti-Semitism, and Friedländer stresses that 'la permanence du stéréotype négatif du Juif exige que l'on élargisse l'explication historique traditionnelle pour y intégrer les données de la sociologie et de la psychologie'.[3] He argues that these three ingredients interact, with particular pressures coming from one or another depending on the specificities of historical circumstance. In the case of France, the specific 'mix' of circumstances was such that the most important explosion of anti-Semitism occurred at the junction of the nineteenth and twentieth centuries in the Dreyfus Affair:

> C'est la France qui, lors de l'affaire Dreyfus, connaîtra la manifestation collective la plus importante [...]. On y retrouvera la

---

1    J. Chardonne, 'Politique', *NRF*, February 1939, p. 208.
2    J. Benda, *La Jeunesse d'un clerc, NRF*, August 1936, pp. 282, 286.
3    S. Freidländer, 'Aspects de l'antisémitisme moderne', in *L'Antisémitisme nazi: histoire d'une psychose collective*, Seuil, 1971, pp. 11-52 (p. 18).

convergence de tous les thèmes évoqués et l'apparition des tendances sociales et psychologiques.[4]

Furthermore, as Pierre Birnbaum has argued,[5] with the election of the Popular Front in 1936 under Léon Blum, factors specific to France gave a further boost to anti-Semitism, and the strident opposition of a minority of fanatical pro-Nazi Frenchmen to Blum's Popular Front helped to pave the way towards the institutionalized anti-Semitism of the Vichy régime. Michael R. Marrus and Robert O. Paxton confirm that

> it is not enough merely to assert that anti-Jewish feeling grew in the 1930s in France. Closer examination reveals an anti-Semitic idiom somewhat different from that of 1920s, to say nothing of the 1890s and the time of the Dreyfus Affair. [...] Anti-Jewish images permeated like a gaseous current beneath the cultural surface, periodically changing [...] then sometimes bursting forth, after having mingled explosively with some economic or social issue.[6]

The susceptibility of some of the French right-wing press and intellectuals to racist ideas and xenophobia inevitably led to their admiration for Nazi anti-Semitism, and this, combined with domestic social problems and the fear of Bolshevism abroad, watered the 'roots of Vichy anti-Semitism'.[7]

It is not surprising, given the extent to which intellectuals associated with the NRF were preoccupied with political and international issues, that Paulhan's review should also be subject to the climatic fluctuations of anti-Semitism. The problems confronting Paulhan as editor were complicated by the fact that the NRF sheltered writers both of Jewish origin (such as Julien Benda, Benjamin Crémieux and André Suarès), and those who expressed anti-Jewish prejudice of varying degrees (such as André Gide, Paul Léautaud and Marcel Jouhandeau). To his credit Paulhan managed to avoid any lasting damage to the review even if, from time to time, there were bitter exchanges between certain contributors. Here we shall attempt to show that despite its reputation for rational argument and high quality literature, some contributors to the NRF were unavoidably permeated with anti-Semitic influences, influences which were part of the cultural ambiance of the interwar Third Republic.

---

4     Ibid., p. 51.
5     In *Un mythe politique: la «République juive»*, Fayard, 1988.
6     M.R. Marrus and R. O. Paxton, *Vichy France and the Jews*, New York: Basic Books, 1981, p. 26.
7     Ibid., chapter two, 'The Roots of Vichy anti-Semitism', and P.-M. Dioudonnat, *'Je Suis Partout', 1930-1944: les maurrassiens devant la tentation fasciste*, La Table Ronde, 1973.

### 'Cultural' anti-Semitism

Whilst they were not mentioned specifically in the exchanges which took place in 1919 in the *NRF* between Jacques Rivière and Henri Ghéon on the Parti de l'Intelligence, Jews were implicated — along with the Bolsheviks and the Chinese — in anything which threatened Western civilization: 'tout le reste est confusion, contradiction, asiatisme',[8] Ghéon had written. Despite the *NRF*'s resistance to the nationalist ideology of the Parti de l'Intelligence, the review still tended to be gallocentric, and perpetuated the immediate postwar view, as Pascal Michon has noted, that

> le Russe, le Juif et le Chinois sont les trois figures de l'anti-Occident, de l'anti-civilisation chrétienne, de l'anti-humanisme. Ils représentent au sein même de la culture occidentale ce point aveugle par lequel échappaient la Culture, le Sens et l'Histoire.[9]

In the specific case of Germany, Mme Mayrisch, writing in the *NRF* under the pseudonym 'Alain Desportes', saw Jewish influence everywhere and called for extra vigilance from the French: her allegation that Jews dominated the cultural sphere in Germany reflects one of the many accepted stereotypes incorporated in the Jewish myth:

> J'ai dit «talmudique» et ceci m'amène à signaler la proportion, j'allais dire la prépondérance de l'élément juif dans la vie intellectuelle allemande. [...] Critique, théâtre, journalisme, production littéraire [...] sont envahis par les Israëlites; *ils sont partout*, avec leur esprit souple tour à tour et incisif, apportant comme un levain indispensable autant que dangereux à l'informe pâte allemande, leur sens critique, le sentiment aigu qu'ils ont du défaut de la cuirasse, leur flair, leur don d'insinuation, de pénétration psychologique, leur sensualité; certains traits de leur caractère ressemblent à ceux du caractère allemand et les renforcent.[10]

This received view of Jewish 'preponderance', a view that was quite common and acceptable in the cultural climate of the time, provides an illustration of one of the major categories of anti-Semite: 'ceux qui sont antijuifs par conformisme et adoptent l'opinion qu'ils croient être dominante'.[11] Such views underlie Gide's more 'literary' anti-Jewish feelings, and led Emmanuel Berl, who believed that the *NRF* had been fundamentally anti-Dreyfusard, to exclaim: 'Je ne peux pas lui

---

8    *NRF*, November 1919, p. 953.
9    P. Michon, *Recherches sur l'idéologie de la NRF, 1919-1924*, Unpublished mémoire de maîtrise, 1981, pp. 161-162.
10   *NRF*, June 1919, p. 159.
11   Freidländer, 'Aspects de l'antisémitisme moderne', p. 25.

pardonner son anti-sémitisme stupide'.[12]  Gide expressed anti-Jewish sentiments on several occasions in his *Journal*, and Berl refers to the often-quoted passage from 1914 on Léon Blum's character and on Jewish literature.  In Berl's view, Gide saw the Jewish writer as 'something on a scale between Bernstein and Rothschild'.  Gide appeared to ignore the lasting achievements of Durkheim, Lévy-Brühl, Bergson and Proust.  What rankled most with Gide was Blum's ambition: 'Un temps viendra, pense-t-il [i.e. Blum] qui sera le temps du Juif'[13]; Gide went on to vent his spleen against the work of French Jews which, he considered, was *not* French, but Jewish:

> Il est absurde, il est dangereux même de nier les qualités de la littérature juive; mais il importe de reconnaître que, de nos jours, il y a en France une littérature française, qui a ses qualités, ses significations, ses directions particulières [...].[14]

These 'directions particulières' were not, or should not be, as far as Gide was concerned, those of the *NRF*, and there is no doubt truth in the assertion that such thinking — equating Jewish literature with second-rate, 'boulevard' or 'right-bank' literature — led to the rejection in late 1912 of Proust's novel by the *NRF*.  Proust was half-Jewish and was considered a 'snob and a literary amateur' by Gide.[15]  Even if, by 1921, Gallimard had bought back Proust's work from Grasset, Gide could still express the opinion that 'en parlant de la souplesse de son style, je pourrais dire que c'est juif'.[16]

Considering Gide's attitude to 'boulevard' literature, it is worth reflecting that the *NRF* would have been quite different had Gide blocked the choice of Gaston Gallimard as publisher.  Indeed Gallimard's influence over affairs in later years was often at variance with Gide's preferences and tastes in what both the review and the publishing house produced under the *NRF* imprint.  Through Gallimard's connections with the Jewish *bourgeois* intelligensia (he had been Robert de Flers' secretary, and was acquainted with Caillavet and Proust), Jewish authors would be considered and brought into the *NRF*.  By 1912 Gallimard had published the work of the poet Henri Franck, a cousin of Emmanuel Berl.  Jean-Richard Bloch was also attracted to the *NRF*, and Gallimard accepted his work, offering a long-term contract.  Later Gallimard employed Louis-Daniel Hirsch as

12    E. Berl with P. Modiano, *Interrogatoire*, Gallimard, 1976, pp. 48, 121.
13    A. Gide, *Journal*, I, p. 396, entry dated 24 January 1914.
14    Ibid., p. 397.
15    G.D. Painter, *Marcel Proust*, Harmondsworth: Penguin Books, 1977, vol. II, p. 179ff, esp. p. 183.
16    *CAG*, 4, p. 72, entry dated 7 April 1921.

his commercial director, and appointed Robert Aron as his secretary.[17] In the 1920s Gallimard encouraged Albert Cohen to set up a review which would promote Jewish interests: this enterprise became *La Revue juive*.[18] Cohen was connected with Chaim Weizmann, head of the World Organisation of Zionists, and this body provided a substantial subsidy; a contract was eventually signed with Gallimard after protracted negotiations. The first issue appeared on 5 January 1925. The review bore a remarkable resemblance to the *NRF*: Hirsch was *gérant*, and Gallimard used the same printers, Paillart, in Abbeville. In his opening declaration, Cohen maintained that if the new review was first and foremost 'une revue littéraire', it was also an 'organe de l'activité et de la reconnaissance d'Israël', and would, therefore, treat the Zionist movement with sympathy. The editors were inspired with optimism when they declared:

> [*La Revue*] estime en effet que c'est par la création d'une résidence nationale que pourra être résolu le problème juif dans le monde entier; et sinon prendre fin, du moins diminuer, l'antisémitisme.[19]

After six issues the review passed to the publisher Rieder, following a number of 'intrigues', according to Cohen himself.[20] In the field of Franco-German relations too, Gide subscribed to received ideas on Jews. He was most surprised that Walter Rathenau did not comply with the conventional stereotype, declaring that 'certaines de ses théories [...] me paraissent si contraires à l'esprit de la race juive que je ne pus me retenir de marquer mon étonnement.'[21] For Gide, Rathenau should have resembled Jews in general because '[il] avait des antennes pour prévoir tout ce qui allait venir'.[22] Gide's comments were not intended to be overtly anti-Semitic, but they certainly attest to the nature of received thinking about Jews.

Despite the success of the *Union sacrée* during the First World War, and the temporary respite in overt or militant anti-Semitism, such as that of the Action Française, the tendency to view the Russian Revolution as a Jewish conspiracy funded by American Jews became dominant from 1917.[23] Although Edouard Drumont died in 1917 and *La Libre Parole* disappeared for lack of readers in 1924, the publication of the infamous *Protocols of the Sages of Zion* provided sustenance

---

17    On Gallimard's connections with Jewish society, see P. Assouline, *Gaston Gallimard, un demi-siècle d'édition française*, Balland, 1984, pp. 41, 42, 50, 53, 125-127.
18    On *La Revue juive*, see Assouline, *Gaston Gallimard*, pp. 180-183.
19    *La Revue juive*, no. 1, January 1925, pp. 8-9.
20    Assouline, *Gaston Gallimard*, p. 182.
21    *Journal*, I, 'Feuillets' [1920], p. 713.
22    *CAG*, 5, p. 63, entry dated 10 November 1929.
23    E. Weber, *Action française*, chapter 4, and B. Philippe, *Etre Juif dans la société française*, Montalba-Pluriel, 1979, pp. 258-263.

for the conspiracy theory.[24]  Although acknowledged to be false, these writings were the inspiration for much anti-Semitic sentiment in the interwar period.  By 1924 in France, the year of the *Cartel des gauches* victory, anti-Semitism seemed momentarily to be on the wane.  By 1927, following the sensational acquittal of Schwartzbard, the Jewish assassin of the anti-Semitic nationalist Petlioura in 1926, 'the French parliament passed a remarkably liberal law on naturalization which later eased the pain of exile for thousands of Jews'.[25]

This period of calm did not last for long.  Committed anti-Semites lost no opportunity to revive anti-Jewish feeling.  In September 1928 *L'Action française* broke the news of a financial scandal which some considered to be a new 'affaire de Panama en réduction'.[26]  This was the 'affaire Hanau', in which Jewish financiers were directly implicated.  A new, younger generation of anti-Semites, led by Jean Drault, Jacques Ploncard and Henry Coston, went on the offensive and launched a revived *Libre Parole nationale*.  And in February 1931, Georges Bernanos gave a lecture entitled 'Edouard Drumont, ou le clerc qui n'a pas trahi'.  As Pierre Pierrard has noted, Bernanos 'faisait ainsi d'une pierre deux coups: en exaltant Drumont, il attaquait le Juif Benda, auteur du célèbre ouvrage, *La Trahison des clercs*'[27]; the result of this and other lectures and articles was *La Grande Peur des bien pensants*, published in 1931 by Bernard Grasset.

### The *NRF* and Bernanos

Bernanos' controversial work, with its reverential treatment of Drumont, attracted the sympathetic attention of Albert Thibaudet.  In an essay for the *NRF* he chose to characterize Drumont's work as an example of 'journalisme de combat'.  The author of *La France juive* should be located with those talented right-wing polemicists whose tradition was much stronger than that on the left.  Thibaudet could 'admire' *La France juive*:

> Je puis admirer *La France juive* sans déjeuner d'un rabbin, dîner d'un banquier, ni souper d'un auteur dramatique.  Encore aujourd'hui, *La France juive* reste un bouquin très fort, fort de style, d'allant, de *pectus*, où le mouvement du coup de poing prend son temps pour se former, se déclenche et s'abat dans une trajectoire impeccable, un bouquin certes romancé apocalyptiquement mais où le romancement s'engrène sur la réalité et produit de l'action, et

---

24    See N. Cohn, *Warrant for genocide: the Protocols of the Elders of Zion*, London: Eyre & Spottiswoode, 1967, and Philippe, *Etre Juif dans la société française*, p. 278f.

25    Marrus and Paxton, *Vichy France and the Jews*, p. 26.

26    See 'Gygès', *Les Juifs dans la France d'aujourd'hui*, Documents et témoignages, 1965, p. 53.

27    P. Pierrard, *Juifs et catholiques français, de Drumont à Jules Isaac, 1886-1945*, Fayard, 1970, p. 256.

où le cadre de l'apocalypse s'adapte en effet à une poésie de la race.[28]

Thibaudet could praise the polemicist's talent, regardless of how Drumont's legacy was being passed on to a newer generation of anti-Semites. He praised it for its style, its 'panache', and went on to stress that it was only its links with the Dreyfus Affair which had 'gangréné l'arbre entier'. Thibaudet located the book within the French historical tradition, for it was based upon the mythical idea that 'la masse du peuple français a été conquise, ou est conquise, ou menace d'être conquise, par une minorité ou par des minorités ou par des minorités ethniques'. By the Third Republic this idea of a cultural or ethnic invasion had had a chance to fuel 'le racisme et le nationalisme terrien de Barrès et de Maurras', and this tradition had influenced Drumont in as much as he was a 'celtiste'. Thibaudet stressed the importance of the *mythical* nature of French racist ideas (equally applicable in the context of anti-Semitism) when he wrote:

> Cette idée raciste n'est ni vraie ni fausse, *elle est viable*. La critique historique ne peut l'attaquer [...] que jusqu'à un certain point [...]. Dès qu'elle a été communiquée à un groupe, elle agit, elle est.[29]

Drumont's racism was in part explicable through his experience of the *Semaine sanglante* of 1871, when Paris had been 'conquered' by the provinces. Drumont, although no *communard*, 'vit aux mains de la République la trace du massacre de 1871': hence the strongly anti-Republican political charge underlying anti-Semitism. This, and the anti-Semitism of the 'République des lettres', conspired to enter 'la République tout court', and Thibaudet criticized Bernanos for not mentioning what he saw as a key to the interpretation of Drumont, 'le krach de l'Union générale'.[30] This banking disaster had prepared the way for an intense phase of Catholic anti-Semitism, as shown by *La Libre Parole* 'et ses milliers d'abonnés des presbytères'. As the Third Republic struggled through the last twenty years of the nineteenth century, so Drumont adapted his polemic, building from the Panama scandal up to its zenith in the late 1890s. If, however, 'le triomphe de Drumont fut le Panama, son désastre [fut] l'affaire Dreyfus'. Thibaudet identified two Dreyfus affairs, one military, the other religious. Drumont's demise was caused by the very success of his campaign in *La Libre Parole*, to the extent that it led directly to *combisme* and the Separation of church and state:

---

28    'Autour de Drumont', *NRF*, June 1931, pp. 904-912 (p. 905).
29    Ibid., pp. 906-907.
30    Ibid., pp. 907-909. On the Union Générale, see J. Verdès-Leroux, *Scandale financier et anit-sémitisme catholique*, Editions du Centurion, 1969.

> L'incroyable fanatisme religieux déclenché dans le clergé régulier et
> séculier, et parmi les fidèles, par l'Affaire, est l'oeuvre de Drumont
> [...]. Le frais de la guerre, Drumont en a payé son obole avec son
> déclin et son ruine. Mais l'Eglise a payé la grosse part, presque
> tout. Elle a payé, parce que le petit clergé, et une bonne part du
> gros, avaient emboîté le pas derrière un journaliste, malgré les
> avertissements de Léon XIII, qui se garda bien de se prononcer sur
> l'Affaire Dreyfus.[31]

Bernanos, a former *camelot du roi*, delighted the Action Française with his paean of praise to Drumont, and shows how easy it was in France to revivify anti-Semitism for political ends. Another form of anti-Semitism was growing in strength in Germany, and the increasing awareness in France of Hitler's anti-Jewish policies led to the creation of the Ligue internationale contre l'antisémitisme (LICA), which was later transformed under Bernard Lecache into the Ligue internationale contre le racisme et l'antisémitisme (LICRA). French Jews, especially those on the Left, rallied behind Bernard Lecache's movement, and, in February 1932, before Hitler's advent to power, their monthly newspaper *Droit de vivre* made its first appearance.[32]

### The *NRF* and Jean-Richard Bloch

At this time the *NRF* began to serialize (starting in May 1932) Jean-Richard Bloch's novel, *Sybilla*.[33] Bloch, recognized as an *NRF* author, was coming close to fellow-travelling during this period, and held a regular rubric at *Europe* in which he commented on a wide range of political and cultural issues. Bloch managed to offend deeply Martin du Gard and Gide in one of his *chroniques* after his novel had finished serialization in the review. Martin du Gard told Gide to read Bloch's article in the April issue of *Europe*. The former's sensibilities had been severely bruised by what Bloch had written:

> Nous désirons n'avoir plus rien de commun avec les parcs à
> Lenôtre, les jardins bien ordonnés, l'apologie niaise de l'héritage
> cartésien, de la mesure et du dépouillement.[34]

---

[31]  *NRF*, June 1931, p. 911.

[32]  *Droit de vivre* eventually became a weekly in 1935; it is of importance because its emphasis was pro-republican and pro-French and did not stridently support Zionism. It provided a forum for many intellectuals who were not practising Jews, or who were not Jewish at all, from the Left and centre-Left of the political spectrum.

[33]  This ran in six parts until October 1932 and occupied over 280 pages of the review. It attracted a wide range of opinion, as shown in a letter from Paulhan to Bloch, in *JPC* 1, pp. 259-261, dated 6 July 1932.

[34]  Quoted in Gide-Martin du Gard, *Correspondence*, vol. I, p. 564, letter dated 30 April 1933.

Martin du Gard was so incensed by this 'nihilism' that he wrote: 'à certains moments [...] j'ai senti bouillonner en moi je ne sais quel jus hitlérien!' Although Martin du Gard could understand Bloch's arguments, he felt most disturbed by the fact that it had been a Jew who had '[porté] des coups d'iconoclaste sur quelque chose de pur et précieux'. Bloch had attacked, by inference, not only the 'national heritage', but also the NRF: 'en le suivant, à quoi aboutirions-nous? A la supériorité de Céline sur Valéry?' Gide replied, advancing the theory that Bloch advertized such feelings because 'his novel Sybilla had been a complete failure', and that this was for racial reasons: 'Ces qualités d'ordre, de mesure [...] qui, *chez lui, n'étaient qu'acquises, sont innées chez nous et ressortissent au plus profond de notre nature.*'[35] Gide feared that western Europe had entered a 'dark age' in which the values they had held so dear were no longer respected; *their* works, *Les Thibault* or *Les Faux-Monnayeurs*, belonged to a different category, and it would have been absurd for either of them to have attempted such an undertaking as *Sybilla*. Bloch's view was iconoclastic because for him the traditional cultural values and political dilatoriness of the victorious European states had led to Hitler's rise to power in Germany: if he called for a *tabula rasa* it was because the Nazis were not slow in showing their true colours. At the time of this exchange of letters, *Droit de vivre* warned that 700,000 Jews were under threat from the Nazi regime, and that the Jewish question had become a central issue not only in Franco-German relations, but also in antifascism.[36] André Malraux, at this time very influential at the NRF and familiar with German-Jewish circles through his marriage to Clara Goldschmidt, rallied to the Jewish-backed antifascist cause later that year, when he responded to a survey in Lecache's newspaper. In his reply, Malraux noted that 'l'antisémitisme en France est toujours une idée subordonnée'[37]: by this he meant that anti-Jewish feeling could be mobilized by nationalist propaganda for ulterior, political, motives. This may have been the case in France until the advent of Hitler, but anti-Semitic racism *per se* was an integral part of *Nazi* policies, and it would not be long before such policies found favour among a small minority of genuine, racist, pro-Nazi Frenchmen.[38] Thus

---

35    Ibid., p. 566, letter dated 2 May 1933 (my italics).

36    *Droit de vivre*, March, April and May 1933; it reported that 'Herriot est avec nous', and that intellectuals such as André Chamson, Jacques Kayser and politicians such as Léon Blum were giving their movement support.

37    *Droit de vivre*, September-October, and November 1933. The survey put the question: 'La France est-elle menacée d'un fascisme générateur d'antisémitisme?'. See my note 'Malraux, anti-Semitism and antifascism', in *Mélanges Malraux*, Vol. 17, Spring-Fall 1985, pp. 46-50.

38    Cf. Dioudonnat, *Je suis partout*, and P.J. Kingston, *Anti-Semitism in France during the 1930s*, Hull: University of Hull Press, 1983, pp. 10-64, where the police report 'La Propagande anti-juive' in reproduced.

Malraux interpreted the Jewish problem at this time as a *political* one requiring a *socialist* solution: 'l'idée de race, en Europe, en 1933, ne peut signifier autre chose que l'oppression des minorités'. In opposing anti-Semitism or fascism, Jews had to unite with one of the only two forces which opposed the racists, 'democracy or the proletariat'; above all, they should not simply assume that they could remain above 'party oppositions'.[39] Malraux's high-profile support for the Jewish cause was appreciated by LICA during 1933 and 1934, as attested by the prominence given to reports of his speeches.

### The *NRF* and Gobineau

One of the authors most responsible for formulating theories of racial superiority was Count Arthur de Gobineau, whose *Essai sur l'inégalité des races*, dating from 1851, had been profoundly influential over successive racial theorists during the second half of the nineteenth century. He had attempted to systematize the confused thinking on race which had preceded him by dividing the Eurasian peoples on linguistic lines into 'Aryan' and 'Semitic', thereby heralding biological racism. As Leon Poliakov puts its, by the end of the nineteenth century the Aryan myth 'had achieved pride of place among men of learning'.[40]

In its February issue 1934, exactly a year after Hitler's coming to power, the *NRF* devoted almost all of its space to a special issue entitled 'Gobineau et le gobinisme'.[41] It coincided with what many saw at the time as a genuine fascist *coup* on 6 February, and some, such as André Wurmser, never forgave Paulhan for publishing this 'tribute'.[42] His correspondence shows that Paulhan had been preparing this issue since March 1933. Contributions from non-*NRF* writers included essays by Robert Dreyfus, Abel Bonnard, Bernard Faÿ, Daniel Halévy, Ernest Seillière and Heinrich von Keyserling. Paulhan cannot have been unaware of the potential damage that the Gobineau 'special number' might do, for Paul Bourget, invited through Daniel Halévy to contribute, did not wish to do so because 'le racisme allemand le gêne, et il ne s'en cache pas. Je ne doute pas que ce ne soit la raison de son silence vis-à-vis de vous'.[43]

Not all the contributions praised 'le gobinisme', however. Etiemble, writing under his pseudonym Jean Louverné, submitted a sharp critique and

---

39    *Droit de vivre*, September-October 1933.
40    On Gobineau and his ideas, see L. Poliakov, *The Aryan Myth- a history of racist and nationalist ideas*, London: Chatto-Heinemann, 1974, chapter IX.
41    *NRF*, February 1934, pp. 161-309. This issue also contained Trotsky's 'Qu'est-ce que le national-socialisme?' (see above, chapter four).
42    See A. Wurmser, *Fidèlement vôtre*, Grasset, 1979, p. 54.
43    Halévy to JP, letter dated 7 May 1933 (AP). In the same letter Halévy mentioned to Paulhan that Jérôme Tharaud was re-reading *Essai sur l'inégalité des races*, finding it 'un des plus beaux romans qu'il ait jamais lus' (ibid.).

alleged that had Hitler not resorted to the Aryan myth, Gobineau's work would still be languishing 'in dusty librairies'. For Etiemble, 'le fascisme a lancé cet avocat prétendu de Goering'. Modern ethnography was beginning to show how fraudulent Gobineau's ideas were: 'la naissance relativement récente de la civilisation aryenne forçait Gobineau à rajeunir la vieille Chine'. Paulhan found this to be an exaggeration, but he did not alter the wording.[44]  In a perceptive essay Heinrich von Keyserling examined how Gobineau's ideas had filtered into Germany through the work of H.S. Chamberlain:

> J'ai eu tort, les faits le prouvent bien: Chamberlain a certainement été l'inspirateur principal de l'Allemagne qui a tenu durant la grande guerre. J'ai eu tort une seconde fois, lorsque j'ai ri, en entendant Chamberlain désigner, dès 1923, Adolf Hitler comme le prophète de l'Allemagne à venir.[45]

The most inflammatory piece, however, and the one most likely to have sparked the indignation of Jewish antifascists such as André Wurmser, was Clément Serpeille de Gobineau's 'Le gobinisme et la politique moderne'. The author asserted unequivocally that *gobinisme* was the direct inspiration for Nazi racism. Summarizing Aryan 'superiority' he wrote: 'parmi les blancs, l'Aryan seul est doué de l'esprit social, est apte à gouverner socialement'.[46]  And this social superiority was fundamental to national-socialism:

> C'est pour retrouver son unité sociale que l'Allemagne hitlérienne s'est cru obligée d'éliminer les Juifs qui, servis par le régime libéral, avaient mis en oeuvre toutes leurs qualités individuelles et leurs attirances raciales pour se tailler dans l'activité intellectuelle, économique et politique de l'Allemagne social-démocrate la part du lion.[47]

Serpeille de Gobineau contrasted the superior organizing abilities of an 'Aryan' nation like England and its colonial empire with Spain, which was, supposedly, so racially debased that it was socially chaotic. He concluded that in Italy (another Latin, equally 'mixed' nation) 'Renaissance heroes' were striving to

---

[44]   'Gobineau sinologue', in *NRF*, February 1934, p. 234. Paulhan wrote to Etiemble: 'Tout de même, Gobineau ne date pas du fascisme: et c'est en 1923 qu'*Europe* lui consacrait un numéro d'hommage'; in Kohn-Etiemble, *226 lettres*, pp. 60-61. In October 1923 *Europe* had published a tribute to Gobineau, who died in 1882.

[45]   'Réflexions sur Gobineau', *NRF*, February 1934, p. 242.

[46]   'Le gobinisme et la politique moderne', ibid., p. 251.

[47]   Ibid., p. 252. It is worth noting that the link is forged here between the unconscious, proto-Nazi, anti-Semitism expressed in the 1919 article by Mme Mayrisch (see above, note 10) and Hitler's deliberate racial policies.

forge a new society, and the fact that Mussolini's Italy was fascist was highly significant:

> L'Italie moderne a senti et vu les rapprochements certains que l'on peut faire entre les idées de Gobineau et les idées sur lesquelles s'appuient les mouvements politiques actuels.[48]

If further proof were needed to show how *gobinisme* had fuelled Hitler's racism, the impressive bibliography provided it: this included a section devoted to 'le mouvement de polémique sur Gobineau et le racisme à l'avènement de Hitler'.[49]

### A clash with Charles Maurras

The *NRF*'s special treatment of Gobineau appeared at a particularly important historical conjuncture: the Stavisky scandal, which seemed to validate so conveniently the extreme right-wing equation of 'radical republicanism plus freemasonry equals Jews', and the ensuing political confusion, violence and reaction, all conspired to make anti-Semitism a dominant issue. The *NRF*'s reactions to the events of February, particularly those of Benjamin Crémieux, sparked a bitter exchange of views in subsequent months. Crémieux opened his April *chronique* with the following sentences:

> Un mois après les journées de février, on constate que tous les partis, loin d'avoir précisé, éclairé leur positions, atteignent au comble de la confusion. A l'extrême-droite, l'Action française, consciente de sa faiblesse, ajourne à 1950 le retour du roi et anathématise la guerre civile.[50]

The next month Crémieux noted that Charles Maurras, in *Action française* for 10 April, had taken exception to these remarks. Crémieux had intended to state quite simply that the February riots had demonstrated the political weakness and ineffectuality of the Action Française movement, that they had not even 'mis en branle le mouvement qui a abouti au 6 février'.[51] Yet there was another reason for writing this letter: Maurras had singled out Crémieux as 'un autre rédacteur de la *NRF*, un Juif celui-là'. Deeply offended, Crémieux wished to know whether 'M. Maurras entend par là que je suis Français de seconde zone, un Français moins Français que lui, moins libre que lui d'avoir et d'exprimer des vues politiques'. He dismissed the negative connotations of the accusation—he was

---

[48]   *NRF*, February 1934, p. 256.
[49]   Ibid., pp. 308-310.
[50]   'Partis à prendre', *NRF*, April 1934, p. 698. For Crémieux's interpretations of the February riots see above, chapter three.
[51]   'Correspondance: question posée à Charles Maurras', *NRF*, May 1934, pp. 882-883.

not a capitalist, he had served his country in the war, he was not on the left politically, nor was he a *métèque*. Neither could he imagine that Maurras was accusing him of deicide. The only alternative was that Crémieux might be a proponent of Zionism, yet he rejected that too, seeing Zionism objectively as a logical consequence of anti-Semitism. Therefore clarification was necessary:

> Alors, pourquoi 'un Juif, celui-là?' Serait-ce parce que je suis de sang juif? Par simple racisme? J'aimerais beaucoup à être fixé sur ce point.[52]

A letter from Maurras arrived too late for quotation in June, so the debate continued in the July number, including Crémieux's own riposte to the Action Française leader.[53] Maurras corrected what he believed to be inaccuracies in Crémieux's representation of Action Française ideas, and answered the specific charge of having singled out Crémieux's Jewish origins. For Maurras, referring to Bernard Lazare, the Jewish tradition was dangerous, and therefore unassimilable, due to 'la présence de certains éléments *conservateurs* et *destructeurs*'. The roots of the problem were traceable to the 1789 Revolution and the republican tradition; democracy was too uniform a system to permit progress. Yet under a 'hereditary monarchy', as Maurras put it, he could easily conceive of a 'Jewish province' in France, so long as, significantly, it could be controlled by statute. Maurras did not believe that French Jews were, or could ever be, assimilable. This he ascribed to the 'nouvelle vague juive, un nouvel arrivage de sang juif [...] venus de l'est ou du midi comme en 1815, en 1870'.[54] One major symptom of this later 'influx' was provided by the action of Isaac-Moise-Adolphe Crémieux, who, Maurras wondered, might have been a forebear of Benjamin Crémieux. He was referring to the Crémieux law of 1870 whereby French citizenship was conferred upon Algerian Jews. He implied that 'seven weeks after Sedan' this action had been treasonable and against the national interest; he wrote:

> Ce Juif nîmois sans doute assimilé depuis des siècles et porté au gouvernement par notre égalitarisme naïf, pouvait songer à tout autre chose que le service de la patrie en danger; il songeait à se retourner vers ses bons frères en burnous!

Maurras drew a direct parallel between this event and the fact that at the time he was writing, 'la croix gammée fait [...] de redoutables conquêtes dans l'Afrique

---

52  Ibid., p. 883.
53  'Divers', *NRF*, June 1934, , p. 1034, and 'Un Juif, celui-là', in *NRF*, July 1934, pp. 100-108.
54  *NRF*, July 1934, p. 101-102.

du Nord'. Once again, referring to the period since 1790, as Drumont had done in *La France juive*, Maurras blamed the republican régime for all the ills visited upon France, particularly by the Jews: 'Israël n'a été si puissant sur la France que parce que la France souffrait des maladies du régime électif'.[55] Crémieux, in his reply, could see little to distinguish Maurras' attitudes to the Jews from those current in Nazi Germany:

> S'il ne dépendait que de M. Maurras, les Juifs seraient en France, comme en Allemagne nazi, soumis à un statut spécial qui en ferait effectivement des Français de seconde zone.

What is more Crémieux noticed that since the imposition of anti-Semitic policies in Germany, Maurras had suddenly stopped alluding to 'l'alliance judéo-allemande'; neither did he mention that the Nazis accused Jews of rationalism, nor did he acknowledge the existence of a Jewish peasantry or proletariat. Crémieux demonstrated that Maurras' doctrine equated the Jewish tradition with a 'Jewishness' that was completely 'innate', and therefore inescapable. Such racist determinism bore very close resemblances to theories underpinning Nazi anti-Semitism. Turning his attention to the example of the naturalization law of 1870, Crémieux corrected Maurras, insisting that Adolphe Crémieux (his distant cousin) had only put the finishing touches to a *'senatus-consulte* dating from 1865'. Crémieux laid bare Maurras' *real* target: 'Le libéralisme français assimilateur, l'égalitarisme, voilà au vrai l'ennemie pour M. Maurras et non pas le Juif'.[56] He admitted in conclusion that assimilation could not provide the complete solution to the Jewish question, but it remained the best and only solution for the time being. Anti-Semitism was an obstacle to assimilation, and that was why Crémieux was determined to highlight 'the inanity of anti-Semitic argument, even if it was signed Maurras'. Finally, Crémieux drew attention to the important problem of immigration into France: at the time he was writing in 1934, the influx of Jews into France from Hitler's Germany was gradually increasing, but by no means was France the only destination—proportionately speaking, many more Jews than those who settled in France found their way to the United States.[57] As the 1930s progressed, however, the question of immigration became ever-more problematic and, by 1939, 'establishment' Jews such as Emmanuel Berl were calling for a complete halt to the influx. In this 1934

---

[55]    Ibid., p. 104.
[56]    Ibid., pp. 106-107.
[57]    For a discussion of these matters, see Marrus and Paxton, *Vichy France and the Jews*, pp. 34-36; cf. V. Caron, 'The Politics of Frustration: French Jewry and the Refugee Crisis in the 1930s', *Journal of Modern History*, 65, June 1993, pp. 311-356.

text Crémieux sounded a cautionary note regarding the level of immigration and, in a footnote, suggested a *numerus clausus* :

> La question de l'afflux continu des Juifs de l'est mérite naturellement d'être posée; elle me paraît entrer dans le cadre des mesures générales à prendre au sujet de l'immigration, mesures très nécessaires, mais portant en temps normal sur la qualité physique et morale des individus, non sur leur origine. Quand il s'agit d'afflux massif comme pour les Russes blancs ou les Juifs victimes de l'hitlérisme, il convient de fixer le maximum digestible et de s'y tenir.[58]

Although Crémieux himself favoured assimilation as an approach, he could understand that some Jews would prefer the Zionist solution to being treated as 'second-class citizens'. Thus the problem of anti-Semitism permeated through to the pages of the *NRF*.

In common with moves towards a united political front supported by moderate and left-wing intellectuals, groups such as LICA incorporated the Jewish question into the struggle against fascism. Malraux, for example, repeated his pro-Jewish pronouncements in May 1934 alongside Bernard Lecache, Jean Longuet, Georges Izard (from *Esprit*) and Léon Pierre-Quint.[59] The activity of right-wing *ligues* after 6 February became more menacing and, although attacks on Jewish persons and property did not begin in earnest until late 1935, it was apparent that the *ligues* had adopted anti-Semitism, and were mimicking Nazi thuggery in Germany. Maurras' observation of the situation in North Africa was proved accurate: anti-Jewish riots in Constantine, Algeria, left twenty-five Jews dead.[60]

### André Suarès and Julien Benda

In the December 1934 issue of *Droit de vivre*, reference was made to André Suarès' latest text in the *NRF*:

> Suarès vient, dans le dernier numéro de la *NRF*, de résumer, avec une magnifique partialité, ce que des millions d'hommes n'osent pas publiquement penser.[61]

---

[58] *NRF*, July 1934, p. 108.
[59] *Droit de vivre*, 25 May 1934: 'Plus de 6.000 auditeurs acclament les mots d'ordre de la LICA et protestent contre les agressions antisémites'.
[60] J. Plumyène and R. Lasierra, *Les fascismes français*, Seuil, 1963, pp. 64-96, and P. Machefer, *Ligues et fascismes en France, 1918-1939*, PUF, 1974. On the 'pogrom' in Algeria, see *Droit de vivre*, August 1934.
[61] *Droit de vivre*, December 1934.

Suarès was a noted germanophobe: in the November issue, much to the annoyance of such as Jean Schlumberger, he had written: 'Depuis deux mille ans, l'Allemagne est la plaie ouverte, l'ulcère de l'Europe. [...] Cette race [i.e., the Germans] est l'iniquité même, comme toute race d'ailleurs.'[62] German barbarism and Nazi racism were condemned as satanic ('de la bête'). *Droit de vivre*, however, did not quote from Suarès' next paragraph, in which Israel was also condemned for displaying extreme nationalism:

> La grande misère d'Israël est d'avoir tourné le sentiment de la justice en raison universelle. Et, par une erreur inverse, d'avoir cru que le savoir et le juste sont fonction l'un de l'autre.[63]

Suarès, himself from Jewish origins, disliked Zionism as much as any other form of nationalism, for he believed *all* racial distinctions were unworthy of his own highly aristocratic conception of humanism. Yet Suarès placed Nazism at the summit of his hierarchy of totalitarian horrors: in the case of Jewish nationalism his antipathy was more redolent of anti-Zionism than anti-Semitism. Thus *Droit de vivre* could only publicize its admiration for Suarès by omitting his more unflattering comments on Israel. Suarès himself recognized that he was open to attack from all sides, a fact that endeared him to Paulhan, who believed that Suarès and the *NRF* were entirely compatible in expressing 'toutes les exagérations', even if this might incur Schlumberger's wrath or cancelled subscriptions.[64]

Although the question of anti-Semitism was never far from his mind, Julien Benda, like Crémieux and Suarès, rejected Zionism as a solution to the Jewish question. Benda had experienced the anti-Semitism of the French literary establishment when, on the insistence of Léon Daudet and Georges Sorel, his novel *L'Ordination* was denied the Goncourt prize in 1912 because Benda was a Jew.[65] Again, after the publication of *La Trahison des clercs*, Action Française and its acolytes never ceased their persecution of Benda, in whom these forces of the extreme Right saw the embodiment of a conspiracy between Jews and the Republic. Although he subordinated his Jewishness to his self-appointed rôle of *clerc*, in the judgement of one of his biographers, Benda 'ranime sa judéité devant l'antisémitisme envahissant'.[66] Due to his strong sense of patriotism and his negative attitude towards Germany, Benda was often cast in the stereotypical

---

62    *NRF*, November 1934, p. 653.
63    *NRF*, December 1934, p. 864-865.
64    JP to Jouhandeau [late 1934] (BD).
65    See *Un Régulier dans le siècle*, Gallimard, 1968 (orig. ed. 1938), p. 209f.
66    P. Chambat, 'Postface' to *La Trahison des clercs*, Pluriel edition, 1977, p. 405.

rôle of the Jew as warmonger. Maurras' calls for his assassination were no less repulsive than they would be later for Léon Blum, and the polemic between them following the publication of *La Trahison des clercs* provided Maurras with numerous opportunities to display his anti-Semitism:

> Il existe un écrivain juif dont l'industrie est florissante, mais à qui, pour ma part, je n'ai pas reconnu la qualité d'un honnête belligérent. Il est à pendre haut et court, comme un simple maraudeur de champ de bataille.[67]

By mid-1935 Benda was indeed drawing attention to his Jewishness, but took care to deflect criticism that he was acting merely out of Jewish self-interest.[68] Moreover in October that year, in the *NRF* Thibaudet also drew attention to Benda's 'Jewish nature'. Taking exception to Benda's insistence (in *Délice d'Eleuthère*) that 'il n'y a pas de vérité juive, il y a la vérité, la vérité du philosophe dans ses concepts', Thibaudet applied his own theory (derived from Taine) that 'Eleuthère ne perdrait-il pas les trois quarts de son intérêt si l'on ne l'expliquait pas par son peuple, si on ne voyait pas son peuple, ou plutôt le sacerdoce de son peuple [...] à travers lui?'[69] Benda replied that his forthcoming memoirs would assist Thibaudet in any clarification he required regarding his background, and emphasized that his family had raised him in an atmosphere where the values were 'purely spiritual'. Benda insisted that not only his *lycée* education, but also his own vocation as *clerc* had inculcated in him 'le culte de l'esprit pur'. Turning specifically to 'the Jewish factor', Benda pointed to the inconsistencies of Thibaudet's argument when he ascribed his moralism to his Jewish origin:

> Peuple sans terre, répondrai-je, mais non sans comptes de banque et, en tant que tel, peu bloqué dans l'Esprit. Ajoutez sa croyance à une vérité juive; [...] sa prétention depuis quelque temps de ranimer l'âme spécifiquement juive, l'âme de la "race élue". Ma religion de l'esprit pur a autant consisté à me nourrir d'un certain sémitisme qu'à me libérer d'un autre, à rompre, comme mon maître, avec la synagogue.[70]

---

67    *Action française*, 5 January 1933, quoted in C. Maurras, *Dictionnaire politique*, La Cité des livres, vol. 3, 1933, p. 461.

68    'Il y a un mois, je souhaitais ici même que la France se tînt armée contre les provocations de l'hitlérisme. D'aucuns déclarèrent que je prenais cette position parce que Juif et qu'Hitler persécute les Juifs. Ils n'examinèrent pas un instant si cette position était sage'; in *NRF*, July 1935, p. 146.

69    'De l'explication dans les lettres', *NRF*, October 1935, pp. 567-572 (p. 572).

70    'Esprit pur et esprit incarné', *NRF*, January 1936, pp. 108-109.

The possibility of further debate on this matter between Benda and Thibaudet was precluded by the latter's death a few weeks later; yet Benda's memoirs would appear in the *NRF* that year, and would contribute to the worst outburst of anti-Semitism from any author within the *NRF*.

### Anti-Semitism and the Popular Front

The prospect of a Popular Front government was becoming more likely during these months, and there were already signs that a government headed by Léon Blum would unleash a wave of anti-Semitism. The hatred for Blum of much of the political Right reached such levels that he was physically attacked by Action Française supporters and *ligueurs*; this led to the dissolution of the Ligue d'Action Française, a ban extended to all *ligues* in June 1936. On 3 May, in spite of the anti-Semitic campaign in the extreme right-wing press (a campaign which included incitements to murder),[71] the Popular Front was elected, and a month later the government was formed. Gide was sympathetic to the Popular Front, but his old adversary Henri Massis lost no time in placing him in an embarrassing position. Massis had sent Gide an advance copy of his forthcoming *Lectures* rubric from *La Revue universelle* dated 1 June 1936, for, on 27 May, 'La Petite Dame' noted her companion's consternation.[72] Massis, prompted by a recent reading of Gide's *Journal* in the newly published *Oeuvres complètes*, had rediscovered the passage concerning Léon Blum, and Gide's view of 'Jewish' literature. Massis could hardly conceal his delight in being able to quote Gide — perceived as an eminent left-wing sympathizer and fellow-traveller — and what appeared to be his long held anti-Semitic sentiments, in order to discredit Léon Blum. Massis pointed to the relevance of his discovery by describing the designated members of the Popular Front government:

> Ce personnel ne sort pas de la classe ouvrière. [...] Il se compose de fonctionnaires, de 'bourgeois socialisants': intellectuels, universitaires, médecins, avocats, qui appartiennent aux profession libérales où sont nombreux *ces Juifs embourgeoisés, dont M. Léon Blum est le type représentatif.*

Massis extended Gide's character sketch of the individual Blum to encompass what he called 'Israel' in general: 'Israël aspire au rôle d'arbitre souverain, de contrôleur de tous les autres éléments du pays, qu'il s'agisse d'art, de littérature

---

71    See P. Birnbaum, *Un mythe politique: la «République juive»*.
72    'Gide est tout occupé des manoeuvres de Massis qui publie un long article où il relève tout ce que Gide a publié sur Léon Blum dans son *Journal*. Il exploite ses paroles tant qu'il peut et *L'Action française* reproduit chaque jour les passages incriminés'; *CAG* 5, p. 540, entry dated 27 May 1936.

ou de politique'.[73] Massis used Gide's comments ('une littérature juive qui n'est pas la littérature française') to illustrate his own view that Jews in France were, in the long run, unassimilable. Referring specifically to a sentence in which Gide implied that he would prefer silence to Jewish domination, Massis commented: 'Cela peut de même s'entendre en bien d'autres sortes de choses', meaning that extra vigilance and opposition would be required, now that French national identity was at stake. Massis' article made Gide appear to attack his political ally on the grounds of anti-Semitism.

The arrival of the Popular Front government in France lent support to the view of some anti-Semites that the Jews were in the process of taking complete control of the country and its interests. Marc Bloch, the historian, noted this in *L'Etrange Défaite*:

> On ne saurait exagérer l'émoi que, dans les rangs des classes aisées, même parmi les hommes en apparence les plus libres d'esprit, provoqua l'avènement du Front populaire. Quiconque avait quatre sous crut sentir passer le vent du désastre.[74]

Political anti-Semitism was indeed being exploited as a focus for opposition to Blum's Popular Front government. As noted by Marrus and Paxton, 'those years re-shaped anti-Jewish sensibility into a political, economic, and social world view, giving it a combative edge, the *cri de coeur* of an opposition movement attempting to defend France against revolutionary change.'[75] It was against this highly charged background that Paulhan arranged to have *La Jeunesse d'un clerc*, Benda's first volume of memoirs, serialized in the *NRF* beginning in August 1936. At the same time, the anti-Jewish animosity of Marcel Jouhandeau, an exclusive *NRF* author, reached such a level that in the early autumn, he demanded that Paulhan should publish in the *NRF* an article which attacked Jewish influence in general, and Benda, in particular. Paulhan refused, arguing that if he were to include Jouhandeau's 'letter', he would betray Benda. He made it clear that as editor he could not allow an *NRF* author to be attacked in such terms, an author whom Paulhan had given much support.[76] Jouhandeau took his article, 'Comment je suis devenu antisémite', to *L'Action Française* instead, and it appeared there on 8 October. Jouhandeau insisted that he had become anti-Semitic through 'patriotism' alone, not for reasons of personal rancour. He referred to an anecdote concerning the young Jewish author Maurice Sachs'

---

73   *La Revue universelle*, 1 June 1936, pp. 472, 474. (my italics).
74   Quoted by P. Aubery, *Milieux juifs de la France contemporaine à travers leurs écrivains*, Plon, 1962, p. 187.
75   Marrus and Paxton, *Vichy France and the Jews*, p. 39.
76   JP to Jouhandeau (Autumn 1936) (BD).

alleged disgraceful behaviour at a reception, and his scorn of France and French history. Dismissing Sachs as a nonentity, Jouhandeau then turned to Benda, supporting his assertions with references to the serialized memoirs. Jouhandeau took particular exception to Benda's tribute to his family and their milieu, where Benda had written:

> Je vois une succession de juifs intelligents, travailleurs ironiques, amis de la science pendant que presque tout autour d'eux croupit encore dans les superstitions, agents de libération humaine, sur qui s'appuient tous les partis de progrès. En vérité, je suis honteux de m'y prendre si tard pour me sentir fier de descendre d'une telle élite, comprendre tout ce que je lui dois.[77]

Jouhandeau, a deeply passionate Catholic, was outraged by this 'free-thinking' attitude, all the more so because its author was Jewish. Benda denied that his father's and his own sense of patriotism had included any instinctive or irrational element. But by denying this emotional attachment to France, Benda could not be patriotic by definition, and in his commentary Jouhandeau, following Drumont's line in *La France juive*, demonstrated that his target was as much the French Revolution and republicanism as the Jews, for it had been the Revolution which had emancipated the Jews. Republicanism had 'opened all the doors', and had encouraged Jewish pride and ambition in obtaining all the prime places in society. In addition to this 'oppression', as he put it, Jouhandeau alleged that Jews now had the temerity to 'hate the French':

> Où M. Benda se démasque un peu plus [...] et devient tout d'un coup intolérable, c'est après nous avoir confié «son culte pour les valeurs posées dans l'éternel», quand il nous exprime «sa haine de ceux qui ne les saluent que dans l'historique».

Jouhandeau could hardly contain his rage, exclaiming:

> Vous entendez? Rien que cela, sa haine, la haine de ce petit clown sémite, et vous savez à qui elle va, cette haine? A vous, à moi, à nous qui avons des traditions...[78]

He was convinced that since the advent of Blum to power ('Blum est le vrai successeur de Louis XVI'), Jews occupied all the primary places in French society: Jouhandeau hoped to tar the Republic and the Popular Front with the same brush. He showed the depth of his feelings when he affirmed that if French

---

[77]     *NRF*, August 1936, p. 285. See also *L'Action française*, 8 October 1936.
[78]     *L'Action française*, 8 October 1936.

Jews decided to leave for Palestine, he would willingly escort them himself; should even one remain, he would not be content until that single Jew were subject to a special statute. It was this type of thinking that prefigured the institutionalized anti-Semitism of the Vichy régime. Much later, during the course of an interview, Jouhandeau argued somewhat disingenuously that his criticisms (as he had expressed them in his tract *Le Péril juif*) had only been aimed at the government of the time, and not the Jews.[79]

Reactions to this controversy were varied: Grenier, never an admirer of Benda, thought that Jouhandeau had been 'très modéré concernant J.B.', while *Droit de vivre* likened him to Julius Streicher.[80] Although Paulhan attempted to give Jouhandeau as much support as he could as editor and as a friend, he admitted to Suarès that he was distressed by this public expression of anti-Semitism: 'Qu'aurez-vous pensé de la brusque violence antisémite de Jouhandeau. Brusque? Non. Je la connaissais depuis près de deux ans. Pourtant son expression m'a étonné, et peiné'.[81]

Jouhandeau continued his anti-Semitic campaign by attempting, during the first half of 1937, to have further articles published; he met with little success. One portion of text which was eventually published in *Le Péril juif* could well have been one such article. It included remarks made to Marcel Aymé on Jewish 'predominance' in the Gallimard publishing house.[82] *L'Action française* rejected another Jouhandeau article, again refused by Paulhan. These refusals explain why Jouhandeau was forced to group the articles together in *Le Péril juif*. Whatever his motivations might have been in these outbursts, in large part he copied his rhetoric from the familiar catalogue of anti-Semitic diatribe. In common with other anti-Semites, he harboured an extreme dislike of the Third Republic which was exacerbated by the political crises and confusion of the 1930s. This dislike was fuelled by Maurrassian 'doctrine', a nostalgia for the *ancien régime*, and a deeply entrenched Catholicism whose earthly embodiment – the Church – had been irreparably handicapped by the radical republic. And

---

[79]     'Les Juifs s'étaient emparé du pouvoir en France, ils conduisaient la France à l'échec que nous avons connu et qu'ils ont partagé. *Le livre était donc essentiellement une critique du gouvernement de l'époque.* Le Juifs vraiment intelligents ne m'en veulent pas de mon attitude.' See J. Denon, *Entretiens avec Elise et Marcel Jouhandeau*, Belfond, 1966, p. 90 (my italics).

[80]     Grenier to JP, letter dated 24 October 1936, quoted in Paulhan-Grenier, *Correspondance* , p. 92, and B. Lecache in *Droit de vivre* , 30 October 1936.

[81]     JP to Suarès, letter dated 29 October 1936, *CJP* 4, p. 152.

[82]     Aymé agreed that the governement might well include 'too many Jews', but he failed to see where else they predominated: Jouhandeau pointed out that 'J'aurais pu lui demander de faire seulement le tour de la maison, de notre éditeur commun où nous venions de nous rencontrer, où presque tous les directeurs de service sont israëlites'; M. Jouhandeau, *Le Peril juif*, Sorlot, 1937, pp. 19-20.

Jouhandeau's visceral antipathy for communism was counterbalanced by an admiration for the 'virile' régime in Germany which, eventually, led him very close to pro-Nazi collaboration.[83]

On 21 June 1937 Blum resigned, giving way to Chautemps' new cabinet. Although an attempt was made to revive it in March 1938, the Popular Front, which had been seen by many as a political 'experiment', began to die a lingering death. Also, anti-Semites believed that the Jewish-led Popular Front had visited ruin upon France, now either dominated by, or at the mercy of, every other European power. In the *NRF* for August 1937, Paulhan placed the first part of *Un Régulier dans le siècle*, the second volume of Benda's memoirs, which contained Benda's recollections of his intellectual itinerary at the time of the Dreyfus Affair. Unlike many 'dreyfusistes', as he called them, Benda believed that the political consequences of the Affair were equally important, if not more so, than the judicial case itself. Too many 'dreyfusistes' had deserted the Republican cause and its campaign against the Army and the Church. He went further:

> La vérité est que ces hommes, qui avaient sans doute été dreyfusistes dans la sincérité de leur coeur, ont très vite compris combien ce passé les gênerait. [...] On peut dire que leur ancien dreyfusisme aura empoisonné la vie de tels de mes contemporains.

Such thinking helps to explain Benda's wish '[qu']il existât comme une affaire Dreyfus en permanence, qui permît de toujours reconnaître ceux qui sont de notre race morale.' The implications for French stability of Benda's view, at least as it would have been understood from this text, were serious, and the expression of these attitudes did much to fuel the right-wing view that Benda was indeed a belligerent subversive. Anticipating the question, 'Que faites-vous de l'intérêt de la France', Benda replied:

> Je réponds que l'intérêt de la France m'est fort peu de chose auprès de la netteté en matière morale, et que cette préférence est une définition de ma forme d'esprit.[84]

Once again, *L'Action française* pounced on these latest statements: extracts were reproduced on 9 August, and the *NRF* reproduced a 'letter' dated 11 August 1937, signed 'A.V.', as a 'document' to accompany the December

---

[83] D. Gascoyne's review of *Journal sous l'Occupation* (see *Times Literary Supplement*, 5 December 1980), which played down Jouhandeau's anti-Semitism, attracted an angry corrective from M. Bowie (ibid., 26 December 1980), with quotations from *Le Péril juif*.

[84] *'Un Régulier dans le siècle'*, *NRF*, August 1937, pp. 196-197.

instalment. This correspondent characterised Benda as an 'esprit démoniaque de dissolution', typical of '80% des Juifs en général, et 95% de l'Intelliguentzia israëlite' [sic]: these were typical anti-Semitic and anti-republican views:

> Les faux semblants, le camouflage intellectuel et politique, grâce auxquels les dirigeants Judéo-Jacobins [sic] de France ont réussi, depuis plus de cinquante ans à manoeuvrer l'opinion de nombreux «bien-pensants», catholiques pour la plupart, ont permis un renouveau de l'activité révolutionnaire en France, menaçant de s'étendre au delà des frontières de ce pays.

The writer extended the Dreyfus Affair back to 1789, and warned that the fatal conjunction of forces, 'Judaisme–Jacobinisme–Marxisme, n'acceptera jamais sa défaite sans combat final'. The letter concluded by thanking Benda for having awakened readers to the true dangers confronting France.[85] It was not Benda, however, who replied, but Drieu La Rochelle, who, in a curious, long text, attacked 'A.V.' for his outmoded Maurrassianism, and his cowardly bad faith for not being willing to die for France on French soil.[86]

### Gide, the NRF and Céline

The literary event of Christmas and New Year 1937-1938 was the publication of Louis-Ferdinand Céline's *Bagatelles pour un massacre*. Céline's stream of vituperation against the Jews provoked a wide range of critical reaction, both in regard to classifying the book, and in how to interpret it.[87] The Jewish view of the text was quite unambiguous: in *Droit de vivre*, Philippe Lamour was convinced that Céline had produced 'un mélange du plus mauvais Gohier et du pire Julius Streicher. Non, ce n'est pas un pastiche', he exclaimed, and accused Céline of directly serving Hitler.[88] Marcel Arland, writing in the *NRF*, labelled the book a 'pamphlet', and also saw it as a prolongation of Céline's 1932 novel *Voyage au bout de la nuit*. For Arland, Céline saw the Jews as the principal protagonists of the Apocalypse. He admitted that he found the book's fierce eloquence and lyricism highly arresting. According to this view, *Bagatelles pour*

---

85    'Lettre', *NRF*, December 1937, p. 985, 986-988.
86    By this time Drieu was an enthusiastic supporter of Doriot's Parti Populaire Français. See *NRF*, January 1938, pp. 117-123.
87    On Céline's anti-Semitism, and the formalistic problems it raises, see P.J. Kingston, *Anti-Semitism in France during the 1930s*, part II; M. Hanrez, 'Le massacre de la Saint-Bagatelles', *Tel Quel*, Summer, 1982, pp. 66-76, and N. Hewitt, 'L'Antisémitisme de Céline: historique et culte de la blague', *Etudes inter-ethniques*, 6, 1983, pp. 55-66. Useful too is J.-P. Dauphin, *Louis-Ferdinand Céline* 1, 'Calepins de Bibliographie' no. 6, tome 1, 1914-1944, Minard, 1977.
88    *Droit de vivre*, 22 January and 5 February 1938.

*un massacre* was everything *but* an anti-Semitic diatribe.[89]  Many anti-Semitic
themes are undeniably present in *Bagatelles*, themes derived both from the 1930s
and from the turn of the century.  Indeed the reader is left with the impression
that Céline — or Ferdinand — is the only non-Jew in creation.  But it has not been
remarked that throughout this work — beginning on the very first page — Céline
also makes numerous references to Gide and other contemporary writers, or 'les
raffinés', as he calls them.  Gide, and by extension the *NRF*, were 'enjuivés', and
on several occasions Céline passes remarks which make *Bagatelles* as much an
attack upon the established (therefore, for Céline, Jewish) literary world of
Paris.[90]  Céline abhorred left-bank 'raffinés', and revels in assaulting them in this
text.  The constant presence of Benda at the *NRF* would only serve to reinforce
Céline's view (he refers to 'Benda-Brothers' and 'PluriBendas').  What is more, it
suited Céline's temperament to combine homosexuality and Jewishness; again,
he only had to look to the *NRF*.[91]  The prejudice that Jews dominated the cultural
scene was nothing new: Paul Morand had already viciously satirized the (Jewish)
film industry, and Eugen Weber notes that Jean Zay, the Popular Front education
minister, rejected one of Céline's ballet projects for the 1937 exhibition.[92]

On 11 March 1938 Gide finished reading this work, and is reported as
feeling that '[*Bagatelles*] *n'est d'aucune portée quant à la question juive* et [...] ne le
trouve pas moins fort intéressant comme document révélateur sur un cas
morbide; et [...] *certains pages sont d'une étonnante réussite'*.[93]  The next day, as
Hitler swept into Austria, and as France languished without a government, Gide,
Pierre Herbart and Martin du Gard discussed the Jewish question which, Gide
considered, was now paramount.  His reading of Céline had inspired him: by the
15th he had finished an essay for the next number of the *NRF*.  This text,
deliberately divided into two parts, reflected his impressions on finishing the
book.  The first part dealt with the work itself: Gide wrote that by including
'Cézanne, Picasso, Maupassant, Racine, etc.' in his catalogue of Jews, Céline was
quite clearly joking: 'Il fait son mieux pour qu'on ne le prenne pas au sérieux'.[94]

---

89    *NRF*, February 1938, pp. 308-310.  Arland's view was seized upon and reiterated by
      *L'Action française*, 3 March 1938.
90    *Bagatelles pour un massacre*, Denoël et Steele, 1937, pp. 11, 82, 83, 166, 214.  On p. 216
      Céline writes: 'J'aime encore mieux Claude Farrère que douze ou treize faux-monnayeurs
      [sic]'.
91    *Bagatelles*, p. 214: 'Je sais nettement que l'art Gidien, après l'art Wildien, après l'art
      Proustien, font partie de l'implacable continuité de programme juif.'
92    See *France-la-Doulce*, Gallimard, 1934, and Weber, *L'Action française*, p. 352.
93    *CAG*, 6, 1975, p. 76, entries dated 11 and 12 March 1938.
94    A. Gide, 'Les Juifs, Céline et Maritain', *NRF*, April 1938, pp. 630-636.  Cf. N. Hewitt, on
      the 'culte de la blague'.  Arland and Gide were not the only critics to express such a view;
      cf. André Thérive, in *La Revue juive de Genève*, June 1938, and J.-G. Tricot, in *La Flèche*, 22

Returning to the Jewish question, Gide separated it from Céline's book and turned instead to Jacques Maritain's lecture 'Les Juifs parmi les Nations'.[95] Here Gide displayed his scepticism of Maritain's view that the Jewish question (or, more accurately, stereotyped attitudes towards Jews) was socially and historically derived rather than racially determined. Gide misread Maritain, reasserting his own conviction that 'la question n'est pas confessionnelle, mais raciale. Il n'y a rien à faire à cela'.[96] Gide went on to discuss the Jewish question in a vacuum as part of the problem of minorities in an alien culture, completely ignoring ideological or political variables or contexts which might give a different charge to the question. Despite the Nazis' policies toward Jews in Germany, Gide adhered to his own long held view that the Jews in France were an alien minority which, if not wholly unassimilable, was widely at variance with his own 'identity' as a Frenchman. Paulhan admitted to Jouhandeau that he suspected Gide of 'un fond d'antisémitisme', and Maritain, in a reply to Gide, corrected Gide's misreading of his lecture and pointed to the fact that it was irresponsible, especially 'in a review such as the NRF', to treat the question frivolously.[97]

It is true that Gide did not comment on what was, given the historical context, the most interesting and apposite part of Maritain's lucid essay. Whatever the interpretation of Céline's book, or, for that matter, however consciously or not Gide was anti-Semitic, the most important thing for Maritain was to remember that

> il y a, dans l'Europe d'aujourd'hui, ceux qui veulent l'extermination des Juifs, car c'est bien de cela qu'il s'agit, n'est-ce pas, en définitive? – et qui, sous l'appareil stupide du scientisme raciste ou des documents forgés [this is a reference to the forgery, *Protocols of the Sages of Zion*], dissimulent aux autres hommes, et parfois à eux-mêmes, l'espoir fou d'un massacre général de la race de Moïse et de Jésus. *Ce massacre reste un songe; les germes de haine dont s'emplit l'atmosphère sont une réalité.*[98]

---

January 1938, who wrote: 'Je suis persuadé que les Juifs seront les premiers à rire du livre de Céline'.

95    This lecture was delivered on 5 February 1938, and published in the February number of *La Vie intellectuelle* as well as by Les Editions du Cerf.

96    *NRF*, April 1938, pp. 634-635.

97    J. Maritain, 'Réponse à André Gide sur les Juifs', *NRF*, June 1938, pp. 1020-1022.

98    'Les Juifs parmi les Nations', p. 46 (my italics).

*Kristallnacht*

If Gide or others remained ignorant or cynical regarding such a view, events later that year were to validate Maritain's assessment of Hitler's intentions.[99] With the 'capitulation' of Daladier and Chamberlain at Munich on 30 September 1938, Franco-German relations entered a critical phase. As shown in the next chapter, Paulhan assembled a 'special number' on Munich which conclusively singled out his review as *anti-Munich* and, therefore, as 'bellicist'; among the essays was Benda's 'Les Démocraties bourgeoises devant l'Allemagne', a text which, conveniently enough for anti-Semites, conformed well with the stereotype of the Jew as warmonger. The anarchistic *Le Crapouillot* displayed its own anti-war attitude by publishing a special issue. In a savage attack on Benda's 'bellicose' attitude towards Germany in the First World War (as described in *Un Régulier dans le siècle*), *Le Crapouillot* characterised Benda as a 'buveur de sang', one of the oldest elements in the anti-Semite's demonology.[100] Such attitudes, although expressed with less violence, extended to the pacifist weekly *La Flèche*, where Claude Mauriac had become embroiled in an exchange with Bernard Lecache of *Droit de vivre*: and Galtier-Boissière, editor of *Le Crapouillot*, repeated his attack on Benda in *La Flèche*.[101]

Following the assassination of Ernst Vom Rath on 7 November 1938, a ferocious wave of anti-Jewish violence broke out in Germany, after what came to be known as *Kristallnacht*. At last the Jewish question began to be taken more seriously, at least to the extent that Hitler's intentions were now clearer to those who were willing to notice them. The *Revue juive de Genève* reported some of the details of anti-Jewish repression in Germany after *Kristallnacht*: up to 60,000 arrests were made, whole Jewish families committed suicide, and 'au camp de Buchenwald (calqué sur le trop fameux Dachau) [sic], le nombre de Juifs passés par les armes est de 200'.[102] In the wake of the violence the same review asked leading personalities to comment on the Jewish question: among the respondents

---

99     That the Jewish question remained in the foreground, and that Gide continued to hold prejudiced views, is confirmed by Julien Green: 'Mais les Juifs, dit Gide, l'Amérique ne les absorbera pas! Il faudra que les Juifs absorbent l'Amérique. Mais si. Et il en sera de même partout. En 1800, il y avait un Juif pour 6.000 habitants à New York. Vers 1890, il y en avait un pour 600. Maintenant, il y en a un pour 60!'; *Journal*, in *Oeuvres*, IV, Gallimard, 1976, p. 471, entry dated 26 June 1938.

100    'Pendant la crise de septembre [1938], M. Benda est une des publicistes qui ont le plus poussé au massacre. Il frétillait à l'idee de revoir ces temps bénis de 14-18 où il pouvait chaque matin déguster un grand bol de sang frais. La paix ne l'intéresse pas, les blessés, les mutilés (...), M. Benda s'en fout jacobinement, à condition que sa petite idéologie soit sauvée, fût-ce au prix de la destruction totale de la France'; *Le Crapouillot*, 'Septembre 1938', pp. 43-44.

101    'Des bellicistes, et en particulier M. Benda, couillon magnifique', *La Flèche*, 28 October 1938.

102    *La Revue juive de Genève*, January 1939, pp. 182-183.

were Benda and Gide. In his reply, Gide seemed to be more concerned about the style and presentation of his opinion than about making any bold pro-Jewish or anti-Hitlerian statement. At least he was sufficiently worried by the repression to declare:

> Indépendamment de toutes considérations diplomatiques, la médiocrité des réactions, en France, devant de tels abus de pouvoir, m'apparaît comme un triste signe de décadence morale et de diminution de vertu. Il importe d'autant plus que quelques-uns du moins fassent entendre leur protestation.[103]

One further sign that anti-Jewish repression across the Rhine had reached higher levels was the renewed influx of refugees fleeing for their lives. This led to a further intensification of anti-immigrant and anti-Jewish feeling.[104] Against this ever darkening background, Paulhan could not avoid the question in the *NRF*, because it was now tied to the ever more likely prospect of war. In this respect Jacques Chardonne submitted a series of personal reflexions to the *NRF* for February 1939. Talking specifically of Germany and changes there since 1918, Chardonne imputed that the Jews there had been responsible for the advent of Hitler:

> Avant l'avènement d'Hitler, les Juifs n'étaient pas très nombreux en Allemagne, à peine six cent mille. Mais depuis 1918, ils détenaient les principaux emplois, et ils ont marqué de leur influence et signé tous les événements: la révolution, l'inflation, la faillite, l'anarchie de l'argent ou de la misère.

Chardonne believed that it was a typical German characteristic to be tempted by catastrophe and despair, and that this was also a Jewish trait. In a simplistic paralogism, Chardonne contrived to congratulate Hitler for providing a cure for 'le mal allemand':

> L'Allemand recèle un Asiatique; c'est la part d'esprit juif qui est en lui. Aussi l'effort de régénération prendra chez l'Allemand la forme d'une révolte contre le juif. Cette victoire sur soi-même, opposée à l'esprit juif, est incarnée par Hitler.
>
> Il n'a rien apporté, qu'une foi au peuple, un remède au mal allemand.[105]

---

[103]  Ibid., December 1938, p. 105 (réponse recueilli par Arnold Mandel). Benda's reply appeared in the issue for March 1939.
[104]  For detailed coverage of this problem, see V. Caron, 'The Politics of Frustration', art. cit.
[105]  J. Chardonne, 'Politique', *NRF*, January 1939, p. 207.

Although Chardonne thought that the attitude of the French towards Jews was different, he was one of a number of intellectuals in France who were convinced that a French 'dictatorship' would prove salutary for the country: later, during the Occupation, Chardonne contributed enthusiastically to Drieu's *NRF*.

During these months leading to the declaration of war in September 1939, Paulhan became increasingly embattled at the review, and found himself caught between conflicting loyalties: furthermore, it is possible to detect lingering anti-Semitism in the *NRF* circle. In his renewed *Chronique dramatique*, Paul Léautaud launched a vicious assault upon what he regarded as the unacceptable demagogy of such as Jean Perrin, Paul Langevin and Joliot-Curie. Léautaud believed that these and others were guilty of charlatanism because they were willing to pronounce on political matters. Léautaud found it intolerable that Charles Dullin, in his new production of *The Marriage of Figaro*, should apply his own personal 'conception' to a 'classic' French drama. 'C'est un scandale', remarked Léautaud, and concluded: 'Il faut que nous ayons un ministre de l'Instruction publique et un sous-ministre aux Beaux-Arts *étrangers à la littérature française*, pour qu'il soit permis.'[106] These were immediately recognisable as the ministers Jean Zay and Raoul Huisman. Léautaud's remarks severely tested Paulhan, because he was divided between his loyalty to Léautaud on the one hand, and to such as Gallimard, Crémieux and Caillois, all of whom objected to Léautaud's view, on the other. The episode was eventually concluded by Léautaud's resignation from the review, and although Paulhan managed to calm the affair down, he had come perilously close to resigning his editorship.[107] Léautaud devoted the last pages of his final submission to the 'Merveilleux effets d'une *Chronique dramatique*', and disappeared from the *NRF* amid a storm of protest from indignant subscribers.[108]

A further problem arose from the renewed presence of André Suarès in the *NRF*, in his *Chronique de Caërdal*. Readers familiar with his polemical work would not have been surprised that Paulhan himself played the role of censor regarding Suarès' attacks on the dictators. Italian anti-Semitism had only recently been made official policy: indeed as late as December 1937 Ciano, Mussolini's foreign minister, had insisted that there was 'no Jewish problem in

[106] P. Léautaud, *Chronique dramatique*, NRF, March 1939, pp. 492-494 (my italics).
[107] For Léautaud's version, see his *Journal littéraire*, XII, pp. 211-215. Cf. R. Caillois, 'Lettre', *NRF*, April 1939, pp. 717-718, and JP to Jouhandeau: 'Orages soulevés, entre autres, chez Gaston, Crémieux, etc., par la critique de Léautaud, qui est violente...'; 'Gaston, Caillois, 50 autres le disent déshonorant pour la revue. Cela fait toute une révolte' (BD).
[108] NRF, May 1939, pp. 868-874. For subscribers' reactions, Léautaud, *Journal littéraire*, XII, pp. 236-238, entries dated 2-8 May 1939.

Italy'.[109] Just one year later, however, a Nazi-inspired anti-Semitic policy was adopted in Italy, as reported in the *Revue juive de Genève*.[110] Suarès, who felt a deep affection for Italy and Italian culture, found such a development grotesquely inconsistent and, against all Paulhan's demands for restraint, unleashed a violent attack upon Ciano: 'Il est infiniment probable que le Chiano et ses Chiani [sic] ont du sang juif dans les veines, comme du vent fasciste dans le cerveau [...]. Noirs bouffons, sacs à mensonges.'[111] As a direct result, Italy countered by banning the *NRF*:

> Mauvaise nouvelle, la *NRF* se voit interdite en Italie. Chiano [sic], moins patient que Mussolini (ou si vous étiez tombé trop juste?). Cela fait 500 abonnés de moins [...] Et plus de mille Italiens, sans doute, qui n'auront plus le réconfort (je pense) que leur donnait la revue.

'Rien de tout cela n'est gai', Paulhan added laconically.[112]

One final incident placed Paulhan in further difficulty, and shows how profoundly this question had penetrated into the very heart of the *NRF* to influence policy and presentation. Paulhan's loyalty towards Julien Benda, despite much opposition and criticism, remained unyielding. In one sense he had always relied on the author of *La Trahison des clercs* to anchor the *NRF* in what was conceived as apolitical, liberal, or uncontroversial territory: although Benda's main adversary was *L'Action française*, he had also opposed the Left in the shape of Jean Guéhenno and Romain Rolland. From 1936-1937, however, Benda inclined increasingly towards the Left, favouring in particular the communists. What is more, Benda stridently opposed appeasement after Munich. These factors combined to render Benda's presence more problematic for some within the *NRF*, especially for Schlumberger. Since 1935 Schlumberger had held the view that Benda occupied too much space. So, in April 1939, Paulhan was obliged to inform Benda that he would not have so much space in the *NRF* as he had enjoyed previously, and in principle Benda did not object to this.[113] In a long letter of self-defence, Benda stressed that in all his time at the

---

109     Comte de Ciano, *Journal politique 1937-1938*, Les Editions de Paris, 1949, p. 75, entry dated 3 December 1937.
110     December 1938, p. 135. This report noted the visit to Italy of the Bevölkerungs-politische Kommission, whose policy imperative was 'remplacer les théories désuètes de l'humanisme latin par le nouvel idéal aryo-nordique [sic], c'est-à-dire de délatiniser l'Italie'.
111     *Chronique de Caërdal*, *NRF*, May 1939, pp. 856-857.
112     JP to Suarès, letter dated 5 May 1939, *CJP* 4, p. 236.
113     'Attendre quelque temps pour un article, voir mon nom moins fréquemment dans *NRF*, être absents des *Airs du mois*, sont des choses que j'accepte sans peine'; Benda to JP, letter dated 25 April 1939 (AP).

review he had always denied having any influence, and suspected that his political stance and his contributions elsewhere were the underlying reasons for Schlumberger's criticisms. Benda appealed explicitly to Paulhan's sense of loyalty:

> Il est clair que si la direction veut ma peau, non pas seulement en raison de mon attitude dans la *NRF* mais ailleurs, et en raison de ma tendance politique générale, ma cause, —notre cause—, puisque vous voulez bien me défendre, devient singulièrement menacée.

In another letter Benda pointed to rather more sinister undertones concerning his 'Jewish' presence in the *NRF*:

> [Schlumberger] me reproche d'avoir, depuis cinq ans, publié dans la revue tous mes ouvrages destinés ensuite à devenir des livres. On dirait vraiment que c'est moi le maître de ces publications; alors que je n'ai fait que proposer les ouvrages, qu'ensuite on a bien voulu prendre [...]. Je suis aussi affecté par l'accusation d'être bien 'de la race juive, avec cette volonté d'occuper toute la place dès que je suis admis dans un lieu...' C'est là rigoureusement l'antisémitisme le plus bas. Il m'est pénible de savoir qu'il siège dans les conseils de la NRF.[114]

Benda was dismayed by such aspersions, and from this time onwards did not dispose of his customary allocation of space in the review. At the time these letters were written, the *loi Marchandeau* (21 April 1939) was introduced to ban overtly anti-Semitic material from the press; thereafter, this law spared the *NRF* any additional public embarrassment.

Unlike the other major issues it had examined, the *NRF* had no particular or predetermined *parti pris* regarding the Jewish question. For the most part this is because it was tangential to other questions, such as Franco-German relations, radical-republican, socialist and communist political cultures, literary judgements and taste, or even immigration. If, for some, the *NRF* had an anti-Jewish reputation, this is principally explained by the unconscious or culturally-acquired prejudices of some within its circle. For others on the Right, the *NRF* was a haven for influential, subversive, 'war-mongering' Jews who represented all that was dangerous in the French Republic. But all those major contributors of Jewish origin – Benda, Crémieux, Suarès – wrote as assimilated Jews,

---

114     Benda to JP, letters dated 24 and 25 April 1939 (AP).

eschewing Zionism and other extreme forms of nationalism.[115]  One further observation arises from this issue concerning the treatment – particularly Gide's – of Céline's anti-Semitism.  By applying purely literary or stylistic criteria to *Bagatelles pour un massacre*, the underlying issue was at best poorly treated, and at worst, dismissed, at a time when the Jewish question had already assumed dimensions of historical significance confirmed by events only months later.  The *loi Marchandeau* put a temporary halt to public expressions of anti-Semitism in France, but the 'roots of Vichy anti-Semitism' had already taken hold.

After Munich, and particularly throughout the phoney war, Paulhan determined to steer the *NRF* away from its supposed neutral course, to adopt instead an attitude which explicitly opposed appeasement, the betrayal of alliances and 'peace at all costs'.  In a phrase, Paulhan and the *NRF* were beginning to resist fascist aggression.

---

115     After the defeat Benda went underground in the Carcassonne region; he survived the war, whilst his library, notes and letters were confiscated by the Nazis and lost. Crémieux eventually joined the resistance, but was betrayed and arrested in Marseille; he was deported to Buchenwald where he died in 1944. Suarès also went to ground, and Paulhan maintained contact with him at different addresses in the Creuse and on the Rhône. Suarès died in 1948, aged 80.

## Chapter 7

## Resisting delusion: the *NRF*
## and the drift into war

*Et personne ne sait mieux que moi l'étrange, l'étonnant retentissement que peut avoir au dehors un article de la* NRF.[1]

*J'ai été, du premier jour, résistant. Il faut avouer que l'horreur, le dégoût que m'inspirait les gouvernements de l'entre-deux-guerres a fait beaucoup pour me jeter—et me maintenir—dans ces bons sentiments (qu'il m'est arrivé d'exprimer, bien avant 1940).*[2]

There is an apocryphal story about the *NRF* which has been used by a number of historians of French intellectual life to demonstrate how the *NRF* dominated the European intellectual scene during the interwar period. One source attributes the story to the newly arrived military governor in occupied Paris, another to Otto Abetz, Hitler's ambassador in the French capital, who is reported to have said: 'il y a trois forces en France: le communisme, la haute banque et la *NRF*'.[3] Leaving the uncertain attribution to one side, it is true that innumerable intellectuals aspired to consecration in the *NRF*. In previous chapters we have examined how the formidable cultural power of the review extended to the political arena and to the domain of international relations, and nowhere is this power more visible than the stand it took in the period between the Munich agreement and the fall of France in June 1940. The Nazis themselves recognized this power and would attempt to mobilize it in support of their propaganda

---

1    JP to Suarès, letter dated 17 [February 1939], in *CJP* 4, p. 223.
2    Jean Paulhan, interviewed in C. Jamet, *Le rendez-vous manqué de 1944*, France-Empire, 1964, p. 257.
3    Cf. P. Ory, *Les Collaborateurs, 1940-1945*, Seuil, 1976, pp. 234-235, and H.R. Lottman, *La Rive gauche*, Seuil, 1981, p. 274, which is the source quoted. R. Debray repeats Ory's version in *Le Pouvoir intellectuel en France*, Ramsay, 1979, p. 164, whilst P. Assouline follows Lottman in *Gaston Gallimard*, Balland, 1984, p. 280. See also D. Rubenstein, *What's Left? The ENS and the Right*, Madison: University of Wisconsin Press, 1990, pp. 103, 184.

efforts during the Occupation. Jean Paulhan was fully aware of this power, as the epigraph to this chapter shows. By 1939 he had reached the peak of his authority at the review, and, in combination with a number of his preferred contributors, in the face of formidable opposition he committed the *NRF* to a line which laid the foundations of intellectual resistance to fascist aggression and Nazi occupation. To understand Paulhan's actions during these difficult months is to understand better the nature of developments in the cultural domain during the first months of Occupation.[4]

## Before Munich

During 1938, but especially after the conclusion of the Munich agreement on 30 September, the increasing prospect of war became the overriding issue for intellectuals in France, including those writing for the *NRF*. History has come to judge the Munich accords as a delusion whereby an obsessive desire for peace at all costs led both Britain and France into a betrayal of their commitments to Czechoslovakia and, therefore, into capitulating to Hitler's expansionist ambitions. Jean-Pierre Azéma underlines the historically pivotal nature of Munich as

> [la] référence-clé de notre histoire contemporaine, injure suprême de notre langue politique, et [Munich] marque une étape décisive dans le destin de l'Europe; on croyait la paix rétablie, on entrait en fait dans la Seconde Guerre mondiale.[5]

The nature and discourse of the Daladier government, appointed in April 1938, suggested at last that the chronic ineffectiveness of French governments throughout the 1930s to contend with problems at home and abroad had been checked, and even partly reversed; Daladier's was proclaimed as a government of 'national unity', and was noticeably more authoritarian.[6]

Those who suspected Hitler's warlike intentions were proved right by his belligerence following the reoccupation of the Rhineland in March 1936, the Austrian *Anschluss* of March 1938, and his exploitation of Chamberlain's appeasement policy. Indeed, international relations throughout western Europe

---

4     For a study of the *NRF* during the Occupation, and its intellectuals 'à la dérive', see P. Hebey, *La NRF des années sombres. Juin 1940-juin 1941*, Gallimard, 1992.

5     *De Munich à la Libération, 1938-1944*, Seuil, 1979, p. 9.

6     'Le long gouvernement Daladier, de 10 avril 1938 à mars 1940 [...] contraste avec l'instabilité des dix années précédentes. [...] Un climat nouveau se fait sentir dans l'opinion. Il révèle une aspiration à être gouverné et l'apparition des nouveaux clivages sur la guerre et la paix'; J.-M. Mayeur, *La Vie politique sous la Troisième République*, Seuil, 1984, p. 360.

were now dominated, if not dictated, by Hitler's every action. In respect of the Soviet Union, the revelations of the show-trials, Stalin's purges, as well as the high-profile disappointment of fellow-travellers such as the *NRF*'s André Gide, seemed to have tarnished for good the projected image of Russian communism as a new form of humanism; the effect of this disillusion was such that in some quarters it was felt that Hitler's Germany should and should provide a bulwark against future Soviet expansionism.

Against this sombre background, and partly too in reaction to the failure of the Popular Front 'experiment', Jean Paulhan determined to alter the course of the *NRF* by taking a harder, more patriotic line. This new stance would be overtly antifascist. The change of direction is illustrated by the insertion of an article by Armand Petitjean entitled 'Dictature de la France' in the April 1938 issue of the *NRF*.[7] Here Petitjean urged that it was time to end the complacency of those in authority, and to 'confront head-on the reality of 1938'; in order to do so, and to counter the threat from across the Rhine, France had to be reunited under a strong government which would establish the nation's military preparedness. Acknowledging their political strength, Petitjean called on French communists in particular to be loyal to their homeland. And on at least another two occasions over the summer of 1938, Julien Benda, the *NRF*'s stalwart defender of the republican faith, asserted that French communists, by now the backbone of French antifascism, were the only genuinely patriotic political party. In July, with sections of the extreme right in his sights, Benda wrote:

> Toute une société, en France, a cessé d'être patriote, juste au moment où Staline a donné aux communistes français l'ordre de l'être. La politique de ce monde-là est commandée entièrement et uniquement par la haine du communisme. Ils mettraient le feu à leur maison si les communistes décidaient de la conserver. Tel est leur bon sens.[8]

As though to reinforce this more patriotic line (with its distinct political overtones), Paulhan determined to signal unequivocally the *NRF*'s indignation at Hitler's annexation of Austria. The opening text in the issue for August 1938 was Pierre-Jean Jouve's 'In memoriam Salzbourg'. Here Jouve used juxtaposition to great effect: opening with an extract from his elegiac poem 'Mozart' dated 1924, he cast a fond glance back on what he considered to be a 'golden period' of

---

7    'Dictature de la France', *NRF*, April 1938, pp. 663-665.

8    'Air du mois', *NRF*, July 1938, p.160. Benda reiterated this line even more forcibly next month in his *chronique* 'Anticommunisme et patriotisme'; *NRF*, August 1938, pp. 307-309.

creativity in musical performance in Salzburg between 1921 and 1937, and contrasted it with Hitler's invasion of April 1938:

> Cette petite fleur fine de l'Autriche, pointe de bien des siècles familiers et graves, cet édifice si proportionné de génie allemand ancien qui s'épanouissait dans de petites villes, —l'envahisseur ne peut que la détruire.[9]

In September, another essay by Petitjean was inserted in which the author pursued further the ideas expounded in his April article. 'Nous [...] sommes, selon toute apparence, au plus bas de notre histoire', began Petitjean. He refused to believe that a civilization like France, if it was truly decadent, would spend so much time and effort meditating on the causes and effects of the process. The Popular Front was not, after all, a total disaster, because it had shown that France was capable of rapid social change, even if certain sectors of society did their best to undermine the results:

> Il a suffi qu'avec l'avènement du Front populaire, la fraction de notre population qui était jusqu'ici tenue à l'écart de toute vie nationale y eût brusquement accès, pour que celle dont la nationalisation date de quelques décades se comportât de la façon la plus contraire aux intérêts du Pays.[10]

In view of the circumstances of the time, Petitjean remained optimistic, because

> nous restons même l'un des pays d'Europe qui ait du champ devant lui, de l'«espace vital», de l'air dans ses idées, et qui ne se laisse opprimer ni par les frontières de son territoire, ni par celles de son âme.[11]

In common with Benda (although he expressed his ideas quite differently), Petitjean affirmed his conviction that Frenchmen might regain their strength through a new version of Jacobin patriotism. Amid so many indications of paralysis, he could detect encouraging signs which proved that the French were coming to terms at last with 'historical reality', as he put it. He had much faith in the youth movements that were springing up, and felt that there was much cultural activity to applaud:

---

9     'In Memoriam Salzbourg', *NRF*, August 1938, pp. 177-86 (quotation from p. 178). Marcel Arland would echo these sentiments in his *Chronique de Vacances* published in October 1938, pp. 636-639.

10    A. Petitjean, 'Après l'après-guerre', *NRF*, September 1938, pp. 478-488 (p. 481).

11    Ibid., p. 481.

> Un movement de jeunes s'est fondé, qui n'a pas adopté d'autres principes que celui du mouvement et de la jeunesse: c'est le mouvement jociste—et ils sont 400.000. Le premier livre de philosophie et de l'histoire qui ait été écrit depuis la guerre vient de paraître: il est d'importance. Un renouveau du théâtre français se prépare [...][12]

His conclusion was forward-looking and positive: 'L'après-guerre est bien morte, deux fois morte. À nous de ne pas nous laisser mourir de cette mort. À nous de quitter le plan des principes, pour vivre et pour bâtir'. All these texts, which appeared *before* the conclusion of the Munich agreement, laid the foundations for what would be even more overt expressions of resistance to fascist aggression in the *NRF*.

### Reactions to the Munich agreement

The signature of the Munich protocols during the night of 29-30 September 1938 produced mixed reactions in France. If, initially, the agreement caused relief among the majority of public opinion, it soon became clear that there were sharp splits between 'pacifists' and 'bellicists'; because of the complex nature of political alignments in France, in fact four 'poles' of opinion on the Munich issue have been identified.[13] Yet for all this it was soon realized that a stark choice — either for or against the agreement, and therefore for or against peace — confronted the French. To begin with, Paulhan had grave misgivings (as he expressed them to Schlumberger):

> La situation demeure trop grave, il me semble, pour que quelque précaution ne s'impose pas. Ne pensez-vous qu'il faut nous interdire à la *NRF* toute attaque contre l'Italie et Mussolini? (J'ai eu plus d'une occasion de voir qu'ils sont diaboliquement sensibles aux critiques de la *NRF*, et le dernier Claudel, entre autres, n'est pas passé tout seul).[14]

Despite these misgivings, and despite the strong pacifist position being adopted by some within the *NRF* circle, Paulhan decided that the *NRF* should take a deliberate, unambiguous stance. The review would back the anti-Munich cause and resist fascist aggression.

---

[12]   Ibid., p. 488.

[13]   These are: 'les pacifistes traditionnelles de la gauche; le nouveau pacifisme de droite; les antifascistes résistants de gauche; la droite nationaliste'. See J.-B. Duroselle, *Politique étrangère de la France. La décadence 1932-1939*, Imprimerie nationale, 1979, pp. 357-364, and G. Vallette and J. Bouillon, *Munich 1938*, A. Colin, 1983.

[14]   JP to Schlumberger [Autumn 1938] (BD). The reference to Claudel concerns the *air du mois* 'Le régime du bouchon', *NRF*, September 1938.

Paulhan informed Schlumberger that he was going to assemble three major texts in reaction to Munich, whereby

> l'on verra bien que la *NRF* est catholique (universelle). Cela fera trois réactions:
>
> Petitjean—25 ans—catholique
> Schlumberger—50 ans—protestant
> Benda—70 ans—juif.[15]

Another letter reveals the extent of Paulhan's conviction, for he repeated to Schlumberger his intention to take a unified, committed, stance:

> L'article de Benda tiendra, je pense, de 10 à 15 pages. Son thème sera: Chamberlain et Daladier ont refusé la guerre, par crainte de la gagner... Je voudrais bien savoir quel sera le sens de votre article. [...] Je souhaiterais qu'il eût le sens d'un engagement de nous tous pour l'avenir. J'ai tout lieu de penser que l'article de Benda—qui sera fin, et, dans l'ensemble, plausible—s'achèvera sur une démission: "la politique des clercs" [...] doit disparaître avec la Société des Nations.[16]

The three texts duly appeared in the issue dated 1 November 1938. Petitjean, who had been caught up in the mass mobilisation of late September, contributed his 'Prière pour les copains'. This is an emotional appeal to God to protect France and the French from impending doom. In a poetic-prose style reminiscent of Charles Péguy, he prayed God to take pity on those who had done so much to damage the nation over the last 20 years, and to endow French men and women with sufficient courage and strength to protect them from death:

> Seigneur, camarades, faites taire tous ces représentants qui, depuis vingt ans, ne représentent plus rien. Et si Vous prenez le temps de Vous apitoyer sur eux, montrez-leur donc un jour ce que c'est que la France, qu'elle est faire de Français; faites-leur faire par exemple un exercice de mobilisation; conduisez-les devant la ligne Maginot, à quelques kilomètres de la Mort, là où j'avais la chance d'être il n'y a pas huit jours avec les copains.[17]

Benda's article was polemical and analysed what he saw as the complicit weakness of 'Les démocraties bourgeoises devant l'Allemagne'. He boldly labelled the Munich agreement as a 'capitulation' to Hitler's ambitions on the

---

[15]   JP to Schlumberger [Autumn 1938] (BD).
[16]   JP to Schlumberger [Autumn 1938] (BD).
[17]   'Prière pour les copains', *NRF*, November 1938, pp. 757-760.

part of Chamberlain and Daladier who, despite 'holding some powerful trump cards', had allowed the Nazis to 'cry victory'. French and British ministers, Benda alleged, had even ignored the resolve of their respective populations earlier that year.[18] The reasons for this capitulation were threefold, according to Benda: 'l'humanitarisme, [...] la crainte de perdre la guerre; [...] la crainte de la gagner'. The motivation behind the third reason was the fact that the British, despising communism and fearing its spread, preferred to appease Hitler and to treat Germany as a bulwark against communism. Benda widened his criticism when he examined why Britain and France did not wish to win the war. These nations' rulers would never allow *true* democracy — the spread of social justice, the recognition of workers' legitimate demands — to damage their class interests:

> De cette démocratie-là, les democraties bourgeoises ne veulent à aucun prix (j'entends si les réformes sont sérieuses). Preuve: leur insurrection contre le ministère Blum en France.[19]

Referring to earlier examples in French history, Benda stressed that bourgeois democrats had always acted to place 'résolûment les intérêts de leur classe au dessus de leur nation', and at Munich there had been no exception to this rule:

> Les ministres de [ces] démocraties ont eu la volonté [...] de ne pas humilier l'homme qui, aux yeux de ces bourgeoisies, incarne la résistance aux montées révolutionnaires.[20]

However, the bourgeois democracies were completely misguided by placing their faith in Hitler's 'order' against revolutionary 'chaos'. Part of the delusion derived from the fact that the democracies wilfully ignored that 'fascism had nothing to do with the 'traditional order of things'. Britain's attitude towards French 'hegemony' in Europe, and a long-standing distrust of France as the 'dangerous country of Revolution', explained British indulgence towards Germany after 1918, especially after the Franco-Soviet Pact of 1935. But the true source of anxiety for Benda was to be found in his anticipation of the Vichy régime:

> La bourgeoisie française poussera-t-elle sa soumission au Reich jusqu'à adopter le régime fasciste, notamment la suppression de la

---

[18]    'Si leur refus de céder davantage eût amené la guerre, ils savaient à cette époque que leurs pays ne le leur reprocheraient pas'; 'Les démocraties bourgeoises devant l'Allemagne', *NRF*, November 1938, pp. 761-771 (p. 762).

[19]    Ibid., p. 763.

[20]    Ibid., p. 765.

liberté d'expression, la destruction du système représentatif, le racisme?

Answering his own question, Benda showed remarkable insight when he suggested that this future régime would cling to some 'vestiges of liberalism' whereby 'l'on ne verra pas en France de fascisme total. [...] Un fascisme larvé me paraît probable'.[21] In a pessimistic conclusion, Benda alluded to his own position as an intellectual, and, despite his pride in republicanism and the occasional triumph of 'universal values', he reaffirmed axiomatically that 'la loi de ce monde déchu est celle de classes qui jouissent'.[22]

Jean Schlumberger, who had on previous occasions made a number of important comments on Franco-German relations in the *NRF*, submitted an essay entitled 'Contre l'humiliation'. Much later he remembered that this 'forthright excursion into politics' was welcomed by friends and commentators as an attempt to restore dignity after the 'shame' of Munich.[23] The true gravity of Munich for Schlumberger was to located in a general feeling of 'shame'; it was impossible to ignore that through her action, France shared responsibility for ceding the fate of Czechoslovakia to the Nazis. France, he argued, had not been equal to the rôle designated by the Versailles Treaty; what was more, at home, underinvestment in armaments (specifically, in aviation) had deprived France of her ability to back treaty undertakings and, by extension, 'quand il s'agit d'un glissement qui a duré tant d'années, et sous tant de ministères, une nation est complice'.[24] Broken French promises and squandered advantages were compensated (if only modestly) by the calm acceptance of the mobilisation which, thought Schlumberger, had been 'miraculous' in the way it had brought out the best in the country. Praise for the coordination of the national effort was the essence of his message: he referred to Petitjean's patriotic appeal ('Dictature de la France') published earlier that year, stressing that *because* it had appeared in the *NRF*, its impact had been all the more forceful. On balance, Schlumberger was less pessimistic than Benda, insisting that peace was a worthy aim, but only if it proved to be an honourable one. Given the circumstances surrounding Munich, however, this would soon prove to be impossible.

These three texts were not the only reactions to Munich in November's *NRF*. The whole of the *airs du mois* section of shorter texts was devoted to the

---

21    Ibid., p. 770. For a discussion of 'Vichy before Vichy', see the second part of P. Laborie, *L'opinion française sous Vichy*, Seuil, 1990.

22    *NRF*, November 1938, pp. 770-771.

23    See J. Schlumberger, *Oeuvres*, V, Gallimard, 1960, pp. 177-178.

24    'Contre l'humiliation', *NRF*, November 1938, pp. 772-783 (p. 774).

crisis. In 'L'Attente', Marcel Arland described his own observations of Frenchmen as he travelled through the provinces earlier in September. All French people could do now was wait, and Arland wondered how many of the million mobilized servicemen and women knew precisely *why* they were being called upon: it was certainly not for Czechoslovakia. Thus the underlying cause of Arland's 'nouveau mal du siècle' took on a renewed importance in 1938: 'un peuple a besoin de dieux pour mourir; et il en a a besoin pour vivre dignement.'[25]

Henry de Montherlant sent Paulhan some pages suppressed by the literary weekly *Candide*; these were ironically entitled 'La paix dans l'honneur'. Montherlant wrote from Lorraine, and lambasted French complacency:

> Que vous le vouliez ou non, lâches imbéciles, un jour viendra où l'odeur de vos cagayes sera étouffée dans l'odeur de votre sang. A moins qu'éternellement vous ne vous préserviez du sang, par la honte.[26]

Denis de Rougemont submitted a text in the form of pages from an imaginary history book. In common with Benda, de Rougemont focused on the 'appeasement' politics of the bourgeois democracies, but differed in his conclusion by envisaging some kind of anti-Hitlerian European union inspired by the Swiss model:

> Personne ne sut opposer au Führer l'idéal qui avait fait jusqu'alors la force et l'équilibre dynamique de l'Occident: l'utopie agissante d'une Fédération des Egaux dont la seule Suisse figurait le microcosme.[27]

Jacques Audiberti's impressionistic contribution described the reactions of the bourgeoisie living around the Champs-Elysées the night after Daladier's supposedly 'triumphant' return to Le Bourget airport: 'les femmes en chapeau pointu et les jeunes hommes en gabardine hurlaient en faveur de la paix. Et ils commençaient à donner la chasse aux Juifs et aux assimilés'.[28] Two shorter pieces by Henri Pourrat and Marcel Lecomte preceded the 'Déclaration du Collège de Sociologie sur la crise internationale', signed by Georges Bataille, Roger Caillois and Michel Leiris. After admitting their 'limited competence' to deal with every aspect of the question, the authors of the Declaration analysed the nature of the 'collective psychological reactions' that the proximity of an outbreak of war had provoked. Daladier had praised the public for their 'sang-

25    M. Arland, 'L'Attente', *NRF*, November 1938, pp. 860-863
26    H. de Montherlant, 'La Paix dans l'honneur', ibid., pp. 863-865.
27    D. de Rougemont, 'Page d'histoire', ibid., pp. 866-867.
28    J. Audiberti, 'Un soir, aux Champs-Elysées', ibid., pp. 868-871.

froid, dignity and determination', but in reality a more appropriate choice of words would have been 'consternation, resignation and fear'.[29] Finally, Paulhan himself — writing as Jean Guérin — gave his own sardonic point of view:

> *Munich*. Par les accords de Munich, la paix est sauvée. La paix dans ce qu'elle a de plus plat et de plus périssable.
> *Paris*. Les tailleurs répandent le slogan: la paix nous donnant la joie de vivre, l'on s'habillera en clair cet hiver.
> *Londres-Paris*. H.G. Wells et Léon Blum demandent que le prix Nobel de la Paix soit attribué au Président Bénès. [...]
> *Paris*. Il est question d'élever un monument à la Tchéco-Slovaquie martyre.
> L'on peut se demander si les Tchèques attendaient de nous tant de prix et de statues.[30]

The impact of this special issue on Munich was widely felt, all the more so because of the reputation of the *NRF* and of the intellectuals to whom it gave a voice. Although it purported to reflect what a broad church the review was, and to show how it could apply its œcumenism to international relations, the special issue proved to be overwhelmingly *antimunichois*, against government policy and, therefore, anti-peace (or 'bellicist'). Within the *NRF* circle, Martin du Gard, by this time an 'integral pacifist' and aligned with Gaston Bergery's *La Flèche*, found himself in profound disagreement. Despite his earlier enthusiasm to see the *NRF* adopt a more distinct political tone, this time his objections and dissociation from the review attest to the strength of his feeling:

> Une revue purement littéraire, et dirigée par vous, se devait [...] de tenir la balance égale entre les tendances opposées. Vous en avez jugé autrement. [...] La *NRF* a pris parti. Et ce parti n'est pas le mien.[31]

As for Gide, because of his proximity to the position of his friend Jef Last at this time, his attitude was certainly closer to that of Paulhan or Schlumberger than Martin du Gard: he confided to his *Journal* that he was completely disillusioned with French foreign policy.[32] And later, in March 1940, Jean-Paul Sartre confided to his notebook just how influential Paulhan's November number, and in

---

29    'Déclaration du Collège de Sociologie sur la crise internationale', ibid., pp. 874-876. This is reproduced in D. Hollier, *Le Collège de sociologie*, Gallimard, 1979, pp. 98-104.

30    'Bulletin', *NRF*, November 1938, p. 877.

31    Martin du Gard to JP, letter dated 24 November 1938 (AP); see also 'Une lettre de Martin du Gard, le 14 octobre 1938', in *La Flèche*, 21 October 1938.

32    A. Gide, *Journal*, I, p. 1326, entry dated 3 December 1938. See also the special number of the *Bulletin de l'Union pour la vérité*, 'Après Munich', October-November 1938, and C. Martin, 'Ce fou de Jef: André Gide et Munich', *Revue des sciences humaines*, January-March 1970, pp. 119-125.

particular Benda's interpretation, had been, for he repeated almost exactly their underlying sentiments about Munich and appeasement:

> C'est la bourgeoisie qui a empêché la guerre en 38 et décidé la capitulation de Munich, plus encore par peur de la victoire que de la défaite. Elle redoutait que la guerre ne profitât au communisme.[33]

Outside the *NRF* there came a storm of protest. Thierry Maulnier was among the first on the nationalist Right to react. In *La Revue universelle*, one of the most important pro-Munich intellectual reviews, Maulnier lambasted the *NRF* for creating a dangerous blend of moralism and politics; he berated such as Benda and Montherlant for interfering and for challenging what was a diplomatic *fait accompli*, arguing that they were not competent to judge. His prime target was Benda, 'ce professionel du *faux* intellectuel', who, according to Maulnier, had for so long proclaimed his political disinterestedness.[34] But one of the most unforgiving counterattacks came from the pen of Emmanuel Berl, in his pamphlet, *Pavés de Paris*. This was all the more remarkable because Berl had once been very close to Gaston Gallimard and André Malraux, and because his publication received a government subsidy through the Quai d'Orsay. Berl opened mischievously:

> Sans doute la *NRF* n'est pas ce qu'elle fut jadis. Elle a perdu la plus grande partie de son importance. Il y a avait au fond de Jacques Rivière un prédicateur; il y a au fond de Jean Paulhan un farceur. Tout cela n'en mérite pas moins un sérieux commentaire.[35]

Taking each text in turn, Berl strove to demolish all their arguments; he too was particularly severe on Benda. In his comments on Benda's prescience of the Vichy régime, in effect Berl proved Benda's thesis: 'Si un fascisme larvé paraît probable à M. Benda, c'est qu'un gouvernement de Front populaire a en quelque sorte fait le lit du fascisme en rendant illusoires et dérisoires les libertés dont la petite et la moyenne bourgeoisie ont souhaité et souhaitent encore la

---

33    J.-P. Sartre, *Les carnets de la drôle de guerre, novembre 1939-mars 1940*, Gallimard, 1983, pp. 375-376. And he continued: 'En septembre 39, au contraire, la guerre est bien accueillie par la bourgeoisie parce que le traité germano-russe a déconsidéré le communisme et qu'on sait à présent que cette guerre, qui se fait, directement ou indirectement, contre les Soviets, s'accompagnera nécessairement d'une opération de police intérieure. Le parti communiste sera dissous. Ce que n'avaient pu faire dix ans de politique, la guerre fera en un mois. Telle est, mne semble-t-il, la raison principale de l'adhésion bourgeoise à la guerre. Sous des allures de guerre nationale, c'est en grande partie une guerre civile.'

34    'Les intellectuels arrivent trop tard', *La Revue universelle*, 15 November 1938, pp. 494-498.

35    'La *NRF* contre la paix', *Pavés de Paris*, no. 23, 18 November 1938, pp. 1-14.

sauvegarde'.[36] Berl was hardly less sweeping in his dismissal of Schlumberger: 'M. Jean Schlumberger est infiniment plus rusé que M. Benda. Il sait, comme la plupart des protestants, tout placer dans le plan moral le plus haut. Chez les protestants, l'inversion elle-même cesse d'être un vice pour devenir un cas de conscience.'[37] But his most searing vitriol was reserved for his former employer Gaston Gallimard, whom Berl alleged was a 'draft-dodger' and 'hypocrite':

> Sur un seul point je l'avais vu ferme et constant: ce point, c'était l'horreur de la guerre. [...] Il n'a pas fait la guerre de 1914 malgré son âge, malgré son excellente santé. [...] Laisser la NRF faire le jeu du bellicisme par une incroyable accumulation d'erreurs et de tricheries, il n'en avait pas le droit [...] [38]

His conclusion went to what he considered to be the heart of the matter:

> Mais je n'attaquerais pas M. Gaston Gallimard sans dire que l'offensive belliciste [sic] menée par la NRF n'est qu'un cas particulier de l'offensive générale menée contre la paix par les chefs d'orchestres invisibles qui veulent à tout prix empêcher la conciliation de la France et de l'Allemagne.[39]

Evidently Berl was happy to propagate the view held by such as Georges Bonnet in the Foreign Ministry that even now, after Munich, Franco-German reconciliation was somehow still possible even if, through the betrayal of alliances, it entailed complicity with Nazi expansionism. Many at the NRF would have been bemused by this *volte-face* of Berl who, having once predicted the 'death of bourgeois thought'[40], was now one of the government's most staunch defenders and was even in their pay.

Antifascists and the communists gave Paulhan's 'special number' their enthusiastic support. Typical is the praise of Georges Sadoul in *Commune*:

> Le numéro de novembre de la NRF est à peu près *un numéro spécial consacré à la honte des capitulations de Munich.* [Il s'y trouve] une violente indignation contre la politique de trahison menée par Daladier au cours des tragiques journées de septembre.[41]

---

36  Ibid., p. 8. These remarks are especially interesting when it is remembered that Berl went on to prepare the drafting of some of Pétain's speeches in 1940.
37  *Pavés de Paris*, no. 23, 18 November 1938, p. 8.
38  Ibid., pp. 13-14.
39  Ibid., p. 14.
40  In his iconoclastic essay *Mort de la pensée bourgeoise*, Grasset, 1929, dedicated to Garine in Malraux's *Les Conquérants*.
41  'Revues françaises', in *Commune*, December 1938, pp. 1911-1917 (p. 1911, my emphasis). This paean of praise sparked a bitter polemic between Sadoul and Berl; see *Commune*, January 1939, pp. 89ff, and *Pavés de Paris*, 27 January 1939.

Such zealous support from these quarters could only reflect upon the *NRF*; there could now be no doubt that Paulhan's review was firmly located in the communist-backed, antifascist camp.

## The drift into war

Paulhan's scarely veiled attack on the government's conduct of policy at home and abroad was reinforced when he inserted in the *NRF* the first of a number of 'political' texts bearing his own name. As a postscript to the November issue, in December he criticised the growing manifestations of paternalism evident among those in authority:

> Les ministres, les percepteurs, et jusqu'au Président de la Société des Gens de Lettres nous prient de devenir de meilleurs Français: plus unis, mais plus travailleurs; plus intelligents, mais plus généreux; par dessus tout, prolifiques et prêts à tous les dévouements. Je regrette de dire (mais je le dis fermement), il ne faut pas compter sur nous.[42]

The ordinary French people were not to blame; rather, it was the manner in which the State and politicians wielded power that had done so much to discredit democracy, and which had done so much to validate anti-democrats' arguments:

> L'on n'a jamais tant parlé d'honneur que durant la chienlit de l'après-guerre. Les Moralistes nous disent encore que toute Démocratie exige, du haut en bas de l'échelle, la vertu des citoyens. C'est une affirmation impudente: car, s'il est naturel d'en conclure qu'il faut supprimer le vice, il est à la fois plus naturel et plus expédient d'en conclure qu'il faut supprimer la Démocratie.[43]

The citizens of France were not to blame for the current state of affairs, because they were only following the counsels of Democracy: 'Ce n'est pas notre faute', wrote Paulhan, and continued: 'Nous sommes précisément, nous n'arrêtons pas d'être ce qu'attend de nous une démocratie libérale, individualiste, paciifque.' The real blame lay with the State: 'C'est l'Etat qui nous invite aux partis, à la division, à la différence'. Citizens were surely being given contradictory advice:

---

42  'Il ne faut pas compter sur nous', *NRF*, December 1938, p. 1065.
43  Ibid. These views are very similar to Alain's conception of 'le citoyen contre les pouvoirs'. A. Clerval notes that 'parce qu'il pose l'excellence de la personne et non celle de l'Etat, de la Nation ou d'une idée, Jean Paulhan n'a jamais été un partisan'; *NRF*, May 1969, p. 936.

> On accuse volontiers la littérature — et la *NRF* en particulier — d'être un nid de réfractaires [this is a reference to Berl's attacks]. Il se peut. Je n'en sais rien. Mais je sais qu'il est de l'honneur du réfractaire, d'abord, qu'il ne se voie pas encouragé. [...] Or notre Démocratie n'a jamais cessé d'encourager ses révoltés, de les honorer, de les nommer ministres — quitte à leur donner de bons conseils.[44]

The essential meaning of this text was that he and the *NRF* would continue to criticize the State whenever the latter risked putting the well-being of the French people in danger.[45] These comments provoked discussion in several quarters, including *L'Action française*, and André Billy, writing in the literary supplement of *Le Figaro*, offered his own interpretation of what he termed this 'new, sibylline, manifesto of the *NRF*':

> Que le gouvernement gouverne, qu'il fasse preuve d'autorité et nous fiche la paix, à nous autres, intellectuels et poètes, dont la mission est de servir un idéal sans commune mesure avec les réalités et les exigences de la vie en société! [...] La *NRF* est-elle pour ou contre Daladier?[46]

The next week Billy revised his view, this time saying that 'j'ai cru comprendre, à relire l'article de Jean Paulhan, que celui-ci ne trouve pas le gouvernement actuel assez jacobin.'[47] Billy was proved right in his interpretation when, in the January 1939 issue, Paulhan issued a further warning about the threats facing France were the government to pursue its 'pacifist' (or 'appeasement') policies. He saw war as a virtually inevitable rite with its conformists, heretics and martyrs, and argued that the more the nation proclaimed its opposition to violence, the more it invited attack.[48] He feared that rather than risk war, the government might even consider the cession of French territory:

> L'Italie, comme l'on sait, nous réclame aujourd'hui Tunis et la Corse. Et il est vraisemblable—si j'en juge par les précédents—que nous allons sous peu les lui remettre. [...] C'est aussitôt le Savoie, la Provence et jusqu'à Manosque, qu'exigeront nos voisins. Et je ne vois point du tout comment cette fois nous éviterions la guerre.[49]

---

44  'Il ne faut pas compter sur nous', pp. 1065-1067.
45  Jean Grenier took a contrasting view in 'Cercle carré', *NRF*, December 1938, p. 1068-1069.
46  A. Billy, 'Propos du samedi', *Le Figaro littéraire*, 10 December 1938.
47  A. Billy, 'Propos du samedi', *Le Figaro littéraire*, 17 December 1938.
48  'Petit traité du pacifisme', *NRF*, January 1939, pp. 170-172.
49  Ibid., p. 172. For Italian claims on French territory, see J.-B. Duroselle, *La Décadence*, pp. 390ff. The reference to Manosque concerns Giono, whose manifesto *Les Seules Vérités* irritated Paulhan greatly; see 'Les revues', *NRF*, January 1939, p. 167.

Because Foreign Ministry diplomats were still attempting to negotiate with the Germans, these were daring criticisms to make. Paulhan was aware that such outspokenness might lead to further government hostility towards the *NRF*, or even censorship. To counter this, in January 1939 he exercised his own policy of censorship when Suarès, invited to renew his monthly *chronique de Caërdal*, went too far in attacking the dictators and, as discussed above, in May the Italian authorities banned the review with the loss of some 500 subscribers. It should be remembered too that during the period 1937-1939, 'le monde de la presse parisienne est «actionné» par des manipulations émérites, comme le célèbre Otto Abetz pour l'Allemagne, [et] les services du *Minculpop* italen représenté à Paris par le consul Landini.'[50] Of course the independence of the *NRF* is not in doubt; but its standing as a intellectuals' forum encouraged fascist propaganda services to approach individual contributors from an early date, as in the case of Benjamin Crémieux.[51]

By late summer 1939 events were moving too quickly for Paulhan to react in any measured, reflective way; on 17 August talks between Britain, France and the USSR were suspended, and on 23 August came the bombshell of the Nazi-Soviet pact. After war was declared on 3 September, Gaston Gallimard moved the whole *NRF* operation to the relative safety of his property Mirande, near Sartilly, in the Manche department.

### The *NRF* in the phoney war

Despite all the inconvenience of the relocation, the *NRF* strove to continue as normal. However, the review was subject to all the vagaries of postal and printing delays and the mobilisation of many of its contributors (including Marcel Arland, Aragon, Jean-Paul Sartre, Raymond Queneau, etc.). In addition Paulhan had to negotiate the official censorship, in the shape of the Commissariat Général à l'Information under Jean Giraudoux, inaugurated by *décret* on 27 August 1939 and based at the Hôtel Continental on the rue de Rivoli. The official

---

50  R. Girault, 'Les décideurs français et la puissance française, 1938-1939', in R. Girault and R. Frank (eds.), *La Puissance en Europe*, Publications de la Sorbonne, 1984, p. 29. *La Revue hebdomadaire*, for instance, was entirely controlled by Landini.

51  As early as 1929, Léautaud reported that 'Crémieux, qui est chargé au Ministère des Affaires étrangères du dépouillement de toute la presse italienne [...] dit que [...] sa fortune serait faite s'il voulait se laissé acheter par Mussolini, qu'il a été sondé indirectement à ce sujet, et qu'on ne lui demanderait pas beaucoup, nullement de célébrer le régime fasciste dans sa totalité, mais seulement de dire qu'à côté du mauvais il y a du bon... Mais il est trop profondément républicain pour accepter de faire ce métier'; Léautaud, *Journal littéraire*, VIII, p. 125, entry dated 28 December 1929.

censorship was a source of much frustration for Paulhan, who found it full of 'defeatists'; later he called it a 'fourmilière inerte'[52].

In October, once it had passed through the censor's hands, the *NRF* opened with a leading article by Paulhan. Already hinting at the peculiar atmosphere of the phoney war, he pointed to the sharp contrast between his experience in 1914 and that of his fellow-citizens in 1939:

> Ceux qui partent aujourd'hui, comme ils sont plus sages—et, je pense, plus sagement dirigés. [...] Silencieux: sans cris ni curiosité. Sans pillages. Sans trop de surprise. [...] Où sont-ils, nous ne le savons déjà plus. Qu'ils vivent tous, que vive notre pays.[53]

He concluded with an admonition, projecting his own hopes on to the ordinary soldier: 'A la question: «Pourquoi te bats-tu?», faites que chacun d'eux puisse répondre: «C'est pour être un jour heureux et honoré».'[54] Jean-Paul Sartre however, posted near the German border, was one of many who found that Paulhan's grasp of realities at the front was sadly lacking.[55] Yet Paulhan was determined not to ignore the fact of the war, despite the disapproval of many readers and personalities who bore an influence on the affairs of the review. Among his preferred contributors at this testing time were Armand Petitjean, still a serving soldier at the front, and Suarès, who continued to pour forth his antifascist invective. In November, surprisingly this passage in Suarès' *chronique* escaped the censors: 'Seul, le plus vil des ennemis, cinq cent mille fois assassin ose vomir l'injure sur ses victimes: il mêle son crachat à la mer immense de sang qu'il fait couler'.[56] And Paulhan would have applauded Petitjean who, writing as "Armand", commented in a text truncated by the censor:

> J'espère que la revue [i.e., the *NRF*] va conserver sa liberté et sa vie, qui deviendront scandaleuses. Pourquoi ne pas discuter maintenant

52    Paulhan's correspondence contains several disparaging comments about the censorship; see *JPC* 2, letters 89, 90, 118, and other unpublished letters to Schlumberger (BD). For details of the Commissariat, see M. Mégret, 'Les origines de la propagande de guerre française: du Service Général de l'Information au Commissariat Général à l'Information, 1927-1940', *Revue d'histoire de la Deuxième Guerre mondiale*, January 1961, pp. 3-27, and P. Amaury, *Les deux premières expériences d'un Ministère de l'Information en France*, LDGJ, 1969.

53    'Retour sur dix-neuf cent quatorze', *NRF*, October 1939, pp. 529-532 (pp. 529-530).

54    Ibid., p. 532.

55    Sartre wrote to Simone de Beauvoir: 'l'article de Paulhan m'a fait littéralement gonfler [...]; s'il savait combien les types d'ici sont loin de penser à être un jour heureux et honorés!'; *Lettres aux Castor*, I, *1926-1939*, Gallimard, 1983, p. 360.

56    *Chronique de Caërdal, NRF*, November 1939, p. 776.

des buts de guerre et des moyens de paix. Du principe même de la guerre? C'est pendant qu'il est bon et courageux d'en parler.[57]

The phoney war induced many behind the lines into stunned complacency, a state of affairs caused by inaction and lack of enthusiasm at the front.[58] Yet the *NRF* intended, explicitly, to combat this lethargy. In January 1940, in a notice calling for their continued support, subscribers read that the problems caused by the war 'seront dans [les pages de la NRF] *l'objet d'une attention constante'*.[59] True to its word, the issue of the *NRF* for February 1940 stands as the phoney war counterpart to the special number on Munich. Out of the 144-page issue, 56 pages were directly concerned with the war. It opened with Pierre-Jean Jouve's 'A la France 1940'. 'Aux armes!', apostrophised the poet, and he went on to liken the struggle of the French soldiery to a battle with the Anti-Christ:

> La face humaine est offensée
> Par le gorille à la casquette noire
> Dieu souffre et la face humaine est offensée
> La bête de la mer est la bête de fer
> Hitlerienne! et le chiffre 666 à son front
> Elle avance contre nos coeurs! À Dieu, aux armes!

And the poem ends with an image which conjures up Delacroix's painting 'La liberté guidant le peuple':

> La croix de Christ encor se voit contre son sein
> Et sur ton front léger le bonnet phrygien:
> Poursuis à mort la guerre au tueur pourrissant
> Tes beaux yeux consacrés par la Liberté pure
> Le sang rouge, le bleu divin, et l'ange blanc.[60]

Benda, in his last major piece in the review, analysed 'La Crise de la morale cléricale'. This text may be read as a 1940 postscript to his famous essay *La Trahison des clercs* dating from 1927. Fascism, and before it the *'faux clercs'* Sorel

---

57    'Lettre', in *ibid.*, p. 780.
58    Cf. J.-L. Crémieux-Brilhac, *Les Français de l'an 40*, 2 vol., Gallimard, 1990, esp. vol. I., *La guerre oui ou non?*
59    Unattributed text in publicity brochure, *NRF*, January 1940, p. 11 (my emphasis).
60    'A la France 1940', *NRF*, February 1940, pp. 145-149 (p. 149).

and Maurras, had contributed to the erosion and debasement of those universal values that Benda had held so dear since the end of the previous century.[61]

The next two articles are remarkable because they stand as invaluable documents bearing witness to the inertia of the phoney war. Firstly Petitjean, writing as "Armand" from the Saar front, returned to a theme he had explored over the last two years. After describing the 'unspeakable sadness' of conditions at the front, and the disenchantment of many combatants after the mobilisation, he lamented the death of his comrade-in-arms Julot, who had been among the first fatalities: his death seemed tragic when viewed in the context of the delusions which were now evaporating, but which had prevailed since Versailles:

> La form idable mythomanie entretenue depuis près de vingt ans, en Allemagne et ailleurs, par une génération d'anciens combattants et des cohortes d'adolescents est peut-être en train de s'épuiser lentement au contact de celle qui reste, malgré tout, la réalité des réalités.[62]

The disenchantment had spread in particular to Petitjean's communist comrades-in-arms at the front, who were left crying with rage by the Nazi-Soviet Pact; some tore up their party cards. At the end of the text, however, he hoped that the war would prove to be a regenerative force and, ominously, he called for a 'Nouvelle Révolution Française' whereby 'la Nation entrera dans notre vie quotidienne'.[63] Secondly André Chamson, to whom Daladier had offered the direction of the Commissariat à l'Information, and who had preferred to fight with the French Fifth Army[64], sent Paulhan extracts from his notebooks. Conscious of the intense experience of 'fraternity' among men under arms, Chamson emphasized the nature of the struggle in which France was engaged: 'nous sommes dans quelque chose de beaucoup plus grand qu'une guerre. Nous sommes dans une métamorphose de la vie humaine'. After all the false hopes of the previous 25 years, Europe had come within the grasp of 'adventurers and gangsters'. The message was simple: only by resisting fascist aggression could France and Europe be saved, so the war had to be prosecuted to its conclusion:

> Guerre ou pas guerre, nous sommes partis, l'enjeu est sur la table. [...] Le peuple le plus pacifiste et le plus pacifique de la terre, le nôtre, refuse la main qu'on feint de lui tendre. Il accepte la guerre,

---

61 'La Crise de la morale cléricale', ibid., pp. 150-161.
62 'Pour l'après-guerre', ibid., pp. 162-173 (p. 163).
63 Ibid., p. 170. Petitjean went on to contribute articles to Drieu's *NRF*.
64 See A. Chamson, *Il faut vivre vieux*, Grasset, 1984, pp. 99ff.

parce qu'il ne veut pas d'une fausse paix, parce qu'il n'a plus
confiance dans la paix.[65]

The *NRF*'s attitude to the war struck a chord, because between June 1939
and April 1940 it gained some 1,700 subscriptions, despite substantial losses in
Germany, Czechoslovakia, Austria and Italy: the *NRF* had thus correctly gauged
the general hardening of public opinion towards the aggression of the
dictatorships.[66] None the less, for some within the *NRF* this 'bellicose' attitude
was too much. Frustrated still by the continuing dilemma he faced between the
'pacifist' and 'bellicist' camps within the review, Paulhan turned to Jean Grenier
for advice. Enclosing a draft text called 'Pour la liberté de l'esprit en temps de
guerre', he asked:

> Crois-tu qu'il faudrait, en tête de chaque *NRF*, une ou deux pages
> [...] qui serviraient de 'prise de position', donneraient à la revue une
> sorte de continuité, serviraient aussi à la justifier des reproches
> bizarres et, heureusement, contradictoires dont on l'accable. Par
> exemple, qu'elle est au fond défaitiste et commet une sorte de
> trahison en donnant Giono [in April 1940]. [...] Ou bien, qu'elle est
> belliciste, et peut-être pas tout à fait innocente de la guerre, avec
> son Benda et son Petitjean.[67]

Such problems diminished in the face of the progress of the war, however. In
April the campaign spread to Denmark and Norway, with the Nazis overrunning
their victims in a matter of hours following a pattern which was becoming all too
familiar: very soon the *Blitzkrieg* would be unleashed against France.

Appropriately enough, in May Georges Bernanos contributed a text from
his South American exile called 'Nous retournons dans la guerre'. These dark
reflexions turned around what Bernanos, deeply affected by his experiences in
the First World War, identified as the unbridgeable gulf between the 'front' and
'behind the lines'. The greatest treachery of all committed 'behind the lines' (i.e.,
by successive interwar governments) was that the 'peace' of 1919 had proved
worthless, and had betrayed the sacrifice of more than a million French
soldiers.[68] And, sure enough, just a few days after this text was published, on 10

---

65    'D'un carnet de route d'un officier de liaison', *NRF*, February 1940, pp. 174-183 (pp. 181,
      183).
66    JP to Schlumberger, letter dated 30 March 1940 (AP). On the development of public
      opinion after Munich, see C.-R. Ageron, 'L'Opinion publique française pendant les crises
      internationales de septembre 1938 à juillet 1939 (Etude de sondages)', *Cahiers de l'Institut
      d'Histoire de la Presse et de l'Opinion*, no. 3, 1974-5, pp. 203-224.
67    JP to Grenier, *Correspondance 1925-1968*, pp. 129-131.
68    'Nous retournons dans la guerre', *NRF*, May 1940, pp. 577-598. This text formed part of
      *Les Enfants humiliés*, published in 1949.

May Hitler began his offensive in the west. As the German armies broke out and swept westwards, reaching the French capital in mid-June, Paulhan and the *NRF* caravanserail struck camp again and left the Manche department to travel south. Eventually they came to rest at Joe Bosquet's house, 'L'Évêché', at Villalier, near Carcassonne.[69] By the end of May the British Expeditionary Force was trapped at Dunkirk. Paulhan anticipated worse to come; on 26 May he lamented to Jules Supervielle:

> C'est une mauvaise journée: Calais et Dunkerque perdus, les Belges nous lâchent. Enfin, plus que jamais, espoir. [...] Tout est angoissant. Pourtant je m'attends à ce que l'Angleterre maintenant étonne le monde.[70]

Paulhan's attitude is summarized here in one crucial word : *'espoir'*. It returns again in the title of his final text in the *NRF*, 'L'Espoir et le silence'. Echoing Chamson, Paulhan equated hope with the struggle to resist 'une des plus grandes forces du monde [...] dressée contre nous'. The greatest hope in the face of the looming Nazi invasion and occupation was, after all, a political one:

> Certes, notre république semble avoir avoué, depuis vingt ans, tous les vices dont les adversaires lui font grief. Pourtant, nous nous battons pour quelque chose qui ressemble à la République: pour la liberté des personnes, contre la servitude volontaire.

In a final, moving, passage which anticipates the spirit of Resistance, he appealed to those who would refuse to be subjugated:

> En vérité, le problème a des termes si clairs qu'il serait fou de ne point espérer une réconciliation française, si chacun de nous, dès aujourd'hui, le pose et s'essaie à le résoudre, dans son secret. Dans son silence.[71]

With these words, Paulhan anticipated his own attitude in the months and years to come under the Occupation.

---

[69]   P. Assouline, *Gaston Gallimard*, pp. 268-269.
[70]   JP to Jules Supervielle, letter dated 26 May 1940, in *JPC* II, *1937-1945*, p. 173.
[71]   'L'Espoir et le silence', *NRF*, June 1940, p. 722.

# In conclusion

The *NRF* was a casualty of the German invasion of France: some of the proofs for the July 1940 issue, as well as other material in various stages of preparation, burned when the printer's premises in Abbeville were bombarded.[1] So ended the review's reign over the intellectual and literary world of the interwar period. Through the stance he adopted, on his own authority Jean Paulhan responded firmly to the threats to France which arose after mid-1938. Unafraid of offending the review's readers or of enraging its enemies, he attacked the delusions of those in authority and sowed the seeds of intellectual resistance. The position of the *NRF* made a considerable impact, judging by the violent campaign against its attitude to the war waged by a number of pro-Vichy newspapers.[2] It was also criticized for the great prestige it enjoyed in the culture of the Third Republic: as early as 10 July, for example, Benjamin Crémieux informed his editor that the weekly *Candide* had attacked the *NRF*, 'which was French in name only'. For twenty years it had been 'too preoccupied with Tibet and Kamchatka, and had never been truly interested in things French'.[3] For Vichyite critics the *NRF* was part of an overall political malaise: like the Third Republic itself, it would have to be replaced. As for Paulhan, he was warned that his own life could be in danger precisely because of the stand he had taken:

---

[1] See the introduction to Armand Petitjean's collection of articles published under the Occupation as *Combats préliminaires*, Gallimard, 1942, p. 9.

[2] In correspondence with his novelist friend Henri Pourrat, Paulhan learned that throughout August and September 1940 an anti-*NRF* campaign was being conducted not only by German radio but also by *Gringoire*, *Candide*, *Le Journal* and *Le Temps* (AP).

[3] Crémieux to JP (letter dated 17 July 1940), referring to an article in *Candide*, 10 July 1940 (AP).

> J[eanne] G[allimard] est de retour. Elle pense qu'il serait imprudent que je rentre (à cause des bavardages d'un colonel qui, trouvant, à Mirande, mon article de juin, aurait proposé de me faire fusiller...) Je ne sais pas trop ce que nous allons devenir, ni la *NRF*.[4]

As the days and weeks of summer 1940 passed Paulhan began to be involved in a number of Resistance activities. He was already in touch with some of the figures who would eventually lead the intellectual Resistance, including Jacques Debû-Bridel, Claude Aveline, Jean Cassou, Jean Blanzat and François Mauriac. The first such group were the 'Amis d'Alain-Fournier', founded on 13 July 1940 by Cassou, Aveline and Pierre Abraham.[5] In December 1940 he became associated with the group of resisters based at the Musée de l'Homme. As he later testified, '[Anatole] Levitsky et [Boris] Vildé avaient fondé, dès 1940, le premier journal clandestin: *Résistance*'; Paulhan was responsible for the group's roneo machine, an involvement which later led directly to his arrest and interrogation at the hands of the Germans in the Santé prison.[6] And looking back at the rôle of the *NRF* during those inauspicious months before and after June 1940, Paulhan himself acknowledged the review's anticipation of Resistance when, after the war, most of the texts chosen for the phoney war section of the anthology *La Patrie se fait tous les jours* were taken from the *NRF*.[7]

Although Paulhan chose silence and resistance, at the same time he kept in close touch with moves being made behind the scenes regarding the future of the review. By September 1940 he learned that Drieu La Rochelle had been called upon by Otto Abetz to relaunch the *Nouvelle Revue française*. In a deposition dating from 1945, Paulhan testified that

> Drieu La Rochelle a confirmé que les Allemands allaient s'emparer de la maison dans sa totalité — éditions et revues — , que celle-ci reparaîtrait de toute façon, qu'on pouvait sauver la maison d'édition, en ne s'opposant pas à la publication [de la revue] — qu'étant un ami de la maison il en prendrait la direction afin qu'elle soit purement littéraire.[8]

4     JP to Pourrat, letter dated 13 September 1940 (AP).

5     P. Hebey, *La Nouvelle Revue Française des années sombres*, Gallimard, 1992, p. 214.

6     See 'Une semaine au secret', published at the Liberation in *Le Figaro* (9 September 1944), reproduced in C. Paulhan, *La vie est pleine de choses redoutables*, Seghers, 1989, p. 264. Paulhan was released after Drieu La Rochelle's intervention with the occupying authorities.

7     J. Paulhan and D. Aury, *La Patrie se fait tous les jours. textes francais, 1939-1945*, Les Editions de Minuit, 1947. The book included texts by Pierre-Jean Jouve, Schlumberger, Suarès, Ramuz, Bernanos, Mauriac, Aragon and Chamson; see pp. 41-94.

8     'Témoignage de JP du 3 novembre 1945, au sujet du comportement de Gaston Gallimard sous l'Occupation', C. Paulhan, *La vie est pleine de choses redoutables*, pp. 255-256.

If the title remained unchanged, it proved, none the less, to be a very different review, despite the insistence that it was to be 'purely literary'.[9] At first Paulhan was invited to join Drieu as co-director, but in November 1940 he confirmed to his friends that he had 'no wish to do so'.[10] Even if the Germans *had* accepted him, he would have been betraying those Jewish contributors he had invited to the review, and whom he had protected for so long, for they were to be excluded from the *NRF* consistent with the new anti-Jewish statutes passed by the Vichy régime before the Nazis' own measures came into effect.[11] For the time being, he was obliged to resign himself to the prospect of relative inactivity: 'Je vais être chômeur', he observed laconically.[12]

The *NRF* published or serialized much of what is now recognized as the most enduring literature of the interwar period in France. In addition, it reflected upon a range of issues which preoccupied many intellectuals at the time, whether they were identifiably on the Left, the Right or the centre of the political spectrum. Its position in the centre as a *revue radicalisante*, and its dislike for rigid, doctrinaire ideology and commitment, appealed to its liberal consituency. Ultimately it displayed an unshakeable respect for the French Republic. Although it may sometimes have seemed that the *NRF* – through the work of its principal essayists Alain, Benda and Thibaudet – maintained a sterile veneration for radicalist ideals, none the less this reverence protected it from being usurped by the extreme-Left or the extreme-Right. Even when it or its contributors were tempted to make unambiguous expressions of political commitment, Paulhan counteracted so that the balance of the review could be re-established. In this way, despite misconceptions concerning the status of its regular personnel, and notwithstanding its location in the liberal centre of the

9    See JP to Leon Bopp, letter dated 30 September 1940, *NRF*, February 1982, p. 181. See also Kohn-Etimble, pp. 203-209. For an introduction to Drieu's review, see L. Richard, 'Drieu la Rochelle et *La Nouvelle Revue Française* des annees noires', *Revue d'Histoire de la Deuxieme Guerre mondiale*, XXV, 97, 1975, pp. 67-84, but especially P. Hebey, *La NRF des années sombres, 1940-1941*. Finally, P. Assouline relates the history of the publishing house under the Occupation in *Gaston Gallimard*, pp. 270-362.

10   'Je n'en ai aucune envie', he wrote, and added: 'Il s'est trouve que les All.[emands] non plus. Nous en sommes là. La *NRF* reparaîtra donc probablement d'ici trois mois, sous la direction de Drieu'; JP to Guillaume de Tarde, *NRF*, February 1982, p. 185.

11   'Je ne pouvais demeurer dans une revue dont on chassait les collaborateurs juifs (Benda, Suares, Wahl) et les antinazis (Bernanos, Claudel, Romains) que j'y avais appelés'; Grover, *MLN*, p. 847. Paulhan witnessed at first hand the anti-Semitism of the French military in an incident concerning Julien Benda while they were dining in Carcassonne; JP to Grenier, *Correspondance*, pp. 138-139, and J. Guéhenno, *Journal des années noires*, Gallimard, 1947, pp. 35ff.

12   P. Leautaud, *Journal littéraire*, XIII, p. 195, entry dated 16 October 1940.

range of periodical reviews, the *NRF* played a leading rôle in the promotion of intellectual debate in interwar Europe. It is for this prime reason that it has merited reassessment.

Jean Paulhan, the review's *éminence grise*, was well suited to take over as editor from Jacques Rivière after the latter's untimely death in 1925. As the interwar years went by, he became more willing to consider texts which were not, strictly speaking, literary. Closer examination reveals that those regularly involved with the review *did* have political preferences and prejudices, including Gide, Benda, Alain, Thibaudet and Paulhan himself. Benda, Alain and Thibaudet, who constituted the pivotal centre of the regular monthly essay section, were considered to be three of the brightest intellectual stars in the radical-republican cultural firmament. They represented the intellectual élite of the mature Third Republic, and, in Thibaudet's phrase, they were among the leading personnel of the *République des Professeurs*. Paulhan's support for Julien Benda in particular betrays the desire at the heart of the *NRF* for the perpetuation of a liberal, idealistic, rationalistic conception of all that was 'just' and 'pure' in the republican intellectual tradition in France. This is illustrated most strikingly by the decision to serialize Julien Benda's celebrated and often reprinted work, *La Trahison des clercs*. Benda, idealist though he was, set out none the less to interpret the rôle of intellectuals within historical terms of reference which explicitly extended back through the tribulations of the radical republic — the First World War, the Dreyfus Affair — to its origins in the French Revolution: as the 1930s progressed towards further, albeit milder, political revolution in the shape of the Popular Front, so Benda aligned himself with the communists, whom he considered to be the contemporary inheritors of the Jacobins. And the long running and multi-facetted debate after the publication of *La Trahison des clercs* opened the *NRF* to intellectual exchange, and directly cleared the way towards the *engagement* or fellow-travelling of some of its most famous personalities, above all Gide, Malraux, and Benda himself.

The implications of these exchanges led to an acknowledgement of the necessity to contrast the idealistic underpinnings of the radical republic with the declining political fortunes of the Radical Party, whose ideas and ideology required modernization. The *NRF* participated in this scrutiny and lent itself as a platform for the discussion of new ideas or doctrine; at the same time, however, Paulhan learned much about the dangers the review incurred in doing so. Here again, despite the temptations of left- or right-wing fellow-travelling (Malraux and Gide on the Left as opposed to Drieu, Jouhandeau or even Maurras on the Right), the liberal 'centre of gravity' of the *NRF* was never really displaced.

The interwar *NRF* had been primed for political considerations through its founders' interest in the Franco-German question, an issue which greatly preoccupied them even before 1914. The status and connections of personalities such as Rivière, Gide and Schlumberger made it difficult to ignore this issue, and in France it continued to be an overwhelming concern. The nature of the question ensured that the treatment of Franco-German relations during the interwar period was bound to be politically sensitive, and it was certainly coloured by preconceived ideas on both sides of the Rhine. These ideas derived from assumptions based on supposed 'national characteristics', as well as from the tensions created by the Versailles Treaty. It was only when the question began to be considered in terms of a clash between fascism and antifascism that a more realistic, or more appropriate, appraisal could be made.

The review dealt with another international issue. Gide's search for a new, non-conformist, anti-bourgeois humanism led him for a while to express sympathy for Soviet Russia. This attraction was, it is true, actively encouraged and abetted by Soviet sympathizers and fellow-travellers both inside and outside the review. Once again, however, we have attempted to show how this fascinated interest towards the 'Soviet experiment' is partly comprehensible within a specifically French radical-republican perspective. Thus, despite Paulhan's strenuous efforts, and through the professions of faith it carried, the *NRF* risked following reviews such as *Europe* and *Commune* into political *engagement* on the Left: it was only Paulhan's decision to commission a critique of Marxian orthodoxy, and Gide's disappointment with Soviet reality itself, which ultimately restored balance.

As the true nature of Nazism began to be realized in France, so the Jewish question became increasingly relevant and controversial. The problem of anti-Semitism was not new in the France of the 1930s: its heritage could be traced back through recent decades, again to the Dreyfus Affair and beyond. But as Nazi racism and persecution spread, eventually finding favour among certain extreme elements of the French intellectual world, it became difficult to ignore the Jewish question in the *NRF*, all the more so since three of the major contributors – Benda, Crémieux and Suarès – came from Jewish backgrounds, even if they all eschewed Zionism. Other contributors too, among them Gide, Léautaud and Jouhandeau, to a greater or lesser degree reflected many of the period's prevailing anti-Semitic prejudices.

After the Munich accords in 1938 an irreversible march began towards a new war. Some writing in the *NRF* had foreseen these dangers as early as the late 1920s. And just as a number of intellectuals and radical-republicans had rallied to the 'defence of the Republic' around the turn of the century, so the *NRF*, true to its constituency, rallied to the patriotic cause and, following Paulhan's lead, opposed appeasement and capitulation to fascism. The stalemate of the phoney war was finally broken in May 1940 when the German invaders overwhelmed France: it would not be long before the Third Republic voted itself out of existence on 10 July 1940. Apologists for the 'new European order' under Nazi hegemony believed that the *NRF* constituted a prestigious and indispensable asset, so the review was appropriated for propaganda purposes. Subsequently, at the Liberation, the *NRF* was liquidated for 'intelligence with the enemy' in a general purge of the Collaboration. It was eventually relaunched in 1953 under the joint editorship of Jean Paulhan and Marcel Arland. But the *Nouvelle Nouvelle Revue française* would only be a pale shadow of its former self, for its soul had perished with the Third Republic.

# BIBLIOGRAPHY

## SECTION I: UNPUBLISHED CORRESPONDENCE AND OTHER SOURCES

## SECTION II: PUBLISHED CORRESPONDENCE

## SECTION III: SECONDARY SOURCES

## SECTION IV: PERIODICALS

## SECTION I:

## UNPUBLISHED CORRESPONDENCE
## AND OTHER SOURCES

N.B.: Reference to unpublished correspondence in footnotes is shown by the letters AP (Archives Paulhan), AR (Archives Rivière), BD (Bibliothèque Littéraire Jacques Doucet), and Fonds RMG (the Fonds Roger Martin du Gard, Bibliothèque Nationale, Département des Manuscrits). Where dates are approximate, square brackets are used.

1.    **Archives Paulhan (AP).** The unpublished correspondence consulted by the author was in the keeping of Mme Jacqueline F. Paulhan, Paris, France. Now much of the Paulhan archive is held by the Institut Mémoire de l'Edition Contemporaine (IMEC), Paris.

Letters from the following correspondents to Jean Paulhan (referred to in references as JP) were consulted: Julien Benda, Roger Caillois, André Chamson, Benjamin Crémieux, Ramon Fernandez, André Gide, Jean Grenier, Jean Guéhenno, Daniel Halévy, Roger Martin du Gard, Henri Pourrat, Jean Prévost and Albert Thibaudet.

2.    **Archives Riviere (AR).** The correspondence between Jean Paulhan and Jacques Rivière is in the keeping of M Alain Rivière.

3.    **Bibliothèque Littéraire Jacques Doucet. (BD)** The following series of letters and documents were consulted at the Bibliothèque Littéraire Jacques Doucet, Paris:

> Paulhan to Franz Hellens: Ms. 7163 *alpha* (1921) to Ms. 7323 *alpha* (1941).
> Paulhan to Marcel Jouhandeau: Ms. JHDC 3366 (1921) to Ms. JHDC 3888 (1940).
> Paulhan to Adrienne Monnier: Ms. 4375 (1920) to Ms. 4479 (16/5/37).
> Paulhan to Jean Schlumberger: Ms. 25001 (1912) to Ms. 25116 (1940)
> Paulhan to Andre Suarès: Ms. 4948 *alpha* (1928) to Ms. 4971/11 *alpha* (7 June 1940).

Dossier de presse, *André Gide et le communisme*, Fonds André Gide, no. A II 4.

4.    **Bibliothèque Nationale, Département des Manuscrits.** The following series of letters are conserved at the Bibliothèque Nationale:

> Paulhan to René Lalou: Nouvelles Acquisitions Françaises, 14692, 'Lettres adressées à René Lalou': Vol. 4.
> Paulhan to Roger Martin du Gard: in *Fonds Roger Martin du Gard*, 'Correspondance à RMG', Vols. CXIII to CXX (8 Vol.), especially Vol. CXVIII.

## SECTION II: PUBLISHED CORRESPONDENCE

Place of publication is Paris unless indicated otherwise.
The *Nouvelle Revue Française* is abbreviated to *NRF*.

'Cent dix-huit lettres inédites', *NRF*, October 1976, pp. 113-123.

Cingria, Charles-Albert, *Correspondance générale*. Tome 3, *Lettres aux amis de la Voile Latine*, Lausanne: Editions l'Age d'Homme, 1977.

Fernandez, Ramon, Rivière, Jacques, *Correspondance, Bulletin des amis de Jacques Rivière et d'Alain-Fournier*, No. 14, 1979.

Gide, André, Martin du Gard, Roger, *Correspondance*, Vol. 1, *1913-1934*; Vol. 2, *1935-1951*; introduction et notes par Jean Delay, Gallimard, 1968.

Gide, André, Giono, Jean, *Correspondance 1929-1940*, édition établie, présentée et annotée par Roland Bourneuf et Jacques Cotnam, Lyon: Centre d'études gidiennes, 1983.

Gide, André, *Correspondance avec Jef Last, 1934-1950*, édition établie, présentée et annotée par C. J. Greshoff, Lyon: Presses Universitaires de Lyon, 1985.

Gide, André, Suarès, André, *Correspondance 1908-1920*, ed. Sidney D. Braun, Gallimard, 1963.

Gide, André, 'Lettres à Jean Paulhan', *NRF*, January 1970, pp. 75-81.

Grover, Frederic J., 'Les années 30 dans la correspondance Gide-Paulhan', *Modern Language Notes*, 95, 1980, pp. 830-849.

Kohn-Etiemble, Jeannine, *226 lettres inédites de Jean Paulhan. Contribution à l'étude du mouvement littéraire en France, 1933-1967*, Klincksieck, 1975.

Paulhan, Jean, Tarde, Guillaume de, *Correspondance, 1904-1920*, *Cahiers Jean Paulhan 1* (referred to as *CJP* 1, etc.), Gallimard, 1980.

Paulhan, Jean, *Jean Paulhan et Madagascar, 1908-1910* [Correspondence], *CJP* 2, Gallimard, 1982.

Paulhan, Jean, *Correspondance Jean Paulhan-André Suarès, 1925-1940*, édition établie et annotée par Y.-A. Favre, *CJP* 4, Gallimard, 1987.

Paulhan, Jean, *Correspondance Jean Paulhan-Giuseppi Ungaretti, 1921-1968*, édition établie et annotée par Jacqueline Paulhan (et. al.), *CJP* 5, Gallimard, 1989.

Paulhan, Jean, *Correspondance Jean Paulhan-Roger Caillois, 1934-1967*, édition établie et annotée par O. Felgine (et. al.), *CJP* 6, Gallimard, 1991.

Paulhan, Jean, *Audiberti-Paulhan, Lettres, 1933-1965*, édition établie et annotée par J. Guérin, *CJP7*, Gallimard, 1993.

Paulhan, Jean, *Correspondance Saint-Jean Perse-Jean Paulhan, 1925-1966*, édition établie et annotée par J. Gardes-Tamine, *Cahiers Saint-Jean Perse* 10, Gallimard, 1991.

Paulhan, Jean, *Choix de lettres*, I. *1917-1936. La littérature est une fête*, Gallimard, 1986. Referred to as *JPC* 1.

Paulhan, Jean, *Choix de lettres*, II. *1937-1945. Traité des jours sombres*, Gallimard, 1992. Referred to as *JPC* 2.

Paulhan, Jean, Grenier, Jean, *Correspondance 1925-1968*, préface de Roger Judrin, Quimper: Calligrammes, 1984.

Paulhan, Jean, Ponge, Francis, *Correspondance 1923-1968*, 2 vols, Gallimard, 1986.

Paulhan, Jean: 'Correspondance', in *NRF*, May 1969, 'Jean Paulhan, 1884-1968', pp. 988-1041.

Paulhan, Jean, Valéry, Paul, 'Correspondance', *NRF*, August 1971, pp. 161-167.

Paulhan, Jean, 'Lettres de Jean Paulhan, 1918-1919', *NRF*, June 1978, pp. 166-179.

Paulhan, Jean, 'Les Lettres de Jean Paulhan', *NRF*, July 1979, pp. 170-192.

Paulhan, Jean, 'Lettres à quelques amis, 1940-1941', *NRF*, February 1982, pp. 177-192.

Paulhan, Jean, 'Lettres à quelques amis', *NRF*, March 1982, pp. 174-191.

Paulhan, Jean, 'Lettres à quelques amis, 1954-1958', *NRF*, April 1982, pp. 169-191.

Paulhan, Jean, 'Lettres à Marcel Jouhandeau', *Cahiers de l'énergumène*, no. 3, Autumn-Winter 1983, pp. 203-215.

Paulhan, Jean, Parain, Brice, 'Correspondance', *NRF*, November 1983, pp. 170-92 and December 1983, pp. 142-148.

Proust, Marcel, Lettres à la *NRF*', *Cahiers Marcel Proust*, VI, Gallimard, 1932.

Ramuz, Charles-Ferdinand, *Lettres*, Vol. II *(1914-1947)*, Grasset, 1959.

Ramuz, Charles-Ferdinand, 'Correspondance', *NRF*, July 1967, pp. 160-192.

210

Rivière, Jacques, Schlumberger, Jean, *Correspondance 1909-1925*, édition établie, présentée, et annotée par Jean-Pierre Cap, Lyon: Centre d'études gidiennes, 1980.

Rolland, Romain, Guéhenno, Jean, *L'Indépendance de l'esprit, Correspondance 1919-1944, Cahiers Romain Rolland* 23, Albin Michel, 1975.

*Romain Rolland et la NRF. Correspondances avec Jacques Copeau et. al., Cahiers Romain Rolland* 27, Albin Michel, 1989.

Sartre, Jean-Paul, *Lettres au Castor*, 2 vol, Gallimard, 1983.

## SECTION III: SECONDARY SOURCES

**Place of publication is Paris unless indicated otherwise.**

Ageron, Charles-Robert, 'L'Opinion publique française pendant les crises internationales de septembre 1938 à juillet 1939 (étude de sondages)', *Cahiers de l'Institut d'Histoire de la Presse et de l'Opinion*, no. 3, 1974-5, pp. 203-224.

Amaury, P., *Les deux premières expériences d'un Ministère de l'Information en France*, LDGJ, 1969.

'André Gide et la *NRF*', in *Sélection*, January 1924, pp. 241-255.

*André Gide et notre temps*, Gallimard, 1935.

Andreu, Pierre, 'Les idées politiques de la jeunesse intellectuelle de 1927 à la guerre', *Revue des travaux de l'Académie des sciences morales et politiques*, 2e semestre, 1957, pp. 17-30.

Andreu, Pierre, *Révoltes de l'esprit. Les revues des années 30*, Editions Kimé, 1991.

Andreu, Pierre, and Grover, Frédéric, *Drieu La Rochelle*, Hachette, 1979.

Anglès, Auguste, *André Gide et le premier groupe de la NRF, 1890-1914*, 3 vol., Gallimard, 1978-1986.

Anglès, Auguste, 'La *NRF*', in *Magazine Littéraire*, February 1983, pp. 20-22.

Anglès, Auguste, 'Le fonctionnement de la *NRF* (1909-1914)', *Bulletin des amis d'André Gide*, no. 61, January 1984, pp. 11-28.

Arland, Marcel, *Essais et nouveaux essais critiques*, Gallimard, 1952.

Aron, Raymond, *Mémoires*, Julliard, 1983.

Aron, Robert, *Fragments d'une vie*, Plon, 1981.

Assouline, Pierre, *Gaston Gallimard (un demi-siècle d'édition française)*, Balland, 1984.

Aubéry, Pierre, *Milieux juifs de la France contemporaine à travers leurs écrivains*, Plon, 1962.

Azéma, Jean-Pierre, *De Munich à la Libération, 1938-1944*, Points-Seuil, 1979.

Bariéty, Jacques, Bloch, Charles, 'Une tentative de conciliation franco-allemande et son échec (1932-1933)', *Revue d'histoire moderne et contemporaine*, 15, 1968, pp. 433-465.

Bellanger, Claude, et. al., *Histoire générale de la presse française*, tome 3, *1871-1940*, PUF, 1972.

Benda, Julien, *La Fin de l'éternel*, Gallimard, 1968 (orig. ed. 1929).

Benda, Julien, *La Jeunesse d'un clerc*, suivi de *Un Régulier dans le siècle*, et de *Exercice d'un enterré vif*, Gallimard, 1968 (orig. eds. 1937, 1938 and 1947).

Benda, Julien, *La Trahison des clercs*,Livre de Poche-Pluriel, 1977 (orig. ed. 1927).

Béraud, Henri, *La Croisade des longues figures*, Editions du siècle, 1924.

Berl, Emmanuel, *Mort de la pensée bourgeoise*, Grasset, 1929.

Berl, Emmanuel, Modiano, Patrick, *Interrogatoire*, Gallimard, 1976.

Bernanos, Georges, *Essais et écrits de combat*, Gallimard, Bibliothèque de la Pléiade, 1971.

Bernard, Jean-Pierre, *Le Parti Communiste Français et la question littéraire, 1921-1939*, Grenoble: Presses Universitaires de Grenoble, 1972.

Bersani, Jacques, *Jean Paulhan le souterrain*, colloque de Cerisy, Editions "10/18", 1976.

Berstein, Serge, *Histoire du Parti Radical*, vol 2, *Crise du radicalisme, (1926-1939)*, Presses de la fondation nationale des sciences politiques, 1982.

Birnbaum, Pierre, *Un mythe politique: la «République juive»*, Fayard, 1988.

Boak, Denis, 'Malraux et Gide', in *André Malraux 3, Revue des Lettres modernes*, Minard, 1975, pp. 31-49.

Bodin, Louis, Touchard, Jean, *Front Populaire: 1936*, Armand Colin, 1972.

Boutang, Pierre, *Maurras: la destinée et l'oeuvre*, Plon, 1984.

Bonnaud-Lamotte, D., Rispail, J.-L., *Intellectuel(s) des années trente entre le rêve et l'action*, Editions du CNRS, 1989.

Bowie, Malcolm, 'Letter to the editor', *Times Literary Supplement*, 26 December 1980.

Brower, D.R., *The New Jacobins: the French Communist Party and the Popular Front*, New York: Cornell University Press, 1968.

Burrin, Philippe, 'La France dans le champ magnétique des fascismes', *Le Débat*, no. 32, November 1984.

Carley, M.J., 'The Origins of the French intervention in the Russian Civil War, January to May 1918: a reappraisal', *Journal of Modern History*, 48, 1976, pp. 413-439.

Caron, Vicki, 'The Politics of Frustration: French Jewry and the Refugee Crisis in the 1930s', *Journal of Modern History*, 65, June 1993, pp. 311-356.

Caute, David, *Communism and the French Intellectuals*, London: Deutsch, 1964.

212

Caute, David, *The Fellow-Travellers: a Postscript to the Enlightenment*, London: Weidenfeld & Nicolson, 1973.

Chamson, André, *Il faut vivre vieux*, Grasset, 1984.

Chavardès, Maurice, *Une campagne de presse: la droite française et le 6 février 1934*, Flammarion, 1970.

Ciano, Comte, *Journal politique, 1937-1938*, Les Editions de Paris, 1949.

Claudel, Paul, *Journal*, I, Gallimard, Bibliothèque de la Pléiade, 1968.

Clerval, Alain, 'Un démocrate, Jean Paulhan', *NRF*, May 1969, pp. 931-937.

Cohn, Norman, *Warrant for Genocide: The Protocols of the Sages of Zion*, London: Eyre and Spottiswoode, 1967.

Cornick, Martyn, 'Jean Paulhan et la censure: la *NRF* à la veille de la guerre', in *CJP* 3, 'Cahier du centenaire, 1884-1984', Gallimard, 1984, pp. 219-227.

Cornick, Martyn, 'Malraux, anti-Semitism and antifascism: his reply to *Droit de vivre* (1933)', *Mélanges Malraux Miscellany*, vol. 17, nos. 1-2, Spring-Fall 1985, pp. 46-50.

Crémieux-Brilhac, J.-L., *Les Français de l'an 40*, 2 vol., Gallimard, 1990.

Danon, Jacques, *Entretiens avec Elise et Marcel Jouhandeau*, Belfond, 1966.

Dauphin, Jean-Pierre, *Louis-Ferdinand Céline* 1, 'Calepins de Bibliographie' no. 6, tome 1, 1914-1944, Minard, 1977.

David, Jean, *Le Procès de l'Intelligence, 1919-1927*, Nizet, 1966.

Davies, J. C., 'Bibliographie des articles d'Albert Thibaudet', *Revue des sciences humaines*, April-June 1957, pp. 197-229.

Debray, Régis, *Le Pouvoir intellectuel en France*, Ramsay, 1979.

Debray, Régis, *Le Scribe*, Grasset-Livre de Poche, 1980.

Debû-Bridel, Jacques, 'Jean Paulhan, citoyen', in Jean Paulhan, *Oeuvres*, V, pp. 483-492.

Decaudin, Michel, 'L'année 1908 et les origines de la *NRF*', *Revue des sciences humaines*, 68, 1952, pp. 347-358.

Decaudin, Michel, *La Crise des valeurs symbolistes, vingt ans de poésie française (1895-1914)*, Toulouse: Privat, 1960.

Decaudin, Michel, 'Formes et fonctions de la revue littéraire au XXe siècle', in *Situation et avenir des revues littéraires*, Nice: Centre du XXe siècle, 1976, pp. 13-22.

*Les Derniers Jours* [Facsimile reprint], J. Place, 1979.

Dhôtel, André, *Jean Paulhan*, Qui suis-je?, Lyon: La Manufacture, 1986.

Dioudonnat, P.-M., *'Je Suis Partout', 1930-1944: les maurrassiens devant la tentation fasciste*, La Table ronde, 1973.

Drieu La Rochelle, Pierre, *Journal 1939-1945*, présenté et annoté par Julien Hervier, Gallimard, 1992.

Droz, Jacques, *Histoire de l'anti-fascisme en Europe, 1923-1939*, Editions la Découverte, 1985.

Du Bos, Charles, *Journal 1921-1923, Journal 1924-1925, Journal 1926-1927*, Corrêa, 1948-1949.

Duchâtelet, Bernard, 'André Gide and Romain Rolland', in *Série André Gide* 7, 'Le romancier', *Revue des lettres modernes*, Minard, 1984, pp. 196-202.

Duclos, Jacques, *Mémoires*, II, Fayard, 1969.

Durosay, Daniel, 'La Direction politique de Jacques Rivière à la *NRF*, (1919-1925)', *Revue d'histoire litteraire de la France*, 77, 1977, pp. 227-245.

Durosay, Daniel, 'Les Idées politiques de Jacques Rivière', *Bulletin des amis de Jacques Rivière et d'Alain-Fournier*, nos. 20-21, 1980, pp. 21-70.

Duroselle, Jean-Baptiste, *Politique étrangère de la France: la décadence 1932-1939*, Points-Seuil, 1983.

Durtain, Luc, *L'Autre Europe: Moscou et sa foi*, Gallimard, 1928.

*Edouard Daladier, chef du gouvernement*, actes de colloque, Presses de la FNSP, 1977.

Epron-Denégri, Madeleine, 'Souvenirs', *Le Figaro Littéraire*, 3 December 1955.

Etiemble, René, *Mes contrepoisons*, Gallimard, 1974.

Etiemble, René, *Lignes d'une vie*, Arléa, 1988.

Evans, Arthur J., *On Four Modern Humanists*, Princeton: Princeton U.P., 1970.

Fauvet, Jacques, *Histoire du Parti Communiste Français*, I. *1917-1939*, Fayard, 1964.

Felix, David: *Walter Rathenau and the Weimar Republic (The Politics of Reparations)*, Baltimore and London: The John Hopkins Press, 1971.

Fernandez, Ramon, *Gide ou le courage de s'engager*, Klincksieck, 1985.

Fini, Marco & Fusco, Mario [scelta e note a cura di], *La Nouvelle Revue Française*, Milano: Lerici editori, 1965.

Finkielkraut, Alain, *La Défaite de la pensée*, Gallimard, 1987.

Foucart, Claude, 'Un hebdomadaire berlinois au service des intellectuels: André Gide et *Die Literarische Welt*', *Bulletin des amis d'André Gide*, no. 58, April 1983, pp. 145-172.

Foucart, Claude, 'La littérature d'exil et ses rapports avec André Gide: Hermann Kesten', *Bulletin des amis d'André Gide*, no. 60, October 1983, pp. 501-517.

Foucart, Claude, 'Ernst-Robert Curtius et André Gide: les débuts d'une amitié (1920-1923)', *Revue de littérature comparée*, July-September 1984, pp. 317-339.

*La France et l'Allemagne, 1932-1936*, actes d'un colloque franco-allemand, Editions du CNRS, 1980.

*La France et les Français en 1938-1939*, actes de colloque, Presses de la FNSP, 1978.

Friedländer, Saul, *L'antisemitisme nazi: histoire d'une psychose collective*, Seuil, 1971.

Garniez, Bernard: *La NRF pendant la période de l'entre-deux-guerres*, Unpublished Ph.D. dissertation, New York University, 1960.

Gascoyne, David, [review of] *Journal sous l'Occupation*, by Marcel Jouhandeau, *Times Literary Supplement*, 5 December 1980.

Geoghegan, C. G., 'Surrealism and communism: the hesitations of Aragon from Kharkov to the 'Affaire Front Rouge'', *Journal of European Studies*, VIII, 1978, pp. 12-33.

Gide, André, *Incidences*, Gallimard, 1924.

Gide, André, *Littérature engagée*, Gallimard, 1950.

Gide, André, *Journal*, I, *1889-1939*, Gallimard, Bibliothèque de la Pléiade, 1951.

Gide, André, *Journal*, II, *1939-1949 (Souvenirs)*, Gallimard, Bibliothèque de la Pléiade, 1953.

Gide, André, *Retour de l'URSS*, suivi de *Retouches à mon Retour de l'URSS*, Gallimard-Idées, 1978 (orig. eds. 1936 and 1937).

Girault, René, 'Les décideurs français et la puissance française, 1938-1939', in *La Puissance en Europe*, Girault, René, Frank, Robert, eds., Publications de la Sorbonne, 1984.

Girault, René: 'Les relations franco-soviétiques devant la crise économique de 1929', *Revue d'histoire moderne et contemporaine*, 27, 1980, pp. 237-257.

Giron, Roger, Saint-Jean, Robert de, *La Jeunesse littéraire devant la politique*, Editions des Cahiers Libres, 1928.

Goueffon, Jean, 'Le radicalisme entre la crise et le Front populaire: la première élection de Jean Zay, 1932', *Revue d'histoire moderne et contemporaine*, 22, 1975, pp. 619-654.

Goulet, Alain, 'Gide à travers la presse soviétique de 1932 à 1937', *André Gide 1, Revue des lettres modernes*, Minard, 1972, pp. 136-178.

Green, Julien, *Journal*, Gallimard, Bibliotheque de la Pléiade, 1976.

Grenier, Jean, *Essai sur l'esprit d'orthodoxie*, Gallimard, 1938.

Grosser, Alfred, 'Jean Schlumberger, l'Allemagne et la morale politique', in 'Jean Schlumberger', *NRF*, March 1969, pp. 334-349.

Grover, Frederic J., 'Malraux et Drieu la Rochelle', *André Malraux 1, Revue des lettres modernes*, Minard, 1972, pp. 61-93.

Grover, Frederic J., 'Les années 30 dans la correspondance André Gide-Jean Paulhan', *Modern Language Notes*, 95, 1980, pp. 830-849.

Guéhenno, Jean, *Caliban Parle*, suivi de *Conversion à l'humain*, Grasset, 1962 (orig. ed. 1928).

Guilloux, Louis, *Carnets, 1921-1944*, Gallimard, 1978.

'Gygès', *Les Juifs dans la France d'aujourd'hui*, Documents et témoignages, 1965.

Hamilton, Nigel, *The Brothers Mann*, London: Secker and Warburg, 1978.

Hanrez, Marc, 'Le Massacre de la Saint-Bagatelles', *Tel Quel*, Summer, 1982, pp. 66-76.

Harris, F. J., *André Gide and Romain Rolland: Two Men Divided*, New Brunswick: Rutgers U.P., 1973.

Haslam, Jonathan, 'The Comintern and the Origins of the Popular Front, 1934-1935', *The Historical Journal*, 22, 1979, pp. 673-691.

Hazareesingh, Sudhir, *Political traditions in modern France*, Oxford: OUP, 1994.

Hebey, Pierre, *L'Esprit NRF*, Gallimard, 1990.

Hebey, Pierre, *La NRF des années sombres, 1940-1941*, Gallimard, 1992.

Hewitt, Nicholas, 'L'Antisémitisme de Céline: historique et culte de la blague', *Etudes interethniques*, 6, 1983, pp. 55-66.

Hewitt, Nicholas, *'Les Maladies du Siècle': The Image of Malaise in French Fiction and Thought in the Inter-War Years*, Hull: Hull University Press, 1988.

Hollier, Denis, *Le Collège de Sociologie*, Gallimard-Idées, 1979.

'Hommage à Alain', *NRF*, September 1952.

Hughes, H. Stuart, *Consci;ousness and Society*, New York: Harvester Press, 1979 (orig. ed. 1959).

Ingram, Norman, *The Politics of Dissent. Pacifism in France 1919-1939*, Oxford: Clarendon Press, 1991.

Istrati, Panaït, *Vers l'autre flamme*, Editions "10/18", 1980 (original edition 1929).

Jamet, Claude, *Le Rendezvous manqué de 1944*, Editions France-Empire, 1964.

Jamet, Claude, 'Le Dreyfusisme radical d'Alain', in *Les Ecrivains et l'Affaire Dreyfus*, PUF, 1983, pp. 177-84.

Jennings, Jeremy, *Intellectuals in Twentieth-Century France. Mandarins and Samurais*, Basingstoke: Macmillan, 1993.

Joll, James, *Three Intellectuals and Politics*, New York: Pantheon Books, 1960.

Jouhandeau, Marcel, *Le Peril Juif*, Sorlot, 1937.

Judt, Tony, *Past imperfect. French intellectuals 1944-1956*, Berkeley, Los Angeles & Oxford: University of California Press, 1992.

Kanters, Robert, 'Le XXe siècle – de 1914 à 1940 – la relève', in *Neuf siècles de littérature française*, Delagrave, 1958.

Kemp, Tom, *Stalinism in France*. Volume 1: *The First Twenty Years of the French Communist Party*, London: New Park Publications, 1984.

Kessler, Heinrich, *Les Cahiers du comte Henri Kessler*, Grasset, 1972.

King, John, *'Sur'. A study of the Argentine literary journal and its rôle in the development of a culture 1931-1970*, Cambridge: CUP, 1986.

Kingston, Paul J., *Anti-Semistism in France during the 1930s*, Hull: University of Hull Press, 1983.

Knei-Paz, Baruch, *The Social and Political Thought of Leon Trotsky*, Oxford: The Clarendon Press, 1978.

Kupferman, Fred, *Au Pays des Soviets: le voyage français en Union Soviétique, 1917-1939*, Julliard-Gallimard, 1979.

Kvapil, Joseph, *Romain Rolland et les amis d'Europe*, Prague: Acta Universitatis Palackianae Olumucensis, 1971.

Laborie, P., *L'opinion française sous Vichy*, Seuil, 1990.

Lacouture, Jean, *André Malraux: une vie dans le siècle*, Seuil-Points, 1976.

Lacouture, Jean, *Leon Blum*, Seuil, 1977.

Lalou, René, *'La Galère d'André Chamson'*, *Les Nouvelles Littéraires*, 1 April 1939.

Léautaud, Paul, *Journal littéraire*, 19 vols, Mercure de France, 1956-66.

Lefèvre, Frédéric, *Entretien avec Julien Benda*, Le Livre-Charmontin, 1925.

Lefèvre, Frédéric, *Une heure avec...*, 6 vol., Flammarion & Gallimard, 1924-1933.

Lefranc, Georges, *Histoire du Front Populaire, 1934-1938*, Payot, 1965.

Leiner, Jacqueline, 'Préface', in *Bifur*, réédition en deux volumes, J.-M. Place, 1976.

Levie, Sophie, *Commerce 1924-1932. Une revue internationale moderniste*, Rome: Fondazione Camillo Caetani, 1989.

L'Huillier, Fernand, *Dialogues franco-allemands, 1925-1933*, Strasbourg: Publications de la Faculté des lettres de l'Université de Strasbourg, 1971.

Lottman, Herbert R., *La Rive gauche*, Seuil-Points, 1981.

Loubet del Bayle, J.-L., *Les Non-conformistes des années 30*, Seuil, 1969.

Machefer, Philippe, *Ligues et fascismes en France, 1918-1939*, PUF, 1974.

Mann, Heinrich, *Sieben Jahre*, Berlin: Zsolnay, 1929.

Mann, Thomas, 'Pariser Rechenschaft', in *Gesammelte Werke*, Band XI, Hamburg, 1974.

Maritain, Jacques, *Les Juifs parmi les nations*, Editions du Cerf, 1938.

Marrus, Michael, Paxton, Robert O., *Vichy France and the Jews*, New York: Basic Books, 1981.

Martin, Claude, *La NRF de Jacques Rivière, 1919 à 1925* [Index], Lyon: Centre d'études gidiennes,1983.

Martin, Claude, *La NRF de Gaston Gallimard, 1925 à 1934* [Index], Lyon: Centre d'études gidiennes,1976.

Martin, Claude, *La NRF de Jean Paulhan, 1935 à 1940* [Index], Lyon: Centre d'études gidiennes, 1977.

Martin, Claude, *La NRF de Drieu La Rochelle, 1940 à 1943* [Index], Centre d'études gidiennes, 1975.

Martin, Claude, 'Ce fou de Jef: André Gide et Munich', *Revue des sciences humaines*, January-March 1970, pp. 119-125.

Martin-Chauffier, Louis, 'Les Clercs sur le pré', *Les Nouvelles Littéraires*, 20 December 1930.

Maurer, Rudolf, *André Gide et l'URSS*, Berne: Editions Tillier, 1983.

Maurras, Charles, *Dictionnaire politique*, ed. Pierre Chardon, vol. 3, La Cité des livres, 1933.

Mayeur, Jean-Marie, *La Vie politique sous la Troisième République*, Seuil-Points, 1984.

Mégret, Maurice, 'Les origines de la propagande de guerre française: du Service Général de l'Information au Commissariat Général à l'Information, 1927-1940', *Revue d'histoire de la Deuxième Guerre mondiale*, January 1961, pp. 3-27.

Mehlman, Jeffrey, *Legs de l'antisémitisme en France*, Denoël, 1984.

Meylan, Jean-Pierre, *La Revue de Genève: miroir des lettres européennes, 1920-1930*, Geneva: Droz, 1969.

Michon, Pascal, *Recherches sur l'idéologie de la NRF, 1919-1924*, Unpublished mémoire de maîtrise, 1981.

Mitterrand, François, [Interview] in *Le Nouvel Observateur*, 18-24 November 1968.

Moatti, Christiane, 'Esthétique et politique: *Les Conquérants*, 1928-1947, ou les aventures d'un texte', in *Andre Malraux 5*, 'Malraux et l'histoire', ed. Walter G. Langlois, Minard, 1982, pp. 117-157.

Morand, Paul, *France-la-Doulce*, Gallimard, 1934.

Morino, Lina, *La NRF dans l'histoire des lettres, 1908-1939*, Gallimard, 1939.

Mourin, Maxime, *Les Relations franco-soviétiques, 1917-1962*, Payot, 1967.

Niess, Robert J., *Julien Benda*, Michigan: Ann Arbor, 1956.

Nordmann, Jean-Thomas, *Histoire des Radicaux (1820-1975)*, La Table ronde, 1974.

O'Brien, Justin, '*La NRF dans l'histoire des lettres*, par L. Morino, Paris, Gallimard, 1939', in *Romanic Review*, Vol. 31. 1940, pp. 190-194.

Ory, Pascal, *Les Collaborateurs, 1940-1945*, Seuil, 1976.

Ory, Pascal, Sirinelli, Jean-François, *Les intellectuels en France, de l'affaire Dreyfus à nos jours*, A. Colin, 1987.

Painter, G.D.,*Marcel Proust*, 2 vol., Harmondsworth: Penguin Books, 1977.

Parain, Brice, *De Fil en aiguille*, Gallimard, 1960.

Parain, Brice, *Entretiens avec Bernard Pingaud*, Gallimard, 1966.

Parienté, Robert, *André Suarès, l'insurgé*, François Bourin, 1990.

Paulhan, Claire (ed.), *La vie est pleine de choses redoutables, textes autobiographiques*, Seghers, 1989.

Paulhan, Jean, *Les Incertitudes du langage*, Gallimard-Idées, 1970.

Paulhan, Jean, *Oeuvres complètes*, 5 vol., Cercle du Livre Précieux, 1966-1970.

Paulhan, Jean, 'Pages de Carnet', *NRF*, August 1979, pp. 183-192.

Paulhan, Jean, 'Une lettre de M. Jean Paulhan à l'universitaire de province', *Combat*, March 1936.

Paulhan, Jean, 'Mort de Groethuysen à Luxembourg', *NRF*, May 1969, pp. 946-976.

Philippe, Béatrice, *Etre Juif dans la société française*, Pluriel-Montalba, 1979.

Pierrard, Pierre, *Juifs et catholiques français (de Drumont à Jules Isaac. 1886-1945)*, Fayard, 1970.

Pistorius, Georges, 'L'Image de l'Allemagne dans la *NRF*, 1909-1943', in *Connaissance de l'étranger, Mélanges offerts à la mémoire de J.-M. Carré*, Librairie Marcel Didier, 1964, pp. 397-414.

*Le Plan du 9 juillet*, préface de Jules Romains, Gallimard, 1934.

Pluet-Despatin, Jacqueline, 'Une contribution à l'histoire des intellectuels: les revues', in Racine, N., & Trebitsch, M. (eds.), 'Sociabilités intellectuelles', *Cahiers de l'IHTP*, no. 20, March 1992, pp. 125-136.

Plumyène, J., and Lasierra, R.,*Les Fascismes français*, Seuil, 1963.

Poidevin, Raymond, Bariéty, Jacques, *Les Relations franco-allemandes, 1815-1975*, Armand Colin, 1977.

Poliakov, Leon, *The Aryan Myth. A History of Racist and Nationalist Ideas in Europe*, London: Chatto-Heinemann, 1974.

Poliakov, Leon, *Histoire de l'antisémitisme*, 2 vol., Pluriel-Calmann-Lévy, 1981.

Ponge, Francis, in 'Portrait de Jean Paulhan', *Cahier des saisons*, no. 10, 1957, pp. 263-307.

Pouey, Fernand, *Un Ingénu à la radio*, Domat, 1949.

*Problèmes franco-allemands*, Librairie Georges Valois, 1932.

Prochasson, Christophe, *Les Intellectuels, le socialisme et la guerre, 1900-1938*, Seuil, 1993.

Racine, Nicole, Bodin, Louis, *Le Parti Communiste français pendant l'entre-deux-guerres*, Armand Colin, 1972.

Racine, Nicole, 'L'Association des écrivains et artistes révolutionnaires (AEAR): la revue *Commune* et la lutte idéologique contre le fascisme (1932-1936)', *Mouvement social*, no. 54, 1966, pp. 29-47.

Racine-Furlaud, Nicole, 'Le Comité de vigilance des intellectuels antifascistes (1934-1939), antifascisme et pacifisme', *Mouvement social*, no. 101, 1977, pp. 87-113.

Racine, Nicole, 'La revue *Europe* et l'Allemagne, 1929-1936', in Bock, H.M. [et. al.], *Entre Locarno et Vichy. Les relations culturelles franco-allemandes dans les années 1930*, Vol. II, CNRS Editions, 1993.

Racine, Nicole, 'La revue *Europe* 1923-1939. Du pacifisme rollandienne à l'antifascsime compagnon de route', in *Matériaux pour l'histoire de notre temps*, no. 30, January-March 1993, pp. 21-26.

Racine, Nicole, Trebitsch, Michel (eds.), 'Sociabilités intellectuelles', *Cahiers de l'IHTP*, no. 20, March 1992.

*Rajeunissement de la politique*, préface de Henry de Jouvenel, Corrêa, 1932.

*Les Relations franco-allemandes, 1933-1939*, actes de colloque, Editions CNRS, 1976.

Rémond, René, *Notre siècle de 1918 à 1991*, Fayard, 1991.

Revah, Louis-Albert, *Julien Benda*, Plon, 1991.

*Revue du cinéma*, [reprint in 5 vols] published by Pierre Lherminier éditeur, 1979.

Richard, 'L'Image de l'Allemagne dans la *NRF* de 1919 à 1939', *Revue de psychologie des peuples*, 25, 1970, pp. 197-210.

Richard, Lionel, 'L'Image de l'Allemagne dans la *NRF* de 1909 a 1914', *Mosaic*, VII, 4, 1974, pp. 71-98.

Richard, Lionel, 'Drieu et la *NRF* des années noires', *Revue d'histoire de la Deuxieme Guerre mondiale*, XXV, 97, 1975, pp. 67-84.

Richard, Lionel: 'Jacques Rivière et l'orientation idéologique de la *NRF* au lendemain de la Première Guerre mondiale', *Ethnopsychologie*, XXX, 1975, pp. 431-454.

Richard, Lionel, 'André Suarès face au nazisme', *André Suarès 2, Revue des lettres modernes*, Minard, 1976, pp. 484-490.

Rivière, Jacques, *L'Allemand*, Gallimard, 1924.

Romains, Jules, *Cette Grande Lueur à l'est, Les Hommes de bonne volonté*, vol. XIX, Flammarion, 1944.

Rouzaud, Maurice: *Où va la critique?*, Editions Saint-Michel, 1929.

Roy, Claude, *Moi je*, Gallimard, 1978.

Rubenstein, D., *What's Left? The ENS and the Right*, Madison: University of Wisconsin Press, 1990.

Sachs, Maurice, *André Gide*, Denoël et Steele, 1936.

Saillet, Maurice: 'La *NRF* va-t-elle disparaître?', *L'Effort*, 29 September 1940.

Saint-Jean, Robert de, *Passé pas mort*, Grasset, 1983.

Schalk, David L., *The Spectrum of Political Engagement*, Princeton: Princeton U.P., 1979.

Schlumberger, Jean, *Oeuvres*, Vols. II, III, & VI, Gallimard, 1958-1960.

Schulin, E., 'Rathenau et la France', in 'Cent ans de relations franco-allemandes', *Revue d'Allemagne*, IV, 3, 1972, pp. 547-557.

Serge, Victor, *Mémoires d'un révolutionnaire 1901-1941*, Seuil-Points, 1978.

Sernin, André, *Alain: un sage dans la cité*, Robert Laffont, 1985.

Silve, Edith, *Paul Léautaud et le Mercure de France*, Mercure de France, 1985.

Sirinelli, Jean-François, 'Le hasard ou la nécessité? Une histoire en chantier: l'histoire des intellectuels', *Vingtième siècle*, 9, January-March 1986, pp. 97-108.

Sirinelli, Jean-François (ed.), 'Générations intellectuelles', *Cahiers de l'Institut d'histoire du temps présent*, no. 6, novembre 1987 (esp. pp. 5-18).

Sirinelli, Jean-François, *Génération intellectuelle. Khâgneux et Normaliens dans l'entre-deux-guerres*, Fayard, 1988.

Sirinelli, Jean-François, *Intellectuels et passions françaises. Manifestes et pétitions au XXe siècle*, Fayard, 1990.

Sirinelli, Jean-François (sous la direction de), *Histoire des droites en France*, 3 vol., Gallimard, 1992.

Soulié, Michel, *La Vie politique d'Edouard Herriot*, Armand Colin, 1962.

Sternhell, Zeev, *Ni droite ni gauche: l'idéologie fasciste en France*, Seuil, 1983.

Suarès, André, *Vues sur l'Europe*, Grasset, 1939.

*Tendances politiques de la vie française depuis 1789*, Hachette, 1960.

Thibaudet, Albert, *La République des professeurs*, Grasset, 1927.

Thibaudet, Albert, *Histoire de la littérature française de 1789 à nos jours*, Stock, 1936.

Thibaudet, Albert, 'The Young Reviews. Letter from France', in *The London Mercury*, vol. 1, 1919-1920, pp. 622-624.

Touchard, Jean, *La Gauche en France depuis 1900*, Seuil, 1981.

Touchard, Jean, 'L'Esprit des années 1930: tentative de renouvellement de la pensée politique française', in *Tendances politiques de la vie française depuis 1789*, Hachette, 1960, pp. 89-118.

Traz, Robert de, *'La Galère'*, Revue hebdomadaire, 18 March 1939.

*Valery Larbaud et la littérature de son temps*, actes du colloque Valery Larbaud, Klincksieck, 1978.

Vallette, G., Bouillon, J., *Munich 1938*, Armand Colin, 1983.

Van Rhysselberghe, Maria, 'Les Cahiers de la Petite Dame', 1. 1918-1929, 2. 1929-1937, 3. 1937-1945, in *Cahiers André Gide* 4, 5 and 6, 1973, 1974 and 1975. Referred to as *CAG* 4, 5 and 6.

Verdès-Leroux, J.,*Scandale financier et anit-sémitisme catholique*, Editions du Centurion, 1969.

Viénot, Pierre, *Les Incertitudes allemandes*, Valois, 1931.

Wall, Irwin M., *French Communism in the era of Stalin*, Westport and London: Greenwood Press, 1983.

Walzer, Pierre-Olivier, *Littérature française*, Vol. 15, *Le XXe siècle*, I, *1896-1920*, Arthaud, 1975.

Weber, Eugen, *L'Action Française*, Stanford: Stanford U.P., 1962.

Wilkinson, James D., *The Origins of Intellectual Resistance in Europe*, Cambridge, Mass.: Harvard U.P., 1981.

Wilson, Stephen, 'The Action Française in French intellectual life', *Historical Journal*, XI, 2, 1969, pp. 328-350.

Winock, Michel, *Histoire politique de la revue Esprit, 1930-1950*, Seuil, 1975.

Wurmser, André, *Conseils de révision*, Gallimard, 1972.

Wurmser, André, *Fidèlement vôtre*, Grasset, 1979.

# SECTION IV: PERIODICALS

The following periodicals – newspapers, weeklies and reviews – were consulted, either in part or in full:

*L'Action française*

*L'Annuaire de la Presse française*

*L'Assaut*

*La Bête noire*

*Bifur*

*Bulletin de l'Union pour la Vérité*

*Cahiers de l'Emancipation nationale*

*Cahiers du Mois*

*Candide*

*Chantiers co-operatifs*

*Combat*

*Commerce*

*Commune*

*Le Crapouillot*

*The Criterion*

*Les Derniers Jours*

*Droit de vivre*

*Les Ecrits français*

*L'Emancipation nationale*

*Europe*

*Figaro Littéraire*

*La Flèche*

*La Grande Revue*

*L'Homme Nouveau*

*L'Humanité*

*Je Suis Partout*

*Journal de Moscou*

*Les Libres Propos*

*Les Marges*

*Marianne*

*Le Mercure de France*

*Mesures*

*La Minerve Française*

*Le Minotaure*

*Le Navire d'argent*

*Nord-Sud*

*Notre Temps*

*Les Nouveaux Cahiers*

*Les Nouvelles littéraires*

*L'Oeuvre*

*Pavés de Paris*

*Revue critique des idées et des livres*

*Revue des Deux Mondes*

*Revue de Genève*

*Revue du cinéma*

*Revue du siècle*

*Revue européenne*

*Revue hebdomadaire*

*Revue juive*

*Revue juive de Genève*

*Revue rhénane*

*Revue universelle*

*Samedi*

*Sept*

*Le Spectateur*

*Le Temps*

*Vendredi*

*Vigile*

# INDEX

Abetz, Otto, 97, 181, 195, 202
Abraham, Pierre, 202
Académie Française, 40
Action Française, 6, 50, 63, 91, 92, 107, 108, 126, 137, 153, 154, 156, 160, 161, 164, 169, 170
*Action française*, 31, 73, 160, 177
*Age des orthodoxies*, l' (Grenier), 87, 89
*Airs du mois*, 29, 41, 42, 44, 80, 81, 83, 86, 142, 188
Alain [i.e., Emile-Auguste Chartier], 26, 32, 36, 48, 70, 71, 72, 73, 82, 89, 93, 203
*Allemand*, l' (Rivière), 100
Alsace, 99, 112
Altman, Georges, 81
'Amis d'Alain-Fournier', 202
Amsterdam-Pleyel (Peace movement), 48, 66, 115
*Année des vaincus*, l' (Chamson), 120
anti-Semitism, chapter 6, passim
antifascism, 69, 97
Aragon, Louis, 17, 24, 28, 40, 74, 93, 142, 195
Arland, Marcel, 22, 27, 43, 44, 60, 93, 171, 188, 195, 206
Arnauld, Michel, 11
Aron, Raymond, 26, 73, 79
Aron, Robert, 76, 152
Artaud, Antonin, 40
*Assaut*, l', 90
Association des écrivains et artistes révolutionnaires (AEAR), 28, 78, 85, 86, 116, 137, 141
Audiberti, Jacques, 38, 40, 189
*Autre Europe, Moscou et sa foi*, l' (Durtain), 127
Aveline, Claude, 202
Aymé, Marcel, 169
Azéma, Jean-Pierre, 182
*Bagatelles pour un massacre* (Céline), 171, 179
Bainville, Jacques, 106, 108
Barbusse, Henri, 67, 137
Barrès, Maurice, 27, 49, 68, 135, 155
Bataille, Georges, 189
Benda, Julien, chapter 2, passim; 4, 26, 28, 38, 44, 71, 81, 85, 86, 89, 92, 93, 120, 121, 125, 131, 132, 146, 147, 150, 163, 164, 165, 167, 168, 169, 170, 172, 174, 177, 178, 183, 184, 186, 187, 188, 189, 191, 197, 199, 203, 204, 205
Béraud, Henri, 18, 71, 102
Bergery, Gaston, 190
Bergson, Henri, 94, 110, 152
Berl, Emmanuel, 32, 57, 58, 76, 129, 133, 151, 152, 191, 192
Bernanos, Georges, 154, 156, 199
Bernstein, Henri, 152

Bernus, Pierre, 110
Bertaux, Félix, 22, 99, 121
*Bête Noire*, la, 38
*Bifur*, 13, 31
Billy, André, 194
Blanzat, Jean, 202
Bloch, Jean-Richard, 142, 152, 156, 157
Bloch, Marc, 167
Blum, Léon, 88, 89, 91, 93, 150, 152, 164, 166, 167, 168, 170, 190
Blumberg, Georges, 117
Bonnard, Abel, 93, 158
Bonnet, Georges, 192
Bopp, Léon, 27
Bordeaux, Henri, 93
Bosquet, Joë, 199
Bourget, Paul, 158
Brasillach, Robert, 3, 37, 42
Brest-Litovsk (Treaty), 124
Breton, André, 17, 93
Briand, Aristide, 107
Briand-Kellogg Plan, 109
*Bulletin* (NRF rubric), 31, 42, 93
*Cahiers de la quinzaine*, les, 28
Caillaux, Joseph, 71
Caillois, Roger, 2, 44, 92, 176, 189
Camus, Albert, 2, 87
*Candide*, 31, 189, 201
Cassou, Jean, 202
Caute, David, 125, 128, 133, 141
Céline, Louis-Ferdinand, 157, 171, 172, 173, 179
censorship, 196
*Cette Grande Lueur à l'est* (Romains), 125
Chamberlain, H.S., 159
Chamberlain, Neville, 174, 182, 186
Chamson, André, 63, 76, 94, 120, 198, 200
Chardonne, Jacques, 137, 175, 176
Chautemps, Camille, 92, 93, 170
Ciano, Count, 177
Cingria, Charles-Albert, 139
*Citoyen contre les pouvoirs*, le (Alain), 72
Claudel, Paul, 3, 20, 33, 94, 139, 147, 185
Clemenceau, Georges, 61, 87
Cohen, Albert, 153
Collège de Sociologie, 189
Combes, Emile, 72
Comité d'information franco-allemand, 104, 107
Comité de vigilance des intellectuels antifascistes (CVIA), 26, 82, 85, 121
*Commerce*, 13, 31
Commissariat général à l'Information, 195
*Commune*, 41, 74, 82, 85, 121, 137, 192, 205
Comte de Paris, 91
Congrès des écrivains soviétiques, 142
Congrès pour la défense de la culture, 88
*Conquérants*, les (Malraux), 59, 129

Copeau, Jacques, 11
Coston, Henry, 154
Crapouillot, le, 174
Crémieux, Benjamin, 19, 22, 80, 82, 119, 145, 146, 150, 160, 161, 162, 163, 164, 176, 178, 195, 201, 205
Crémieux, Moïse-Adolphe, 161
Croisade des longues figures, la (Béraud), 102
Croix-de-Feu, les, 87
Curtius, Ernst Robert, 99, 100, 101, 108, 109, 124
Dabit, Eugène, 42, 144
Dada, 126
Daladier, Edouard, 93, 174, 198, 200
Dandieu, Arnaud, 76
Danton, 87
Darré, Walther, 117
Daudet, Léon, 164
Daumal, René, 41
Debray, Régis, 3, 48
Debû-Bridel, Jacques, 35, 202
Demartial, Georges, 109, 110
Desjardins, Paul, 52, 115
Desportes, Alain (pseud.), 100, 151
Détective, 32
Diderot, Denis, 7
Dimitrov, 118, 140
Doriot, Jacques, 28, 81
Doumergue, Gaston, 80
Drault, Jean, 154
Dreyfus Affair, 45, 49, 71, 81, 131, 149, 150, 151, 155, 156, 170, 171, 205
Dreyfus, Robert, 158
Drieu La Rochelle, Pierre, 28, 41, 70, 81, 84, 93, 119, 120, 121, 129, 171, 176, 202, 203
Droit de vivre, 156, 157, 163, 164, 169, 171
Drumont, Edouard, 153, 154, 155, 156, 161, 168
Du Bos, Charles, 19
Duhamel, Georges, 127, 128, 129
Dullin, Charles, 176
Dunkirk, 200
Durkheim, Emile, 152
Durtain, Luc, 127
Echo de Paris, l', 136
Eclaireur de Nice, l', 102
Ecole Normale Supérieure, 5, 26, 74
Ehrenburg, Ilya, 138, 142, 144, 145
Eléments d'une doctrine radicale, (Alain), 72
Eluard, Paul, 93
Emancipation nationale, l', 28
Enlightenment, 125
Esprit, 43
Essai sur l'inégalité (Gobineau), 158
Essais (NRF rubric), 27
Etiemble, René, 44, 92, 140, 158
Europe, 6, 12, 33, 41, 43, 56, 62, 63, 65, 69, 85, 88, 89, 114, 121, 133, 135, 156, 205

Fabre-Luce, Alfred, 90, 129
Farbman, Michael, 133
Fargue, Léon-Paul, 38
Faÿ, Bernard, 158
February 6th riots, 1934, 80, 119, 141
Fénéon, Félix, 42
Fernandez, Ramon, 4, 22, 26, 27, 51, 54, 56, 61, 76, 78, 79, 81, 82, 83, 84, 86, 93, 114, 129, 135, 141
Figaro, le, 194
Fin de l'éternel, la (Benda), 53, 54, 109
First World War, 1, 11, 15, 47, 50, 53, 68, 70, 97, 124, 153, 174, 199
Flèche, la, 174, 190
Flers, Robert de, 152
France juive, la (Drumont), 154, 161, 168
Franck, Henri, 152
Franco-German relations, 34, 97, chapter 4 passim
Franco-Soviet Pact (1935), 187
Friedmann, Georges, 89, 92
Galère, la (Chamson), 94
Gallimard, Gaston), 12, 14, 16, 18, 19, 22, 24, 32, 33, 59, 70, 72, 77, 83, 87, 104, 105, 127, 128, 139, 152, 153, 169, 176, 191, 192, 195
Galtier-Boissière, Jean, 174
Gambetta, Léon, 87
Garniez, Bernard, 40
Ghéon, Henri, 11, 126, 151
Gide, André, 2, 4, 11, 12, 15, 17, 20, 22, 24, 27, 28, 32, 33, 34, 39, 40, 41, 43, 48, 51, 58, 59, 62, 67, 70, 71, 82, 89, 91, 94, 99, 101, 102, 107, 108, 115, 116, 117, 118, 120, 122; chapter 5, passim; 150, 151, 156, 157, 166, 167, 171, 172, 173, 174, 183, 204, 205
Giono, Jean, 93, 199
Giraudoux, Jean, 22, 24, 195
Gobineau, comte Arthur de, 118, 119, 158, 160
Goebbels, Josef, 120
Goering, Hermann, 120, 158
Goethe, 116
Goldschmidt, Clara, 157
Grand Jeu, le, 31
Grande Peur des bien pensants, la (Bernanos), 154
Grande Revue, la, 101
Grasset, Bernard, 59, 152
Grenier, Jean, 2, 19, 21, 26, 30, 32, 37, 41, 42, 43, 64, 80, 85, 87, 88, 89, 90, 91, 92, 131, 141, 142, 145, 169, 199
Groethuysen, Bernard, 22, 99, 100, 107, 117, 133, 135, 139
Grosser, Alfred, 99
Guéhenno, Jean, 33, 55, 56, 57, 58, 65, 66, 68, 88, 101, 135, 137, 177

Guillain, Alix, 117, 135, 139
Guilloux, Louis, 28
Halévy, Daniel, 40, 158
Hanau Affair, 154
Hellens, Franz, 41, 103
Henriot, Emile, 137
Herbart, Pierre, 172
Herriot, Edouard, 32, 63, 71, 72, 75, 103, 115, 124, 127
Hirsch, Louis-Daniel, 152
*Homme mûr et le jeune homme*, l' (Drieu), 84
Hugo, Victor, 7
Huisman, Raoul, 176
humanism, 49, 55
*Humanité*, l', 131, 137
Istrati, Panaït, 130, 132, 147
Izard, Georges, 163
*Je suis partout*, 136
Jews, chapter 6, passim
Jouhandeau, Marcel, 2, 87, 150, 167, 168, 169, 205
*Journal des Débats*, le, 89
Jouve, Pierre-Jean, 183, 197
Kafka, Franz, 100
Kanters, Robert, 17
Kayser, Jacques, 70
Kérillis, Henri de, 121
Kessler, Heinrich, 116
Keyserling, Heinrich von, 158, 159
Komintern, 123, 140, 142
Kristallnacht, 173
Lalou, René, 31
Lamour, Philippe, 77, 171
Landini, 195
Langevin, Paul, 82, 176
Last, Jef, 190
Lazare, Bernard, 161
Léautaud, Paul, 13, 20, 35, 40, 73, 137, 145, 150, 176, 205
Lecache, Bernard, 156, 157, 163
Lecomte, Marcel, 189
Lefebvre, Henri, 77
Léger, Alexis, 38
Leiris, Michel, 37, 189
Levitsky, Anatole, 202
Lhote, André, 22
liberalism, 75
Libre Parole, la, 153, 154, 155
Ligue d'Action Française, 166
Ligue internationale contre l'antisémitisme (LICA), 156, 158, 163
Ligue internationale contre le racisme et l'antisémitisme (LICRA), 156
Locarno Pact, 106
Longuet, Jean, 36, 163
Louverné, Jean (Etiemble), 140, 158
Madagascar, 14

Malraux, André, 2, 24, 57, 58, 59, 62, 70, 84, 87, 89, 99, 118, 123, 129, 133, 139, 142, 144, 157, 163, 191, 204
Mann, Heinrich, 112
Mann, Thomas, 99, 106, 107, 114, 120
Marcel, Gabriel, 22, 51, 54, 64, 144
Marchandeau (loi), 178, 179
*Marianne*, 32, 33, 41
Maritain, Jacques, 173
Marsan, Eugène, 47
Marteau, Jean, 42
Martin du Gard, Roger, 2, 25, 26, 27, 30, 32, 34, 35, 41, 42, 43, 59, 64, 66, 67, 113, 114, 133, 134, 135, 139, 144, 156, 172, 190
Martin-Chauffier, Louis, 34, 62
Masereel, Franz, 127
Massis, Henri, 18, 31, 166
Mauclair, Camille, 102, 109, 136
Maulnier, Thierry, 93, 137, 191
Mauriac, François, 34, 136, 202
Maurois, André, 33, 38
Maurras, 27, 31, 49, 91, 92, 95, 106, 121, 155, 160, 161, 162, 165, 197
Mayrisch family, 100, 103, 116, 151
*Mesures*, 14, 31
Michel, Henri, 97
Ministère de l'Instruction Publique, 15
*Minotaure*, le, 31, 38
Mirande (Gallimard's property in Normandy), 44, 195
Mitterrand, François, 3
Montaigne, 73
Montfort, Eugène, 11
Montherlant, Henry de, 73, 189
Monzie, Anatole de, 8, 172
*Mort de la pensée bourgeoise*, la (Berl), 58
Mounier, Emmanuel, 77
Munich, 4, 13, 23, 29, 44, 68, 93, 122, 147, 174, 177, 179, chapter 7, passim; 181, 182, 185, 188, 190, 192, 205
Musée de l'Homme, 202
Nazi-Soviet Pact (1939), 195
Nietzsche, Friedrich, 49
Nizan, Paul, 27, 77, 78, 142
*Nord-Sud*, 15
notes (NRF rubric), 21, 30, 43
*Notre Temps*, 62, 115
*Nourritures terrestres*, les (Gide), 140
'nouveau mal du siècle', 61, 189
*Nouveaux Cahiers*, les, 33
*Ordination*, l' (Benda), 164
pacifism, 97
Paillart, 20, 21, 153
*Pamphlet*, 90
Parain, Brice, 57, 117, 124, 127, 132, 133
Parti communiste français, 125, 140, 141, 147

Parti de l'Intelligence, 50, 106, 126, 151
Parti populaire français, 28, 81
Patenôtre, Raymond, 32
Patrie se fait tous les jours, 202
Paulhan, Frédéric, 14
Paulhan, Jean, passim
Pavés de Paris, 191
Péguy, Charles, 28, 49, 85, 186
Péril juif, le (Jouhandeau), 169
Perrin, Jean, 176
Petitjean, Armand, 44, 183, 184, 186, 188, 196, 198, 199
phoney war, chapter 7, passim
Pierre-Quint, Léon, 163
Plan du 9 juillet, le, 83
Ploncard, Henri, 154
Poincaré, Raymond, 107, 124, 127
Poliakov, Leon, 158
Ponge, Francis, 2, 29, 41
Popular Front, 32, 35, 68, 70, 82, 85, 86, 89, 91, 92, 94, 95, 121, 123, 144, 150, 166, 170, 183, 184, 204
Pourrat, Henri, 189
Pozner, Vladimir, 142
Pravda, 130
Prévost, Jean, 22, 27, 59
propaganda (for the NRF), 17
Propos (NRF rubric), 32, 73, 89
Protocols of the Sages of Zion, 153, 173
Proust, Marcel, 24, 94, 152
Quai d'Orsay, 102, 191
Quart d'heure de la NRF, 33-34
Queneau, Raymond, 195
Radek, Karel, 142
Radical Party, 4, 5, 32, 63, 71, 82, 87, 121, 124, 140, 204
Radicalism, chapter 3, passim; 128, 203
Radio-37, 34
Raillard, Georges, 24
Rambaud, Henri, 22
rapprochement, 124
Rathenau, Walther, 100, 153
Réflexions (NRF rubric), 27, 51, 74, 109, 142
Renouvier, Charles, 112
Résistance, 202
Resistance, 200, 202
Retouches à mon retour de l'URSS (Gide), 146
Retour de l'URSS (Gide), 145
Revue blanche, la, 28
Revue critique des idées et des livres, 2
Revue des Deux Mondes, 14, 39
Revue des revues (NRF rubric), 30, 31, 32, 65, 139
Revue européenne, la, 104
Revue hebdomadaire, la, 14
Revue juive de Genève, la, 174, 177
Revue juive, la 153

Revue universelle, la, 6, 166, 191
Rhysselberghe, Maria van, 133
Rivet, Paul, 82, 86
Rivière, Isabelle, 19
Rivière, Jacques, 4, 11, 14, 15, 16, 17, 20, 27, 30, 48, 98, 99, 100, 102, 103, 105, 122, 125, 151, 191, 204
Roi Candaule, le (Gide), 140
Rolland de Renéville, André, 40
Rolland, Romain, 56, 66, 67, 120, 130, 177
Romains, Jules, 22, 83, 125
Rougemont, Denis de, 77, 78, 92, 189
Roussakov Affair, 129, 130, 131
Roussel, Raymond, 37, 40
Roy, Claude, 70
Ruhr, 100, 111, 124
Ruyters, André, 11
Sachs, Maurice, 167
Sadoul, Georges, 192
Santé prison, 202
Sartre, Jean-Paul, 2, 26, 35, 44, 50, 190, 195, 196
Saurat, Denis, 73
Schloezer, Boris de, 22, 127
Schlumberger, Jean, 2, 4, 11, 12, 13, 15, 18, 20, 22, 27, 29, 32, 35, 37, 39, 40, 42, 63, 71, 77, 83, 98, 99, 102, 104, 105, 108, 113, 118, 120, 122, 126, 133, 143, 144, 163, 177, 185, 186, 188, 190, 191, 204
Serge, Victor, 130, 132, 139
serializations in NRF, 23
Serpeille de Gobineau, 159
socialist realism, 142
Sorel, Georges, 49, 164, 197
Souday, Paul, 101
Soviet Union, 23, 28, 31, 34, 97, 115, 116, 122; chapter 5, passim; 182, 205
Spectateur, le, 14
Stavisky Affair, 79, 160
Streicher, Julius, 169, 171
Stresemann, Gustav, 107
Strowski, Fortunat, 71, 101
Suarès, André, 20, 30, 33, 120, 150, 163, 164, 169, 177, 178, 195, 196, 205
subscriptions (to the NRF), 12, 13, 23, 199
Supervielle, Jules, 200
Sybilla (Bloch), 156, 157
tableau d'ordre, 20
Tarde, Alfred de, 14
Tarde, Guillaume de, 14
Tardieu, André, 130
Temps, le, 121, 137
Thibaudet, Albert, 22, 26, 36, 43, 47, 48, 51, 54, 71, 72, 74, 75, 84, 89, 101, 109, 111, 112, 141, 154, 155, 165, 203
Third Republic, 4, 49, 70, 150, 155, 201, 204, 205, 206
Thomas, Jean, 84

Thorez, Maurice, 140
Touchard, Jean, 69, 79
*Trahison des clercs*, la (Benda), 28, 31, chapter 2, passim; 85, 102, 107, 132, 146, 154, 164, 177, 197, 204
Trotsky, Leon , 118, 119, 129, 139
Union intellectuelle française, 106
Union pour la Vérité, l', 52, 83, 84, 114, 143
Vaillant-Couturier, Paul, 137
Valéry, Paul, 16, 39, 64, 94, 135, 157
*Vendredi*, 32, 41, 90, 91
Vermeil, Edmond, 121
Versailles Treaty, 111, 112, 114, 121, 188, 198, 205
Vichy régime, 150, 169, 191, 201, 203
*Vie Contemporaine*, la, 14
*Vie*, la, 15
Viénot, Pierre, 103, 104, 105, 106, 108, 111
*Vigilance*, 26
Vildé, Boris, 202
Vitrac, Roger, 22
Voltaire, 7
*Voyage au bout de la nuit* (Céline), 171
*Vues sur l'Europe* (Suarès), 120
Wall Street Crash, 111
Weizmann, Chaim, 153
Wells, H.G., 120, 190
Wurmser, André, 158, 159
Young Plan, 111
Zay, Jean, 172, 176
Zola, Emile, 4, 9, 86